School Improvement Through Drama

Also available from Network Continuum

With Drama in Mind – Patrice Baldwin
Making a Drama out of a Crisis – Tommy Donbavand

Available from Continuum

100 Ideas for Teaching Drama – Johnnie Young
Learning to Teach Drama 11–18, 2nd Edition – Andy Kempe

School Improvement Through Drama

A creative whole class, whole school approach

Patrice Baldwin

network
continuum

Continuum International Publishing Group
Network Continuum
The Tower Building
11 York Road
London, SE1 7NX

80 Maiden Lane, Suite 704
New York, NY 10038

www.networkcontinuum.co.uk
www.continuumbooks.com

British Library Cataloguing-in-Publication Data
A catalogue record for this book is available from the British Library.

ISBN: 1855394561 (paperback)

Library of Congress Cataloguing-in-Publication Data

Baldwin, Patrice.
   School improvement through drama : a creative whole class, whole school approach / Patrice Baldwin.
        p. cm.
   Includes bibliographical references.
   ISBN 978-1-85539-456-8 (pbk. : alk. paper 1. Drama--Study and teaching (Elementary)--Great Britain. 2. Drama in education--Great Britain. 3. Interdisciplinary approach in education--Great Britain. 4. School improvement programs--Great Britain. I. Title.

   PN1701.B35 2009
   371.39'9--dc22

2009006858

Typeset by Fakenham Photosetting Limited, Fakenham, Norfolk
Printed and bound in Great Britain by Ashford Colour Press Ltd.

Contents

Foreword

This book helps us to understand how exploiting the present will prepare children for the future. Good drama offers all of us the chance to be someone else, somewhere else, at another time with other people ... and to explore what might happen, what did happen and how we feel about it!

Patrice Baldwin plunders her experience, expertise and contacts to offer a treasure trove in this book. It is full of examples to help the novice to get going and the experienced to keep going. It is backed by a clear and logical analysis of why drama matters, how to offer the best provision, and where drama can help the aims, purposes and outcomes of learning.

Do take the chance to dip into the book; you will become absorbed. After that, use the book as a trusted friend to help you build drama into the learning lives of the young people you work with and for ... they will become absorbed in their own learning. There are many books on school improvement and how to achieve dramatic results. This book will deliver ... good drama and school improvement.

Mick Waters

Director of Curriculum
Qualifications and Curriculum Authority

Acknowledgements

I would like to acknowledge the enormous commitment and professionalism of the many teachers and headteachers in Norfolk who have successfully and determinedly improved their schools through drama and continue to do so. They have given generously of their time to provide evidence of their school improvement through drama and share their experiences across the UK and abroad. Thanks to Fred Corbett, the Deputy Director of Norfolk County Council Children's Services for his ongoing support of and belief in D4LC (Drama for Learning and Creativity).

Thanks also to National Drama and especially to Pam Bowell and Kate Fleming who are my good friends and have worked with me tirelessly for many years to improve drama learning and teaching in the UK. Thanks also to Dave Simpson, who externally evaluated the D4LC initiative. Also a special thanks to Mick Waters, Director of Curriculum at QCA, who has been a consistent and important ambassador for Drama and has so generously supported my work in many ways.

Finally I would like to dedicate this book to my friend Howard Reid, who many years ago, as my English and Drama Adviser, gave me my first opportunities as a young teacher to work outside my own school and help others to teach drama. He also enabled me to publish my first book. Despite Howard being long since retired and suffering terminal illness while I was writing this book, he always remained truly and selflessly interested in my work and writing.

Introduction

This book aims to support headteachers, subject and curriculum leaders and teachers to see the importance, value and potency of drama as a very effective vehicle for school improvement at many levels. This book is not just about drama. It is about the impact of drama and what drama can holistically achieve for children, teachers, schools and the citizens of tomorrow.

The book is mainly practical and thoroughly rooted in real drama taking place in real schools that are successfully achieving improvement through it. The testimony of headteachers and teachers is presented, who have set about systematically improving their schools through drama in ways that link clearly to achieving a wide range of school improvement priorities, e.g. improving writing, speaking and listening, creativity, attitudes to learning, pupil engagement, behaviour, personal, social and emotional development, inclusion, cross-curricular links, etc. High quality, whole class drama can contribute to achieving almost any school improvement priority, once headteachers and teachers understand what whole class drama in schools can achieve and are committed to making it happen well.

Every school is individual and ever changing. This book offers schools a Drama Self Evaluation Framework (Drama SEF) that is a starting point for a whole school drama self-review. Using the activities in this book as tools, schools will be guided towards agreeing their vision for drama and helped to identify their priorities. The activities will support the planning process and help schools to identify the practical steps needed to achieve a school's improvement in and through drama. The audit and activities will also yield very useful evidence of self- review and development that can be referred to in the Self Evaluation Form (SEF) and presented to Ofsted. More importantly it will hopefully lead to all children and teachers in the school enjoyably and beneficially experiencing and making good drama together in a sustained way.

This book is timely in relation to the new National Curriculum in both primary and secondary schools and its approach fits well with both. It explores and specifically exemplifies drama as a means of developing successful learners, confident individuals and responsible citizens and promotes and exemplifies drama as a cross-curricular learning and teaching medium as well as a subject that needs to be learned and taught in its own right. There is reference made to the Drama curriculum in some other countries and readers are pointed towards online materials that might help inform their own Drama curriculum planning and assessment.

Models of Continuing Professional Development in drama are considered and suggestions for continuing support are offered. The pros and cons of different types of CPD provision are considered. Attention is also paid to managing positively teachers' insecurities and their probable initial lack of Drama subject knowledge and drama teaching skills. Guidance is also provided on observing and improving drama lessons and lessons that use drama.

This book also considers the implications for schools in relation to drama and the cultural entitlement agenda, the Extended School day and the changing workforce. There is advice offered to schools on leading and managing these changes and accessing and keeping high quality external drama/theatre providers who are willing to work in partnership.

There is an extensive Glossary of Drama strategies and conventions within this book, many of which are used in the practical Drama Units. The Glossary lists many Drama strategies and conventions, briefly describes them and explains when they might be used and for what purpose.

The tried and tested Drama Units all show the way that drama can be creatively used to meet a broad range of learning outcomes across many curriculum areas. The units are structured in such a way that any teacher can (at the very least) pick up the lesson and follow it practically (rather like a recipe). The learning objectives provided and the teacher guidance are intended to support teachers in understanding why the lesson is structured as it is and how to set up the various drama activities. This should therefore place teachers in a better position to ideally plan their own Drama lessons in the future, as they gain in confidence.

PART ONE

Improving your school through Drama

■ What do we mean by school improvement?

School improvement quite simply means making your school better in every way! It's much more than improving exam and SAT results (although this is important to schools). It's about making your school a better place all round, a better place for children, staff, parents and carers, governors, the local community and any other 'stakeholders', but most importantly, *a better place for children* to learn in and to develop in holistically and humanistically, securely and with fun and enjoyment. Attaining well in tests should never be at the expense of children getting on well together and developing as thinking, feeling and caring individuals, able to thrive and survive both in and out of school. Happy, emotionally healthy pupils will be well placed to achieve and attain better, so teaching in ways that children enjoy and which will help them developmentally is a win/win situation. Children who are taught in ways that are formulaic, dull, repetitive and assessment driven are more likely to become stressed, demotivated, underachieve and not enjoy school and are therefore unlikely to attain particularly well in tests anyway. On the other hand, children who are taught by teachers who understand how children learn and understand child development and are alert to the personal, social and emotional impact of a range of teaching methods (including the use of the imagination and working in role) are particularly fortunate.

School improvement is often defined and approached too narrowly. This is mainly due to the continuing pressure on schools to improve test results with a focus on narrowly defined, measurable targets in a few subjects that have been given a relatively high status. It seems certain that the emphasis on literacy, numeracy and ICT will continue, even if systems of assessment change but there is a strengthening recognition now of the importance of personal development and a stated intention to place the child at the heart of education.

School development priorities and efforts are compellingly and clearly focused for the school by Ofsted, who start out data focused and during the inspection are able to decide for schools the main areas they must focus on. However Ofsted can and do also accurately identify and define broader areas for school improvement than just continuously improving Maths and English results. Also it seems that drama is being highlighted increasingly within primary inspections, either for praise where it is found to be good (often as a way of improving speaking and listening and/or writing) or else as an area requiring development where it is found lacking. Inspections of early years settings are quick to ensure there is adequate role-play opportunity in place with skilled interventions by adults but increasingly the use of imaginative approaches to teaching, e.g. through drama, is being promoted within Ofsted reports. There are many schools that have systematically and effectively implemented national strategies but lack spark and imagination in the ways they teach and drama can certainly enliven the learning and teaching in such schools. This will lead to improvement in children's and students' attitudes to learning, resulting in higher levels of pupil engagement, which will raise standards.

PART ONE

'When taught well drama is hugely appealing to children in its own right, before, throughout and beyond the primary years.'

The Independent Review of the Primary Curriculum: Interim report (Reference 1) ∎

The way a school decides to actively respond to and address any Ofsted issues is up to the school. As long as improvement takes place, the ways in which it is achieved are becoming less prescribed. If a school is told it needs to raise standards in English for example, then using drama more often is an approach that is known to engage and motivate children to speak and listen and can provide meaningful contexts for writing with a powerful purpose.

'The recent priority to develop these skills for writing, particularly through the use of drama, is paying dividends, and the school is rightly continuing to emphasize these areas as a key to strengthening writing standards further.'

What the school should do to improve further

'Embed the current good plans to strengthen pupils' speaking and listening skills, and, in particular make use of drama activities to extend communication skills.'

Ofsted Report, Cecil Gowing Infant School (November 2008) (Reference 2) ∎

'It is stretching all abilities. The least able are not really able to sustain writing long enough in one go to either express their imaginations fully nor to practise writing a well-structured story, as they tire too easily. With a structure already worked out through drama it means they have practised this skill in its entirety and can then work on the mechanics of recording it all in a written way or to the level that is appropriate to their ability.'

Year 2 Class teacher, Aldborough Primary School (Reference 3) ∎

If a school is required to make its curriculum more interesting and creative rather than simply following a combination of the strategies and the QCA Programmes of Study, then drama is a way of supporting vivid learning and teaching in and across other subjects.

Through drama, children can actively and flexibly imagine themselves to be anyone, anywhere, at any time in history. They can imagine themselves in another place in this world or beyond it.

'I think it makes you a better thinker and improves your imagination. It can also help you learn. For example, at school we did a Charles Dickens drama session when we pretended we were paying our respects at his funeral. I learned so much more in one session than I could have learned in a week of lessons.'

A pupil's voice (D4LC External Evaluation) (Reference 4) ■

Drama is a curriculum gift! The engagement and learning through drama will be made vivid and memorable through working in role.

'Many lessons are lively and the teachers use a broad range of styles, for example, role-play activities, to promote pupils' interest and involvement. This leads to pupils enjoying learning, as reflected in many of their comments.'

Ofsted Report, Great Hockham C of E Primary School (Reference 5) ■

■ Excellence, enjoyment and Drama

'Drama is one of the key components of our five-year plan. We are aiming for a curriculum that emphasizes creativity, investigation and discovery in order to raise standards and provide a curriculum that truly fosters excellence and enjoyment.'

Deputy Headteacher, Reepham Primary School (Reference 6) ■

Since *Excellence and Enjoyment* (DfES 2003, see reference 7) primary schools now feel increasingly that they have been given permission to 'do different' and now have greater individual freedom and autonomy. Secondary schools are also being encouraged to curriculum plan and teach across subjects more creatively since the new Key Stage 3 curriculum (see reference 8) has been introduced.

The answer to school improvement is often to 'do different' rather than 'do more of the same'. If present approaches are not having sufficient impact then a change of approach is clearly needed. Too often the reasons that schools give for lack of improvement are placed, by the school, at everyone else's door. This can so easily lead to apathy: 'Ofsted got it wrong', 'The local authority made us do it this way', 'These children are not very able', 'This is a poor cohort', 'They aren't getting support from home', 'There are a lot of children with special needs in this cohort', and so on. Even if there is truth in any or all of these justifications the question remains, 'So what are you doing about it?' Every school needs to take ownership and responsibility for improvement and Drama as an approach is worthy of exploration. There is a growing body of evidence from Ofsted and from externally evaluated initiatives such as Drama for Learning and Creativity (D4LC) that drama can improve learning and schools (see www.d4lc.org).

PART ONE

1. Most children clearly enjoy drama.

Schools can effect immense change and improvement but not if they have adopted a blame culture and have halted themselves with a host of reasons they see as conveniently outside their control. The school itself is the main agent of change and improvement on a daily basis and has to take main ownership and responsibility for its own improvement for the benefit of every child.

Even when schools are primarily focusing on raising standards in maths and English, they can nonetheless approach this imaginatively through the use of drama as pedagogy as part of a multi-dimensional, multi-sensory, multi-intelligent approach. Increasingly there are examples of Ofsted applauding creative approaches, as long as they result in evidence of improvement. Some improvement is measurable and quantitative but qualitative improvement is also valuable and valid.

■ Case study

This primary school is a new school in a deprived area of a city. It was created by bringing together three schools (two First schools and one Middle school) that were each very different. Year 7 went to the High School as a result of the restructuring. Two of the three schools had already started focusing on whole class drama approaches to learning and teaching across the curriculum just before merging. The newly appointed headteacher then gave her full support to continuing and further strengthening this approach and the school joined with five other local schools to form a Primary Learning Network that was match funded by the local authority through the Primary Strategy to develop drama for learning and creativity as a key way of improving teaching and learning and thereby raising standards. They decided to measure drama's impact on writing.

The school bought in a specialist drama adviser to help them plan a programme for improvement of writing through drama and arranged whole staff INSET. They enabled the key member of the leadership team to attend a long-term drama course run by the local authority, so that she was better able to lead and support the whole staff to improve their drama teaching. The school bought in a drama for learning specialist to work in classrooms alongside teachers with their own classes. They acquired the services of an Advanced Skills Drama teacher to do drama lessons in partnership with teachers and ensured that all teachers had resources and teacher handbooks in drama that helped them plan lessons. They also bought in a specialist drama adviser to plan a term's drama with teachers from individual year group teams. Two terms later, Ofsted reported as follows:

> 'Across the school drama is used well to stimulate pupils' imagination and to make learning exciting ... New teaching strategies, such as a programme that uses drama to enhance writing skills, have had a positive impact on standards. The good provision on the language development centre, with its emphasis on "speaking, listening and vocabulary, through a drama rich curriculum", helps pupils with specific needs to achieve well ... Imaginative teaching, such as when magic dust is used to transport the class to the woods where the three bears live, encourages enjoyment in learning.'
>
> Ofsted Report, Heartsease Primary School, Norwich (March 2008) (Reference 10)

■ Teacher survey (2004)

A survey carried out among nearly 2,500 teachers in 2007 by the General Teaching Council (see reference 11) provided evidence that teachers believe that pupil achievement is multi-faceted and cannot be stereotyped to mean just doing well in national tests. Only a quarter of teachers surveyed across England considered that good results in national tests counted as 'achievement'. They considered that achievement in relation to pupils becoming lifelong learners and being able to work collaboratively and creatively was more important. These skills once developed have long-lasting benefits. The survey also revealed that 70 per cent of teachers felt that schools over-emphasize national-test-focused achievement.

The percentages of teachers who answered 'reflects completely' or 'quite closely' their view that each aspect counted as achievement

Achievement across the whole curriculum* – 74%
Becoming lifelong learners – 81%
Capacity to be active citizens* – 79%
Capacity to work collaboratively with others* – 84%
Capacity to work creatively* – 84%
Good results in national tests – 27%
Learning to learn – 82%
Progression to the next stage of education or training – 67%

* These aspects of achievement link particularly closely with working in and through drama.

With reference to this survey, drama ticks many of the boxes. Whole class drama requires children to work collaboratively and communally with others and provides opportunity for using and developing children's and teachers' creativity. It is a teaching and learning medium that can support achievement across the whole curriculum.

Through the taking of roles, drama supports, models and enables active citizenship through the children as a community working in role in imagined contexts that draw from and transfer back to 'real life' contexts.

> *'Drama is different from anything else at school because you get to really experience real life things and problems.'*
>
> A pupil's voice (D4LC) (Reference 4) ∎

> *'It (drama) also helps you get confidence and get over your nerves. It also teaches you how to deal with situations in role so if they happen in real life you know how to deal with it.'*
>
> A pupil's voice (D4LC) (Reference 4) ∎

∎ How does drama link to Every Child Matters?

Drama also has much to offer in helping schools achieve the Every Child Matters outcomes. The ECM aims for every child are that they will:

∎ Be healthy

∎ Stay safe

∎ Enjoy and achieve

∎ Make a positive contribution

∎ Achieve economic well-being

Be healthy

Drama enables personal and social issues that are concerning and stressing children to be communicated, explored and possibly resolved in a safe way through the use of role. Used sensitively and professionally, working in role can lead to improvement in individual children's mental health but teachers should not deliberately dabble in psychodrama without specialist training.

Drama usually involves physical movement and some forms of drama and theatre can be made physically very demanding, e.g. physical theatre. Drama therefore contributes to physical health.

Drama can be used specifically to focus on helping children make healthy choices, e.g. healthy eating, not smoking, etc. With older children drama and role-play can be used in sex and drugs education and through role children can practise ways of asserting themselves, not giving in to pressure and learning how to say 'No' in a range of situations.

Stay safe

In drama lessons children are protected and supported by the group and working in role provides a safe emotional distance.

Drama lessons can deal specifically with personal safety, e.g. the prevention of accidents. In an imagined environment children can deal with pretend safety issues that occur in the real world. Drama is often used to approach conflict resolution and/or bullying issues. The learning will be real and can be transferred to real situations once the drama is over.

> *'I use drama to re-enact the types of upset which occur in the playground and to try out strategies to resolve them. This gives children the chance, the skills and confidence to have a go at sorting out problems before they escalate. I have found that they are surprisingly good at working out these strategies.'*
>
> *A teacher action researcher (D4LC) (Reference 4)* ■

Through drama they can try out alternative endings and consider the possible outcomes of different courses of safe/unsafe actions. They may also reveal much of their own real-life experiences and attitudes during the drama process.

2. Children can be very supportive and caring of each other in drama and keep each other safe.

Exemplar

A 7-year-old child who lived in a care home himself in real life, when creating a role for himself in a fictional town stated that his job was to look after the children of the town when the parents of the town were at work. Effectively he had created a day care centre for children for which he was responsible. In the drama he spontaneously challenged a child in role as a mother when she asked if she could leave her child in his care for longer than the working day. He told her that she had to pick up her child at the end of the day and take the child home as she was the child's parent, not him, and the child was her responsibility. The teacher watching the lesson (taken by a visiting drama specialist) was amazed and afterwards wrote:

'Drama has allowed a looked after child to become fully involved, giving him an opportunity to indirectly speak about his experiences through another medium. Instead of being withdrawn and distant, he is now willing to join in and is totally absorbed with the drama. He spoke more in the last drama session than he has ever done in any other lesson. This then gave him the confidence to come back to the classroom and contribute to a "Show and Tell" time, when normally he passes on this activity. He found his voice through drama.'

The class teacher ■

Enjoy and achieve

Children enjoy drama. In a fictitious world they are fairly invincible and are able to confidently achieve highly as a character. This feels good as they rehearse being successful.

'I feel more grown up, clever, by being another person.'

A pupil's voice (D4LC) (Reference 4) ■

The Mantle of the Expert approach (which is rooted in drama) enables children to see themselves as accomplished at achieving tasks that are for an imaginary external client. They are empowered by being respected and being given important tasks to do in role as aspiring 'experts'.

Also there are children who achieve more easily when working in role than they do when more traditional or formal approaches are used (particularly if they have already acquired a sense of failure in other lessons).

'Drama is great. It's my favourite lesson. I think that teachers should do more drama with us and we should learn more things in drama. When I do things in drama I can sort of see them, it's like they are a picture and it comes alive and you actually do it. It's not like reading and writing. They are just loads of words on a page. In drama you can actually do it and you can really understand it.'

9-year-old boy with learning difficulties ∎

Make a positive contribution

Drama relies on everyone positively supporting and contributing to the drama in order to keep the make-believe going and enable it to work. Children's own positive ideas are used and shape the evolving drama. Those who try to mess up a drama when most children want it to work become subject to peer group pressure that encourages positive contributions and whole class co-operation. When positive contributions are made in a drama, there is immediate response from classmates and whole class acceptance and approval raises the self-esteem of the contributor. In drama performance, children soon realize that everyone's positive contribution and full co-operation are crucial for the success of the performance.

'Recently some children were in conflict during a drama session, about how they would portray a group image. The rest of the class were ready to show their sculptures, so we went round looking at these. I left the group with the dispute until the last. When it was their turn, I asked them if they would like to have a go at sorting it out and showing something to everyone else, or, if they could not, then we would move on. They quickly and quietly made an image – without any fuss and without anyone trying to dominate.'

A teacher action researcher (D4LC) (Reference 4) ∎

3. Through drama, children are contributing and sharing their own ideas and taking account of each others'.

'One thing I thought was really good in that drama lesson was Amy, because she was trying really hard and she just wouldn't give up but in other lessons she sort of gives up really easily but in that drama lesson she just kept on trying and trying and she wanted it to work out ... and it did.'

10-year-old girl

Achieve economic well-being

Fictitious worlds can provide a real imperative for dealing with business matters. The Mantle of the Expert approach is an example of this. The children are operating as a successful and motivated workforce with tasks to do for external customers and clients.

The skills that are required by drama and developed through it are closely aligned to those that employers most seek. In drama and in the real world of work children learn to work together towards agreed goals, they co-operate, negotiate, compromise, discuss, explain, communicate ideas, tolerate others and learn to accommodate their ideas; they learn to present with confidence, to problem solve, to think and act creatively. They learn to understand body language, consider situations and ideas from another person's viewpoint, they empathize. They learn to carry out tasks in teams of differing sizes under a time pressure. These are all life skills honed through working in and through drama.

'I then formulated a drama session which would give the children some sense of the fast-paced creativity of the advertising industry. I told each child to get into groups of four or five. Each group was then given one of the following items: a packet of value cornflakes, a tin of value baked beans, value biscuits, value noodles and a bottle of value washing up liquid. The children were also given sticky labels and pens to name the product as they wished. Each group had only two minutes to produce an advert to promote their product. ---------, an observer, would play the part of an advertising executive who would feed back to the groups on the merit of their advert.'

A teacher action researcher (D4LC) (Reference 4)

4. Drama requires and strengthens teamwork, which is a skill valued later by employers.

The creative industries are the fastest growing employment area. By supporting children to operate in the 'what if' world of drama we can value and promote creative thinking and behaviours that will help them in future employment. We might also be helping them towards jobs in the creative industries or help them to create employment for themselves that will contribute towards their future economic well-being.

> 'What I like about drama is that the teacher usually makes it about something that you need to learn about and it's usually about something that has really happened or is probably going to happen in real life, so in drama we learn about things that are going to be useful to us.'
>
> 10-year-old girl

ECM and Drama

The following grid was presented by QCA at a School Improvement Through Drama Conference in 2007.

Table 1 ECM and Drama

Be healthy	Stay safe	Enjoy and achieve	Make a positive contribution	Achieve economic well-being
Exploring my emotions and feelings through imaginary settings.	Challenging others and being challenged myself.	Through imagining and realizing my ideas and intentions.	Appreciating traditions and developing sensitivity to cultural differences.	Communicating and expressing myself effectively and in a range of ways appropriate to needs.
Understanding and interpreting myself and others through role-play.	Understanding how others see me.	Developing a confidence in different unusual situations.	Learning new ways to communicate and share ideas and feelings.	Learning to lead, manage and support.
Developing a sense of identity and self-worth.	Considering the impact of myself on others around me.	Becoming enthusiastic, creative, critical; developing a taste for performance.	Expressing myself imaginatively and creatively; joining a dramatic group.	Developing an awareness of opportunities in the creative and cultural industries.
Being exposed to possible situations, e.g. anorexia, pregnancy.	Knowing what to do in dangerous situations.	Learning to appreciate a wide range of dramatic experiences.	Communicating my thoughts, ideas and feelings.	Seeing possibilities in career paths.

PART ONE

Why schools might make Drama a priority

To understand why drama in schools is so important, we need to consider the roots of drama and its purpose in relation to the holistic development of children as humans and learners. The roots of drama lie in dramatic play, which is a very important universal human activity and one that does not need to be confined to the very young. The ability to pretend starts young but stays with us throughout life and can be kept active through drama.

Before children even come to school they have already voluntarily spent a great deal of time creating imaginary worlds and/or imitating the 'real' world. They have taken on roles alone and sometimes with playmates and siblings and they have probably

5. Through dramatic play, children are practising and developing drama skills, such as taking roles.

experienced playing dramatically with an empathetic parent or carer. They have probably created imaginary playmates and animals, imagined themselves having dangerous adventures as successful super-heroes and pretended they are adults coping admirably in many familiar and less familiar situations. They will have imagined that real objects such as cardboard boxes and sticks are other things, e.g. a car or a gun, a cot or a spoon, etc. They will have created imaginary objects and mimed using them. In short, they have quite naturally used imagined experience as a way of revisiting real experiences in a way they can control and succeed in and will have created imaginary scenarios.

Through dramatic play they are trying out and practising different ways of relating to each other in 'pretend' situations and experiencing what it feels like to act successfully as an adult. Some of these situations will have been observed by them in real life and others may be inspired by the media and/or fiction. If a situation has engaged and aroused them or created a concern for them, then dramatic play enables it to be safely visited and revisited in role and dealt with effectively.

The young child that is developing normally has quite a high level of drama skills before they start school and is already naturally tuned in to the idea that there is value and pleasure in pretending. Early years teachers and teachers of children with special needs are usually quick to acknowledge that the children who cannot imagine and play dramatically also have difficulty learning.

We now bring very young children into the education system earlier and earlier. We have extended school days and give increasing amounts of homework to children. For a multiplicity of reasons, children getting together to play imaginatively and informally to their own agendas and using their own imaginations seems to have diminished. Increasingly children spend time interacting with computers and interactive computer games in often violent and competitive virtual electronic worlds rather than physically and emotionally interacting with each other in the real world and in imagined worlds of their own creation.

In every culture in the world, a child who is developing normally is able to create imagined worlds and play seriously within them. These worlds are often imitations of the real world or worlds they would like to (or need to) exist or practise being in. The brain is able to engage powerfully with and learn memorably through imagined experiences. It is designed to do so! When children are pretending, they are using the neural pathways that support memorable and effective learning. In 'as if' games and in role activities, the same neural pathways are being activated as would be if the situation was real. Also in 'as if' activities such as dramatic play and drama there can be a strong emotional engagement that makes learning memorable, even when children know it is just pretend. As adults, we might have a good cry in a film, even though we know it is a fiction, because good drama awakens and touches us emotionally.

'It (drama) allows you to see a situation through someone else's eyes and from their point of view. It can make you sad or joyful. It can help you discover more about yourself or other people.'

A pupil's voice (D4LC) (Reference 4)

In pretend worlds children are empowered. They usually take the roles of adults they admire or fear and get a sense of what it feels like to be successful and in control. They will play these games together to give them credibility and strength. Joint pretending with friends is highly engaging and enables the children to practise and improve social skills too. If they don't abide by the implicit (and sometimes explicit) rules of pretending then the game will break down and they want their games of make-believe with each other to work.

Young children need to experience the freedom and disciplines of active make-believe, alone and with each other. If schools do not value or enable pretend as entitlement then effectively they deprive children of an approach to learning and life that the brain needs. What starts out as free dramatic play before they come to school may gradually need to shift to a time and place within school when such activity is enabled and encouraged, e.g. role-play time, the drama lesson, etc. What may have been pretending alongside an empathetic parent or carer before starting school might shift to supported play in the role-play area and to active storytelling and whole class drama with a teacher or teaching assistant.

Human beings of all ages will pretend and certainly most primary-aged children do, it is just that it seems to go underground and they stop making it explicit and talking about it when it is not accepted as the norm. But in schools that value and promote drama, you will find older children starting to tell about their current self-initiated imagined worlds, e.g. pretending to live alone without adults, pretending to be doing a job they aspire to, pretending to be a famous pop idol, building dens in woods and pretending to live in them.

It would be easy to say, 'Of course they do this because they enjoy playing but when they come to school they need to settle down to work', but this misses the point. School is a man-made institution but learning is natural, yet we can enable or hamper it. The real skill is to find humanistic ways to enable children to carry on using the imagination and role-play for learning in schools (and other educational settings).

■ Case study

A local authority (Norfolk County Council Children's Services) decided to work in partnership with the leading subject association for drama and theatre educators, National Drama, to develop a sustainable school improvement initiative called D4LC (Drama for Learning and Creativity) (www.d4lc.org). They wanted to work strategically to:

■ enable drama teaching across the curriculum to be improved and developed with specialist support across a significant number of schools simultaneously

■ link drama as active and vivid learning directly to school improvement outcomes

■ help schools to develop a creative curriculum

■ strengthen the local infrastructure, e.g. drama teaching networks.

Headteachers had to apply for their schools to be involved and to give up to six reasons why they wanted to focus on developing drama as pedagogy across their

6. Norfolk teachers meeting with a higher education drama specialist, to evaluate learning and to plan.

schools and explain how it would fit with and help achieve their current or forthcoming school improvement priorities.

- Why did the headteachers want their schools to be involved at this time?

- What were they hoping whole class drama would achieve?

- How did drama for learning and creativity fit into their current or future development priorities?

- How would they know if the initiative was successful?

Headteachers decided to make drama a school priority because ...

School A

- We want to develop creativity in our curriculum and feel that drama plays an essential part in that creative process, across the whole curriculum.

- We believe that drama can hugely improve pupils' engagement with, and response to, the curriculum as well as being a really exciting subject in its own right.

- Drama will be led by me (the headteacher) in our school. I have the experience and seniority to make sure that new ideas will be shared among all staff.

- Our School Improvement and Development Plan identifies writing as an area to develop further; from our own experience to date, drama techniques can lead to more empathic and exciting writing, thus raising standards.

- As a school, we are open to new ideas, having worked collaboratively with partner schools within a Comenius project for the last three years and also a Network Learning Community based on 'Do different' approaches to learning.

PART ONE

■ Drama was identified as an area for development necessary to support an Artsmark application.

School B

■ Drama is underdeveloped at our school – we wish to increase its prominence.

■ We want to enrich our curriculum – to make it more creative and enjoyable.

■ To raise standards in writing, we need to develop greater drama opportunities.

■ We were awarded Artsmark this year and want to develop the arts in school still further and apply for silver and then gold.

School C

■ To use drama as a tool to develop children's self-expression and creativity.

■ To give children a sense of self-worth and support the inclusion of every child.

■ To raise self-esteem in children.

■ To be able to express feelings through a creative approach to learning.

■ To use drama as a tool to enable children to access the curriculum.

■ To raise teachers' confidence and competence.

School D

■ To improve speaking and listening skills that will directly have an impact on our pupils' learning.

■ To enable our less able pupils to access the curriculum in a memorable, enjoyable way, thus raising standards.

■ To enable our non-specialist teachers to grow in confidence so that they can look at the curriculum in more creative ways.

■ To increase the range of teaching styles in our school so that every child can be reached, showing that every child matters.

School E

■ To use drama to raise standards across the curriculum without sacrificing creativity, enthusiasm and fun!

■ Ofsted 2006 identified the need for less able children at our school to have more time to reflect on their answers during lessons. I believe drama will provide excellent opportunities for less able children to reflect on their learning and develop their understanding.

7. Drama enables speaking and listening in role, for many imagined purposes.

■ Ofsted 2006 identified the need for high achieving pupils at our school to have challenging tasks. I believe drama will provide stimulating activities for high achieving pupils and provide them with strategies for independent learning.

■ I would be keen to carry out action research into the impact of drama.

School F

■ We have been working to make our curriculum more cross-curricular. Drama offers the perfect opportunity to work in this way.

■ We want to give our children active learning experiences, really doing things!

■ We want to benefit from skilled drama input to help increase our expertise as teachers.

■ We want to make learning fun for everyone.

■ We have begun working through the Mantle of the Expert and drama supports this work perfectly.

■ Our staff are enthusiastic and keen to try new things.

School G

■ A flexible and creative curriculum is central to the ethos that will drive school standards forward and is a key priority on the School Improvement Plan. As a school that is on a trajectory of improvement, we feel that drama will support and invigorate that process.

■ We have been an Intensive Support Programme school and have identified writing as a priority for school improvement. We believe that drama has the potential to enrich writing skills.

■ Staff have a great deal of enthusiasm for drama. They have an open mind and a desire to find new ways to improve their skills.

■ As a school, we have identified the importance of bringing in outside expertise to raise standards. The opportunity to work with drama specialists is an exciting one that the school is keen to embrace.

School H (in Ofsted 'special measures' category)

■ I want to make sure that the children (in addition to achieving as well as possible) also ENJOY learning. Even though we have moved ahead well with our curriculum and making learning more fun, drama is not yet something that is used effectively to support learning. This is due to lack of confidence and understanding among the staff (and myself).

■ We are currently reorganizing our whole school curriculum, taking a much more integrated and creative approach – making strong planned links between subjects – making learning relevant – drama will fit into this approach well.

■ We are a 'Forest School'. My early years teacher works on Outdoor Learning projects. I think the integration of drama into the projects we already do would support our philosophy of learning through practical, real and relevant experiences.

■ Drama is a natural extension to the 'practical' approach we take to learning – using 'imagined' experiences and stimulating pupils' imagination is something we would like to develop.

■ Our writing standards were identified as being low and with a trend of downward decline. This year we have had an enormous emphasis on improving writing standards through outdoor learning and our integrated curriculum. Incorporating drama would build upon the good practice already in place.

■ Finally, because I feel sure that the staff and children would find drama fun and we want to make learning 'irresistible'.

School I (a Junior school)

- We have already made a commitment to enhance and enrich the curriculum, focusing on making learning fun. This forms part of the SIDP. We are moving towards more theme-based learning. All of the staff are keen to use drama to aid teaching across the curriculum. Hall space has been timetabled in for drama lessons from September.

- Before redesigning the curriculum for September because we have become a Junior instead of Middle school, all Subject Leaders carried out an audit of Teaching and Learning in their subject. Questionnaires and interviews with the children showed how much they enjoyed drama and how they felt it was a very successful vehicle for learning. Staff are keen to develop this enthusiasm through greater expertise, gained through CPD. Some staff have already attended drama INSET this year and some have identified this area to develop and consequently have this identified as a Performance Management Target.

- The School has a high level of special needs (Learning Support Centre and almost 10 per cent of the whole school hold a Statement of SEN). Staff believe that drama provides a means for all children to access the curriculum and we are proud of our inclusive ethos, which was commented on in our recent Ofsted Inspection. Drama fits in well with our aim to include Visual, Auditory and Kinaesthetic (VAK) provision in every learning opportunity.

- The use of drama also fits in well with the SIDP target of improving writing.

- We are part of a Primary Strategy Learning Network developing the quality of children's dialogue and drama approaches will contribute towards this.

8. Drama can inspire writing and give it a meaningful context.

School J

- Our current Y5 cohort has a significant number of pupils (some with special educational needs) who, despite various school-organized intervention programmes and teaching assistant support, still have very low speaking, listening, reading and writing attainment. Teaching through drama may provide the 'key' to raising this attainment.

- There are a significant number of pupils, across the school but especially in the present Y5, with difficult behaviour issues linked to low self-esteem. Drama is an area that teachers are less confident about so it does not feature prominently in the curriculum yet. We want to enable all pupils, regardless of ability, to begin from a 'level playing field'. We anticipate that drama will support those pupils with low self-esteem, giving them the confidence to 'have a go' in much the same way as we have found introducing a modern foreign language has done. Raising self-esteem and confidence, in this way, we believe will have a positive effect on the behaviour of these pupils and improved behaviour should lead to an improvement in attainment for this cohort.

School K

- We are designing an innovative, mixed-age, cross-curricular curriculum for September with enquiry at its heart. Drama would enhance and contribute to this innovation.

- Literacy remains a key priority for the school and drama is at present underdeveloped as a tool for raising standards.

- We are embracing the SEAL curriculum across the school and drama contributes to helping children listen to others, to speak with confidence and empathize with others.

- The school vision and ethos is one that promotes the importance of self-esteem, self-confidence and giving children a voice and a forum to use it. Drama facilitates this.

- We want drama to become an integral part of teachers' delivery and children's experience rather than a special event.

- Governors are keen to assess the effectiveness of role-play/drama in the teaching of foundation subjects. They want evidence that it is as effective as traditional approaches.

School L (in Ofsted 'special measures' category)

- We are currently reviewing the curriculum to provide the children with a far more stimulating curriculum. Drama as an approach would be an excellent support to this.

- Attainment in speaking and listening is below national averages and drama could provide a valuable tool for developing children's speaking and listening skills.

- Many of the children need to learn through doing and drama would enable a much more dynamic approach to traditional subjects.

- The children generally have poor self-esteem probably due to them perceiving themselves as failures because test results do not meet national expectations. Drama would be an opportunity for the children to succeed and to demonstrate that they are able to articulate their ideas, be original thinkers and solve problems – without having to write their answers!

- Staff are aware that the school needs to move forward and that current practices are not necessarily meeting the needs of the children. Developing drama approaches may give us a much needed morale boost.

School M (a Special school)

- Drama is an excellent way of increasing engagement and communication skills in those with severe and complex learning difficulties.

- The school is preparing a bid to achieve Specialist Special School status for Communication and Interaction, and we would use the teaching of drama across the curriculum as a means of increasing communication and interaction.

- The school has an increasing role in supporting the needs of pupils in mainstream school, and drama is a key aspect to include in all children's learning.

9. Children with learning difficulties and disabilities often find drama accessible and exciting.

When 150 schools' aspirations for school improvement through drama were gathered, analysed and categorized, it emerged that drama was seen as a way of improving the following:

Standards

'We are very keen to extend our use of drama across the curriculum as we have found that using it has a direct impact on raising standards.'

Deputy headteacher, Reepham Primary School

'This group of children are working in pre-level 1, from P level 3 to 8. In the drama lesson they were able to work to higher levels in speaking and listening and PSHCE.'

Year 5/6 teacher, Hall Special School

PART ONE

Drama gets children interested in a fiction they co-own and start to care about. While the children's interest lies primarily with the drama itself, the teacher's interest may lie also with using it as a context for learning. The teacher can make sure that the drama requires the children to use and develop their real skills, knowledge and understanding, albeit within a fictitious context. The children are motivated to succeed in order to meet the needs of the drama but in the process of grappling for the sake of the drama, they are at the same time rehearsing and improving a range of competencies that can be linked directly to desirable and often measurable learning outcomes. Drama is very flexible and lends itself to being fashioned towards certain outcomes directly linked to standards. For example, a teacher wanting to help her children improve their ability to subtract, pretended to be a princess who was unable to remember how to do it. Her father the king was getting impatient with her and the children in role helped the princess to find different ways of remembering and approaching subtraction. She was very grateful of course and during the lesson the children were improving their own ability to subtract through explaining methods and approaches to her. The teacher assessed their success in subtracting before the lesson, at the end of it and a month later and found significant improvement in attainment after the lesson.

Achievement

> 'The children who are reception and Year 1 could take on quite sophisticated drama strategies, which surprised me.'
>
> *Infant teacher, Snettisham*

> 'The students (particularly the boys) improved dramatically during this drama unit of work. Some raised their National Curriculum levels from Level 3 to 6 and all students made good progress.'
>
> *Year 9 High School Drama teacher*

Drama in school should be a reasonably regular experience for all children. A one-off experience may have a significant and immediate impact but regular and sustained engagement with learning through drama supports continuity and progression in learning. If children become familiar with drama and better at it then what can be achieved through it will become greater.

> '... on this occasion I was amazed to see that the children had created their own small world out of shells and building blocks, what they had in fact created was their own island. What was more surprising was the fact that the boy/girl divide that was so clearly evident at the beginning of the year had totally disappeared and they were working together collaboratively and harmoniously.'
>
> *A teacher action researcher (D4LC) (Reference 4)*

Drama can reveal a great deal to teachers about what children can do, know and understand through observing and interacting with them in a broad range of imagined contexts. Drama lessons can be a rich evidence base that has much to contribute to formative assessment for learning.

Learning and teaching

> *'I can see that the children love drama and can learn from it.'*
>
> **Year 1/2 teacher, Blenheim Park Community Primary**

> *'Since I have begun teaching through drama, the children are enthusing about lessons instead of forgetting them!'*
>
> **Village Infant School teacher**

> *'Wow! That really worked well. I must try to stretch them like this some more.'*
>
> **Costessey High School, Year 8 teacher with higher ability students**

> *'The multi-sensory nature of the drama lesson means it has high impact and high impact equals learning.'*
>
> **KS3 Special School teacher**

> *'We believe that VAK learning styles can be greatly enhanced through the use of drama strategies across the KS3 curriculum, which relates to the aims of our School Improvement and Development Plan.'*
>
> **Drama teacher, Thorpe St Andrew High School**

Drama teachers have many skills and approaches that will be of benefit to all teachers in any subject or phase. Drama teaching is interactive and collaborative and alters the traditional role and function of the teacher in lessons. The teacher becomes a co-participant in the learning, a mediator of the drama experience. The teacher supports the children's learning by offering an enabling structure that helps participants to construct meanings and express their own thinking and ideas, aesthetically and collaboratively. In drama, children's own thinking and creativity is stimulated and kindled and the teacher may fan the flames. The children have shared ownership of the drama and its direction. The teacher is alert to what learning is required and aimed for and as a co-participant can steer it from within the fiction but should not move it away from the interests of the children. The skill is to maintain a shared learning and teaching agenda, where the drama travels the path the learners want it to and at the same time achieves the learning the teacher wants for them and the children want for themselves.

PART ONE

*'I placed three chairs at the front of the class and asked for
volunteers to play the elderly people. The three children
who volunteered first sat in the chairs and giggled. I realized
that this drama session was not going to work without my
intervention so I motioned to a boy, sat near the front of the
class, to put an extra chair next to the elderly trio. I then
picked up a plastic counting stick (to be used as a walking
stick) and began to shuffle painfully towards the front of the
class. I stopped briefly to rest, breathing heavily. The children
began to giggle but I drew out my laboured approach and the
children became silent. When I reached the front of the class I
asked, using a rasping voice, if I could sit down. I then sat for
several moments, my hands uncontrollably quivering before
quietly relating a fictional tale of meeting David Beckham
when I was a small child. I then asked one of the 'elderly'
ladies if they remembered David Beckham. What followed
was a wonderful, almost genuine reflective conversation
between four elderly people about David Beckham.*

*Afterwards it dawned on me that my role as an elderly man
inspired the children to believe in what they were attempting
to perform. My sudden arrival sanctioned and legitimized
their total immersion into the role of another character and
identity. Even the children observing the role-play were able
to engage with and suspend their disbelief. I believe that this
was an important moment in my professional development.
Through dramatic role-play, I can inspire!'*

A teacher action researcher (D4LC) (Reference 4)

Teachers now have more freedom to teach in innovative ways as long as they are
effective. The problem is that for so many years now teachers have been given
prescriptive lesson plans and have had little opportunity to be innovative. Being
innovative does not entail exchanging one set of lesson plans for another that seem
freer but this could be one step on the teacher's own professional development path.
It is rather as if the teachers' cage door is open but many teachers feel safer staying
inside the cage or maybe cannot yet see that the door is ajar. The headteacher may
now be seen as holding the key and can open or close that door for the teachers.
Maybe it is just that some teachers need to be enticed or accompanied out of the cage
a few times to find new paths and views.

In recent years there has been a great deal of research and discussion into different
teaching and learning styles. There is a general acceptance that some approaches
may benefit particular groups of children, e.g. approaches to writing that favour girls
who tend to be more linguistically developed and are more able to sit and listen for
long periods (and tend to be more compliant when bored). The National Literacy
and Numeracy Strategies at one time had a clock that divided the lesson firmly
into sections and prescribed 'top down' activities, regardless of what the children's
preferred learning styles were or the length and quality of their responses. However,
the shift now is to look at the learning rather than the teaching and approaches are
becoming more active, interactive and personalized. Drama fits well with this and

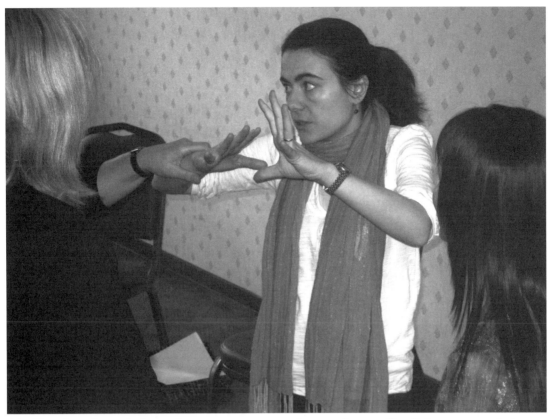

10. Teacher in role is an important, engaging and very flexible approach to learning and teaching

its prominence as a pedagogy in literacy is more evident now. Drama helps integrate the aspects of literacy, i.e. reading, writing, speaking and listening.

> *'There seemed to be a seamless run from need, to thought, to speaking, to writing and then back to reading in role. All children were clear about what they had written, including four children who have been working on IEPs to support their writing, and the three children in the focus group.'*
>
> *A teacher action researcher (D4LC) (Reference 4)* ■

Children learn in a range of ways and have different preferred learning styles. If teachers teach repeatedly in the same predictable ways they consistently advantage the same types of learner and conversely disadvantage others. Children who find learning difficult to access consistently will give up and become disengaged. Drama can be a method enabling re-engagement.

At the simplest level we hear reference to children being categorized as learners who prefer and need visual, auditory, kinaesthetic or tactile (VAKT) approaches in order to access learning. Drama is visual, auditory, kinaesthetic and tactile, so if the VAKT approaches are being considered, then drama has an important place as it enables access to all types of learner.

> *'It (drama) is also different because it's not like any other subject because in most subjects you have to write and sit down but in drama it's more exciting.'*
>
> *A pupil voice (D4LC) (Reference 4)* ■

PART ONE

*'It helps my learning because you get to use your body more
– it makes me concentrate.'*

A pupil voice (D4LC) (Reference 4)

Howard Gardner, an American psychologist, has also influenced the way that teachers look at approaches to learning. Gardner postulated the Theory of Multi-intelligences in his book, *Frames of Mind* (Gardner 1983, see reference 12). He believes that everyone has a range of intelligences.

Gardner originally suggested seven intelligences:

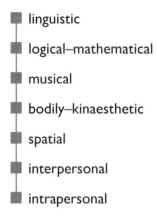

- linguistic
- logical–mathematical
- musical
- bodily–kinaesthetic
- spatial
- interpersonal
- intrapersonal

Later additional intelligences Gardner suggested were:

- naturalist
- spiritual
- existential
- moral

Whether or not one subscribes to Gardner's theory, it is nonetheless an interesting theory to consider in relation to drama (Baldwin 2004, see reference 13). Drama can holistically be seen to utilize, contribute to and help develop all these intelligences. It uses verbal and non-verbal communication, gesture, stillness, movement, music and sound. It involves children knowing themselves and working knowingly and sensitively with each other. It uses space and logically and intuitively ascribes meaning to space. It can evoke feelings of spirituality and is a forum for exploring and practising morality and for developing moral understanding. Drama's focus can be on anything at all and easily on naturalistic issues, e.g. environmental sustainability.

Inclusion

*'A child with English as an Additional Language drew me a
picture of the Fire of London during free choice, a fortnight
after a series of drama lessons on it.'*

Year 2 teacher

'I have one EAL child who at the beginning of the year was very quiet and passive but now is confidently joining in with all drama lessons and wants to play a major part.'

Year 1 teacher, Drake Infant and Nursery School

'Drama was a new way for me to work and it has enabled the whole class to access the lessons in a completely inclusive ethos and helped to develop sensitivity towards the feelings of each other through interaction.'

Year 5/6/7 teacher, Hall Special School

'A statemented student really went to work in role play, watching episodes of The Bill and other documentaries to get into character.'

Year 9 High School drama teacher

'I am doing an MA in Applied Theatre and carrying out research on inclusion. I am finding that using drama strategies helps some students access their learning more effectively.'

Subject Leader for Drama, Methwold High School

'We wish to continue to develop creative teaching and learning approaches for our Gifted and Talented students and drama is an important part of this.'

Drama teacher, Thorpe St Andrew High School

Whole class drama needs to be an inclusive activity. For a whole class drama to work well, it requires everyone to take part (including the teacher). If a child or adult excludes themselves and just sits out and watches as a non-participant, then the dynamics change. Also, with a whole class drama happening, the person watching but not participating could appear more obviously excluded than in many other types of lesson. There may be times when the teacher shifts from being a participant to an observer for a while in order to reflect on what teacher-move to make next, but unless there is a drama-specific reason for a child not to be actively participating at any point in a whole class drama lesson, then all children should be.

Most children want the whole class drama to work and are likely to feel the difference when everyone is involved. In devising and presenting performance work particularly, it is imperative that everyone is included at their own comfort level, in order to succeed at the task.

PART ONE

'...a reluctant participator and talker is fully engaged in what is going on, is giving his ideas to the group and is listening and taking on board ideas and thoughts from the rest of the group...'

A teacher action researcher (D4LC) (Reference 4)

'...the specific child came out of her shell and with support from her peers was able to contribute ideas in a small group. One element of story-land that she created was a magic castle, which could move away if anyone came near it. This and other quotes from this child were used in her Foundation Stage Profile as evidence of her speaking and listening.'

A teacher action researcher (D4LC) (Reference 4)

The key is to ensure that all children feel safe and protected enough in drama lessons to include themselves willingly. If not, then they need to 'contract in' on the understanding that they will not be personally placed 'on the spot' and that they will stay present in the drama, with opportunity to contribute, but will not be forced to contribute.

Being physically present is more likely to lead to involvement than just sitting out and watching (which would reinforce exclusion). Reluctant children are likely to gradually get drawn in emotionally and actively if they stay physically present in the drama and are not put under pressure.

11. Whole class drama encourages and supports inclusion, with everyone actively and supportively involved.

Communication

> 'Children who cannot communicate verbally were actively involved in the drama lesson with minimum adult intervention. Our drama work has helped the children to communicate ideas and feelings through language, expression and movement.'
>
> Teacher, Hall Special School ■

Drama is a vibrant and live form, integrating both verbal and non-verbal communication. It involves live action and interaction and makes and communicates meaning through the use of word, movement, sound, space, lighting, focus, tension, symbol, etc. In drama, children become engaged and stimulated and soon come up with ideas and understandings that they want to express and communicate clearly to themselves and to others through drama and a range of flexible theatre forms. In drama, we make sure we communicate clearly, with the intention of having a cognitive and emotional impact on others. In the process of making drama, we find that we become clearer about what is important to communicate and why, and thereby become clearer ourselves.

> 'The Monday morning that we were due to start this module dawned with a marvellous hard, sharp frost that lasted most of the morning. Some tweaking of plans completed, we dashed out into the playground and took in this frosted experience. When we were all blue to the tips of our noses we returned to start thinking about the poems that we would write.
>
> Prior to D4LC I would have taken a list of the children's descriptive words, compiled them onto the SMART board and begun to compose some of them into a piece of shared writing from which the children could develop their writing. This time, we started to think about what we had seen and the children worked in groups to create tableaux to show others what they had particularly noticed about the frost and its effect on the landscape.
>
> I was amazed that although we were no longer working on our 'Alice in Wonderland' work, the children brought some of their experiences from this to their new work. They are kinaesthetic learners and they appear to find using their bodies to translate their learning so valuable. They also demonstrate that their aspects of learning are continually overlapping.
>
> ... the collaborative work that then followed was a true example of the way that drama provides many different aspects of learning. The children translated things that they had seen into freeze frames, using physical theatre and adding sound effects.'
>
> A teacher action researcher (D4LC) (Reference 4) ■

PART ONE

In drama lessons we present our work to each other (a knowing audience of fellow co-participants), who have insider understandings and can evaluate and challenge how effectively they have been communicated with as a knowing audience involved in creating parts of the same drama. We also in drama may communicate to an external audience that has no prior knowledge of or involvement in the drama, and this has other challenges.

Engagement (pupil and teacher)

> *'That drama lesson was the best lesson I have seen in the last five years. Every child was engaged.'*
>
> **PGCE tutor and an ex-Primary headteacher**

> *'I want to excite and engage children to develop their confidence and the quality of their talk.'*
>
> **Year I teacher**

> *'It was a fun morning. I found it easier than expected to move the children on with the drama. Most children remained focused and in role. It was difficult to get them out to play at break time as they were so keen to carry on with what would happen next.'*
>
> **Year 1/2 teacher, Blenheim Park Community School**

> *'We found much higher levels of engagement for those that are easily distracted. A 15-minute observation by a teaching assistant of our two most easily distracted pupils compared their engagement in the history lesson and then the drama lesson on the same history topic. They were looking, listening, participating twice as much in the drama lesson.'*
>
> **KS3 Special School teacher**

Good drama grabs children's interest and if they can see that what they think and say is making a difference to the way it develops, their interest will be maintained. Children are predisposed to be cognitively and emotionally engaged by stories (all drama is story) and can enter into 'storydrama' through dramatic play, and later drama.

It may involve re-enactment (which is engaging) but drama teachers will move drama well beyond straight re-enactment and support deeper engagement (through working in role and using drama forms). Teachers help keep a focus on what is of underlying human importance and relevance. Moments of significance can be held still in drama (e.g. using 'freeze frame') for deeper and shared consideration and exploration. Deeper levels of engagement and understanding can result.

'Freeze frames also help me learn. When we see the other groups' freeze frames I can see how that character says things and hear other people's views.'

A pupil voice (D4LC) (Reference 4) ■

There will probably be differing levels of activity displayed by each child, which may or may not represent differing levels of engagement. Some children are more confident, extrovert and forthcoming, whereas others may be highly engaged but saying or doing less. In drama less action can ironically sometimes mean more engagement. Sometimes it is weeks later when a child's comment, picture or writing reveals just how deep was engagement during the drama lesson.

Whole class drama actively involves the teacher (hopefully often in role) alongside the children. Children find teachers working in role with them fascinating and uniquely engaging. For teachers also, it is unique as an approach and relies on continuing high levels of teacher engagement for the drama to work well.

'One drama technique I have found that works particularly well is teacher in role as either an unpleasant character or someone who is about to do something foolish. Children have a strong, innate sense of justice and will become incensed at the idea of unfair behaviour. They will do all they can to convince the person that they must change their ways, thus developing good powers of persuasion and reasoning. Some can be very convincing.'

A teacher action researcher (D4LC) (Reference 4) ■

Good drama teachers are constantly involved as either participants or alert observers with a learning and drama purpose. Good drama teaching involves some risk taking and much thinking on the spot and changing course according to what the children offer. High levels of engagement of both teachers and children and between teachers and children are key to making highly effective drama and memorable learning.

Staff morale

'Getting better at teaching drama has given me the confidence to 'have a go' and rekindled my excitement in teaching.'

Year 2 teacher who has been teaching for 25 years ■

'It's like being taught to teach all over again. I am flying by the seat of my pants and loving every minute of it. I had no idea that drama would make teaching such fun again!'

Primary Advanced Skills Early Years teacher ■

Most teachers have become very proficient at repeatedly delivering the same lessons around the national strategy frameworks (their own or else those nationally offered online). When seeing the same lesson plan delivered in several schools it is interesting that some teachers teach the same prescribed lesson well and others follow their plans slavishly and often unenthusiastically with a poor result. Some teachers, however, make the lesson their own, adapting it to the children's needs, tuning in to the children's responses with an eye on what learning they are aiming for but not closed to other learning opportunities that arise. Some teachers prefer the security of delivering a lesson they haven't written and can abdicate some responsibility for. Some teachers think it is just easier for them not to have to plan it. Some teachers hate having to deliver a lesson that they have not created or at least adapted. From teacher to teacher and from school to school it varies, but one thing is certain – some teachers are happy in their work and others are not. However the reasons for this are complex and won't all relate to school and the job. But for many teachers, having professional responsibility and ownership of their lessons is important to them and has a positive impact, increasing their sense of personal and professional worth and well-being. Being a teacher is not about delivery and only measurable outcomes. It is about knowingly influencing and supporting the development and learning of impressionable young humans as learners and people and this is an awe-inspiring and important task.

In recent years many teachers have felt undervalued and deskilled when so much has become centrally prescribed but there is a sense that schools and teachers are being encouraged to take more ownership again of the curriculum and ways in which they teach it (as long as they can prove impact and achieve at least satisfactory outcomes). Taking ownership of what you teach and the way you teach it is often good for morale. Teachers become demoralized when they feel that they are just having to respond to or follow directives and are not considered capable or trusted to devise their own lessons. In contrast, they feel exhilarated and inspired when they can create and achieve for themselves and will have a greater sense of personal and professional pride when it goes well. Children enjoy drama and when it is successful the teacher will get a great buzz and positive feedback from the children.

Thinking skills

'The children were putting forward their own ideas about how to help the character and determining how the untold part of the story would unfold.'

Teacher, Hall Special School ■

'As a whole staff we are keen to support work in drama as this fits closely with our work in developing thinking skills and philosophy as a way to promote cross-curricular learning.'

Headteacher, Falcon Middle School ■

'Their concentration in that lesson was amazing. They just didn't give up. They were thinking so hard about what to do with the man and the different ideas and reasoning they were coming up with showed real depth of thought.'

Year 6 teacher ■

'In drama you do have to think really hard sometimes because it's up to us what happens and we really want it to be alright.'

Year 4 girl ■

'We are hoping to extend using role-play and other drama strategies to develop children's thinking and learning, as good practice across the school.'

Arts Director, Sprowston High School,
Specialist Performing Arts College ■

Drama involves using and developing different types of thinking, including creative and critical thinking. It also involves individual thinking and thinking together (inter-thinking). It involves slow thinking and quick thinking. It involves using the body and voice as well as the mind to think. It allows distancing through role that can be calming, enabling, therapeutic and support reflective thinking.

'It (drama) helps you by making you think really hard. You have to think hard because in role-plays you have to think what your character is feeling and what their emotions are like.

You can let your mind go and clear your head full of worries, you can think better when you're relaxed and I think that's what drama does to you.

Drama for me is mentally calming.

Letting us get up and act and maybe show other people, could release stress so you would have less things on your mind, so you can think straight.

Drama can extend your imagination, allowing you to think within seconds.

Drama helps me think of good things to put in my writing and good words.'

Pupils' voices (D4LC) (Reference 4) ■

Drama has a set of conventions and strategies see pages 124–140 that can be seen as combinations of visual, auditory, kinaesthetic and tactile thinking frames. Different drama strategies and conventions can be seen as organizers and scaffolding for thinking. Some of these strategies' names imply types of thought, e.g. 'Conscience Alley' and 'Thought-tracking'. Some hold moments still so that everyone can speak their personal thoughts or collectively 'inter-think' in role, e.g. Collective Role.

The characteristics of high level thinking (as defined by Resnick) fit closely with those of high quality drama (Baldwin 2004, see reference 13). When teachers begin

PART ONE

12. High quality drama can support and develop high quality thinking.

to understand how the various drama strategies, conventions and forms work singly and together and how they can link directly to requiring, supporting and developing different types of thinking, this is likely to positively influence the teachers' decisions about which types and combinations of drama strategies and conventions to use and when.

Some schools have started to use Mantle of the Expert as an approach to the curriculum. Many drama specialists see Mantle of the Expert as a drama strategy. It uses role and engages the children 'as if' they are experts in some field, e.g. advertisers, film-makers, archaeologists, museum curators, etc. The children work on tasks that need to be achieved, with the mindset of an expert and become involved and immersed in enquiry in order to find out necessary information and develop the necessary skills to complete the task. They are treated by the adults as experts and the children treat and respect each other as experts. They start to believe in themselves and each other as experts and begin to use the language and style associated with their expertise.

Imagining yourself as successful (rehearsing success) and thereby increasing the chances of actually being successful is a well-known technique in the competitive sports world, i.e. 'Imagine yourself winning', or before interviews, 'Imagine the job is already yours'. Drama lets self-belief build up in imagined worlds that enable us to think of ourselves differently, as a first step to maybe becoming different. In drama we put ourselves in someone else's shoes, empathize through working in role and can think ourselves into different roles, times and places.

Creativity

> *'I had to be ready to change and adapt the lesson*
> *throughout as the children came up with answers that were*
> *unexpected and not obvious.'*
>
> **Year 9 drama teacher, Attleborough High School** ■

The definition of creativity that was presented in the report *All Our Futures: Creativity, Culture and Education* (NACCCE 1999, see reference 9) is:

> Imaginative activity, fashioned so as to produce outcomes that are original and of value.

Drama fits with this, exactly. Drama *itself* is imaginative activity that is fashioned so as to produce outcomes that are original and of value. The children in a whole class drama work together to create original, imagined worlds within which learning of value can happen. They imagine and pretend that they are someone else, somewhere else, with something happening that is not really happening but can seem and feel as if it is. They support each other to keep imagining and creating the fiction. They respond imaginatively and creatively, sharing ideas through improvization and they devise original performance.

> *'At the start of every drama lesson before anyone is in*
> *role I talk to the children about imagination and reassure*
> *them that drama is pretend. I believe that it is because the*
> *children feel secure using their imaginations together that so*
> *many of the drama lessons have been as successful as they*
> *have. This security has enabled the children to speak freely*
> *in safety and comfort that what they are going to say is not*
> *going to be wrong because anything is possible when you use*
> *your imagination.'*
>
> **A teacher action researcher (D4LC) (Reference 4)** ■

Drama always involves imaginative activity. The imaginative activity in drama involves and makes explicit the creative process. There are times when drama involves a free-flow of ideas and times when these have to be selected from, mulled over and maybe repeatedly changed, synthesized, adapted and also given focus and form. In focusing, and giving ideas drama form, the process leads to an outcome or product. As drama happens in the moment the outcome is always to some extent original. Even if you repeat a piece of performance or re-play what was just created, or enact a script, it will not ever be the same twice.

All Our Futures (reference 9) recognizes and promotes a democratic view of creativity. It suggests that being creative is a human ability that all people have (assuming normal development). There will be some people that demonstrate high levels of creativity and produce unique, highly original outcomes, for example, Eddison inventing the light bulb, Shakespeare's plays, but most people are capable of creating.

PART ONE

The definition of creativity in *All Our Futures* states that the outcome needs to be 'original and *of value*'. Shakespeare's plays and Eddison's light bulb are of course highly original outcomes and have value to all mankind but this does not diminish what children can achieve creatively in whole class drama lessons that may have high personal value. They come up with ideas and ways of presenting their ideas in and through drama that are compellingly original to them and of value to themselves at the very least. The outcomes also are of value to the teacher. Whole class drama gives moments of significant insight about children to teachers.

> *'When the children were required to perform the adapted script for an Easter play, they asked if their parents could have a go at joining us with the Conscience Alley. They showed a great deal of pride in their achievements and with having another go, thought of different arguments if they were on a different side to before.'*
>
> *A teacher action researcher (D4LC) (Reference 4)* ∎

Curriculum

> *'I have been given "permission" to spend an hour a week on drama so now other curriculum leaders can't argue that their subject is more important.'*
>
> *Year I teacher* ∎

> *'I want to use and see drama as an essential part of the curriculum.'*
>
> *Year R1/2 teacher, William Marshall Primary School* ∎

> *'We have been given the "green light" to extend the use of drama across the curriculum.'*
>
> *Special School teacher with Excellent Teacher Status* ∎

> *'We are now looking for drama ways of delivering different curriculum objectives.'*
>
> *Primary School teacher* ∎

Drama has to have content and a focus. It can be used flexibly to teach any subject and can also be used as a method and pedagogy for linking or integrating any subjects. When children play dramatically before coming to school they know nothing of subjects or areas of learning. The dramatic play flows where their interest lies and is usually child led. It is possible to design a curriculum to support the continuation of this child-led approach or to organize it in other ways, e.g. skills led, content led, assessment led. There is no one and only way to 'correctly' organize a curriculum and the Primary Curriculum has been reviewed and redesigned to enable schools to design the organization and detail of their own curriculum more, using a slimmed-down National Curriculum with less subject content laid down (see Chapter 4). This should enable schools to more easily take ownership of and develop a curriculum that best fits their own children, school and local contexts.

Curriculum models

Subject based: *England, Norway, Slovenia*
This approach sets out the curriculum in subject disciplines. The subjects are not a finite list and the weighting that different subjects already have could be changed. Subjects could be added to or lost.

Areas of learning based: *Northern Ireland, International Baccalaureate*
This approach brings together subjects in ways that link them by the type of thinking and learning the subjects involve. This means that subjects could have elements that would appear within more than just one area.

Skills based: *RSA, Enquiring Minds, Opening Minds*
This way of designing the curriculum focuses on creating programmes of study that are skills based and contexts are offered for developing and progressing in the various skills and their application.

Theme based:
A range of subject content and skills are brought together thematically with each having an identified focus on specific skills.

Whichever way a curriculum is organized, drama should have a place, maybe as a subject in its own right (in a subject-based curriculum), and/or as a way of developing important skills (e.g. functional skills, key skills, communication skills, life skills). As part of a theme based curriculum it is likely to be used as a pedagogical approach.

There is an increased curriculum emphasis emerging on outdoor play (e.g. Forest Schools, the Outdoor Classroom, etc.), on creative learning (e.g. Creative Partnerships), modern languages and social and emotional aspects of learning (SEAL), etc. Drama can be woven through all these as an approach and provide a meaningful and engaging context. Drama outdoors is a natural extension of dramatic play outdoors, modern foreign languages can be taught effectively through working in role and providing imagined contexts, scenarios and reasons to speak in another language. The links with SEAL and drama are also very strong and this is reflected in the materials for SEAL. Drama encourages empathy through working in role, as well as through reflection. Drama has always been a medium for developing the social and emotional aspects of learning. Another common aspect of the school curriculum nowadays is 'Circle Time'. Again, this has direct links with drama, as it was started by Jacob Moreno, the founder of socio-drama and psychodrama. He used it in industry and Jenny Mosely, a drama specialist, took the model and adapted it for schools.

No curriculum should ever be seen as complete and finished, as it needs to be flexible and constantly evolving and adaptable so that it does not become rapidly outdated. There is a more detailed consideration of drama and the National Curriculum in Chapter 4 (see pages 70 to 95).

PART ONE

Speaking and listening

> *'Speaking and listening is one of our priorities (particularly with the youngest children) as the children arrive with a limited vocabulary and role-play and drama is a way forward to developing language acquisition.'*
>
> Headteacher, St Peter and St Paul C of E Voluntary Controlled School, Carbrooke ∎

> *'I was surprised at some of the very strong and mature answers during discussion.'*
>
> Year 9 drama teacher, Attleborough High School ∎

Many teachers use drama specifically and very successfully to raise standards in speaking and listening. In drama children can pretend to be anyone, anywhere, in any situation, with an imagined compelling, dramatic reason, to speak and listen in role.

> *'Using a range of different expressions and language and with her ability to ad-lib she has surprised herself and us! She is much happier and this new-found confidence is having a positive effect on her involvement in other lessons.'*
>
> A teacher action researcher (D4LC) (Reference 4) ∎

Drama can conjure up any imagined speaker or audience and provide many different types of speech for different purposes and audiences, e.g. a parent explaining to a child why they need to be evacuated (Unit 3, World War 2 (Evacuees)), or a bystander reporting when a child is being bullied (Unit 5, The Bystander).

Within a drama there can be situations that require the children to consider their listening audience and to adjust the style and content of their speech accordingly. They may be motivated to adjust their speech so as to appear convincing in role, or maybe to influence, manipulate, instruct, explain to, or inform, their audience. In drama we are stimulating children to speak in role as fictitious characters to other fictitious characters but of course the skills they will call upon and develop in doing this are very much their own and the drama provides a safe forum to practise using and responding to different types of speech.

> *'...a reluctant participator and talker is fully engaged in what is going on, is giving his ideas to the group and is listening and taking on board ideas and thoughts from the rest of the group.'*
>
> A teacher action researcher (D4LC) (Reference 4) ∎

13. Drama lessons provide many opportunities for purposeful speaking and active listening.

If the teacher knows that the children need to experience or practise specific types of speech, then characters and situations can be introduced to give opportunity and support for this. In role alongside children teachers themselves can model ways of speaking in different contexts to different audiences.

The National Primary Framework for Literacy now provides lesson exemplars that have drama more extensively used and more explicitly evident than in the previous framework. The next Primary Curriculum looks likely to have drama as an effective way of developing speaking and listening in English and for teaching Modern Languages. It is also expected to be with the Arts and Design area of learning. With a stronger emphasis on personal development in the Primary Curriculum and a strengthening of SEAL, drama looks well placed to develop across the curriculum and within the arts in its own right.

Writing

> *'A child who had been absent for most of the drama work but present for writing the sequel, had access to a planning map and words to help her. She used the key incidents on the sheet but didn't develop these or describe them like children of similar ability present for the drama work did.'*
>
> *Year 3 teacher, Aldborough Primary School)* ◾

> *'Drama gives you ideas and it helps with expressive words. When you are trying to write an expressive word, things come to you from the drama.'*
>
> *Year 3 pupil* ◾

> *'There has been some very strong, analytical writing in role, that has been recorded in my action research journal.'*
>
> *Year 9 Drama teacher, Attleborough High School)* ◾

PART ONE

'Lower ability writers were more confident and more focused during writing lessons linked to the drama. They were keen to get their ideas from the drama, onto the paper.'

Year 10 High School Drama teacher ∎

Many teachers already use drama specifically to raise standards in writing. Drama often provides a context and a compelling reason to write within the drama, e.g. a message found inside a bottle, a letter written by a character, a character's old school report, a newspaper report on an incident in the drama, etc.

'All children wrote independently, including those children who previously had been quite resistant to writing. They worked with purpose and pace, wanting to reach the point where they could read it back in role.'

A teacher action researcher (D4LC) (Reference 4) ∎

Teachers can set up writing opportunities within a drama but should be on the lookout for some that may arise naturally as the drama unfolds. When there is a genuine, rather than forced, reason arising in a drama that compels children to write (a reason that matters to the drama), they are usually motivated and keen to write because they are emotionally engaged and have an immediate purpose and audience. Their writing becomes important to the drama itself and can feed back into it. A vivid and emotionally charged drama experience can lead to children brimming with ideas that inform and guide their writing.

'It (drama) helps you write – it's easier to do it and then put it on paper.

It (drama) helped me do my Hansel and Gretel book – I knew the story and only had to write it down … I didn't have to think what to write – just how to do it well.'

A pupil's voice (D4LC) (Reference 4) ∎

However, teachers would be wise not always to connect drama with writing, as it may make children think that drama is just a context to get them writing, and this is not all it should be. Also, it may be that during the lesson any writing done should be focused on getting the ideas down without worrying about grammar and punctuation until later. The prime purpose of the writing in the drama lesson relates to its significance for the drama, not to the technical aspects of writing. A drama lesson that is intended to inspire writing is not the same thing as a writing lesson that uses some drama strategies and approaches. Both are valid, but the latter is not a drama lesson.

If helps if the school lesson timings are flexible enough to enable drama to happen when the need arises in the lesson, rather than retrospectively, as of course the motivation will be higher and the writing more immediate. However, if drama is happening in the hall and hall time is limited, then writing may need to be done afterwards, back in the classroom.

> *'It (drama) helps me to make sense because I already know what is going to happen in my writing.'*
>
> *A pupil's voice (D4LC) (Reference 4)* ■

Much drama happens in classrooms anyway, but of course it again depends how rigid the school timetable is as to whether longer sessions can happen within which the children write at the moment the drama requires it and can then continue the drama lesson for as long as the drama requires it.

> *'Empowering children to have the confidence to share their thoughts and ideas verbally, will then inevitably lead to the development of their confidence to commit their ideas to paper.'*
>
> *A teacher action researcher (D4LC) (Reference 4)* ■

Confidence (teacher and pupil)

> *'I want to do drama because it will develop my self-confidence.'*
>
> *Year 1 and 2 teacher, William Marshall School* ■

> *'Drama has made me braver.'*
>
> *A Primary School teacher* ■

> *'Yes this is very daunting when I realize how little I do outside hot-seating in literacy.'*
>
> *'The children had more confidence in role as another person and were therefore more willing to share their ideas.'*
>
> *Year 1 and 2 teacher, Blenheim Park Community Primary School* ■

> *'Meeting the (statemented) student's parents at options evening suggested that his confidence has really grown since doing drama, so much so that he is now taking Drama as a GCSE option.'*
>
> *Year 9 High School Drama teacher* ■

In dramatic play worlds children succeed and so imagined experience for most children has been a success story for them already before coming to school. There

PART ONE

is almost a look of relief on some children's faces when they know they are doing drama because they know they can do 'pretend'. It is something they are already familiar with and enjoy.

> *'A very shy, withdrawn child always sitting at the back of the carpet and looking to hide, wanted to play a very high profile role in our drama work.'*
>
> **A teacher action researcher (D4LC) (Reference 4)** ■

When schools move from dramatic play to drama they make greater 'in role' demands on the children; they 'up the stakes' and increase the level of challenge. This needs to be done in ways that enable success and build on children's current levels of confidence to actively participate 'in role'. To be in role with a whole class has some different and additional challenges to those already experienced when children choose to role-play spontaneously out of school with a friend or parent.

Some children will be immediately confident in Drama lessons and others may need to be helped to feel secure about role-play with a whole class before fully and actively engaging. If teachers are sensitive to the emotions of the learners and understand how to support them working in role, then children will become increasingly confident.

No child should be put on the spot and forced to contribute. They need to trust the teacher and trust their classmates in order to feel confident. A drama contract will help this (see pages 100–101).

Drama enables children to rehearse success. In a fictional world they can achieve anything. In drama worlds you cannot be wrong and anything is possible. You can behave as if you have competencies that you aspire to in real life and be treated as someone who already has those competencies. This gives a real *feeling* of competence and builds confidence. Through pretend worlds children safely use, practise and develop real skills, e.g. speaking to an audience, group problem solving, negotiation, generating ideas, team work, perseverance, communication, etc. Although they are developing these skills in a fictional context the skills development itself is nonetheless real and lasting. So a child in a drama might be involved in solving a fictional problem, e.g. 'I have to survive alone on this desert island. What must I do first?' (Unit 1, Whatever Wanda Wanted). Although in real life this is not going to happen, the problem-solving skills used and developed in solving this imaginary problem are real. So, the child becomes more competent and confident at problem solving.

Drama is full of 'What if?' situations and provides opportunity for children to rehearse and achieve in ways that can benefit them later in real life situations. Drama involves a great deal of social interaction and encourages empathy. Through drama, children can become more socially confident and better able to work with others in a team. In many learning situations in school, it is possible to be solitary or be in a group, but working in parallel rather than truly working together. In drama, children have to work together and support each other and will gradually become more confident and braver about taking personal risks in relation to what they say and do.

'It (drama)'s a very useful skill to have and it improves my
confidence by making my nerves much less. In a way it helps
my co-operation with other people.'

A pupil's voice (D4LC) (Reference 4) ∎

Teachers often see drama as 'risk teaching'. To some extent this is true, but risk is what makes it highly engaging, surprising and exciting, and risk is not the same as danger! Some teachers have the personality and/or experience to try drama anyway and some avoid it due to their own personal or professional insecurities. There are CPD implications here that will be dealt with later (see pages 63 to 66). When teachers have the necessary subject knowledge they will feel more secure. All teachers will benefit from an understanding of drama as pedagogy and it should be part of every teacher's toolkit even if they don't teach whole class drama. Role-play and working in role is part of every normally developing child's learning repertoire and needs to be part of every teacher's teaching repertoire. If there is an expectation set that teachers will use drama pedagogy as part of other lessons then they are likely to get the taste for it and be spurred on by the positive responses of children. This will lead to increased teacher confidence. The more drama that teachers do the better and more confident they will become at teaching in and through drama, as long as they are given training and support and are evaluative and reflective practitioners who are open to changing practice with the focus on children and their learning.

The teacher's relationship with the children often feels different in drama lessons (which is why less secure teachers sometimes avoid it). In drama, the teacher and children can feel as if they are more equal as co-participants exploring and creating together. In a fictional drama-world the teacher may choose to take on a lower status role than those of the children and this can be enlightening. When the drama is over, the fact remains that teachers and children may have seen each other in a different light during the drama, while nonetheless knowing it to be a fiction. Drama can have a lasting and positive impact on pupil attitudes to teachers and vice versa. Research by Harland (Harland *et al.*, see reference 14) suggests that drama teachers are the most popular teachers in secondary schools.

Pupil voice

'Can we carry on doing this at playtime?'

Year 2 pupil, Ormesby Village Infant School ∎

'Can we use our imaginations today?'

Year I pupil, Tunstead Primary School ∎

'You can be anything you want in drama and you can learn
how hard it is to be someone else.'

Year 2 child, Alpington and Bergh Apton C of E Voluntary Aided
Primary School ∎

PART **ONE**

'I was scared when the eagle landed in the classroom.'

Year I child

Whole class drama is done *with* children, not *to* them. Their voice is pivotal to the drama. The teacher supports and enables. The teacher offers focus, structures and scaffolds but it is the children's ideas that are the most important aspect of drama. The drama helps provide an aesthetic form for communicating their ideas, voices and understandings. In many lessons children are passive recipients of information but in drama they are the makers of meaning. When drama is well taught, the teacher is listening intently to the children (and the children listening intently to each other), and their ideas and responses are what drives the direction of the drama. Good drama is not about the children enacting the teacher's ideas, it is about the teacher ensuring the children's ideas are used and are able to be given space and drama form.

Drama usually involves actual voice. The voice may be 'in role' at times, or 'out of role', but in drama lessons children should be doing a great deal of talking and listening to each other, sharing their ideas for a range of reasons, and to a range of imagined audiences. What they say should be respectfully listened to and considered and their ideas valued even if not all end up being carried forward and developed in the fiction. Whole class drama won't work well if it is hijacked by the few or dominated by the teacher. Children begin to realize that the power and momentum in whole class drama is fed when everyone is highly engaged, and, for everyone to be so, everyone needs to be able to be actively involved and empowered to contribute. One of the reasons children enjoy drama is because they are listened to and it is a genuine forum for pupil voice.

Children ask for drama. Once they have tasted whole class drama they usually get the class drama bug and ask for more of it.

'I think that when we are all in the same room doing the same thing, it makes it easier to do and we all understand each other's point of view. To me that is what makes drama enjoyable.'

A pupil's voice (D4LC) (Reference 4)

So, if we are listening to and responding to pupil voice, we should be talking with children *about* drama as well as *in* drama.

Behaviour

'In drama the children were on task all the time.'

Teacher, Manor Field Infant School

'A reception child in my class who is on the point of exclusion is able to express himself best through role-play.'

Reception Class teacher

> *'The main improvement was within the disruptive boys of the class. They found the tasks engaging and stimulating so their behaviour improved dramatically.'*
>
> **Year 9 High School Drama teacher** ■

Drama is not a panacea. Doing drama will not ensure that all children behave well. Children do misbehave, for a range of often complex reasons, but drama can help. Boredom in lessons is often a trigger for some children to misbehave in order to liven things up for themselves and to entertain others. When children are interested in the lessons, they are much less inclined to misbehave.

> *'This child is a Year 1 pupil, who came into the class as one who perceived himself as a naughty boy. He had previously spent many of his playtimes outside the headteacher's office due to his very physical and rough play outside. He had a negative self-image and was initially difficult to engage in class.*
>
> *He began to engage with drama sessions as they caught his imagination. And he was able to contribute ideas and suggestions. As his ideas were being taken seriously by his peers and myself, he engaged more with the strategies and began to take ownership of the drama developments. His ideas became more linked with what was going on and he was able to show and connect this to his wide range of general knowledge. During this process his peers were taking on board his ideas and they began to perceive him as a boy who had useful ideas and would help move the drama forward. His peers became keen to play with him as they realized he has good ideas for play (they have found this out through the drama work).'*
>
> **A teacher action researcher (D4LC) (Reference 4)** ■

The positives of staying engaged with the drama and making it work can outweigh the kick some children might get from messing it up. In drama, when most of the class is engaged and wants the drama to work, they will often apply peer pressure on certain children who are messing the drama up.

The fact that children are active in drama can also help with behaviour. Some children genuinely find it very difficult to sit still for long periods and need to move. They fidget, ask to go unnecessarily to the toilets, find an excuse to move around the room. In drama there are periods of stillness but also periods of action and this is more natural and helpful to most children. Children often find it difficult not to talk for long periods of time. Also, drama is a legitimate vehicle for much interaction and talk. Teachers may avoid drama because they are worried about whether drama will have an adverse effect on pupil behaviour, whereas ironically it is more likely to have a positive effect.

PART ONE

> *'When we started the project (D4LC), there were four children who found it difficult to involve themselves in role-play, preferring instead to distract the others. However, these children are fully engaged, motivated and are actually enjoying the various drama activities I have planned.'*
>
> **A teacher action researcher (D4LC) (Reference 4)** ∎

Whole class drama is not a free for all. It has an accompanying set of very clear behavioural and operational expectations (see pages 101 to 102). Drama is highly disciplined. It is when teachers have had no training, have insufficient knowledge of drama strategies and conventions and just set up long improvizations that problems may arise. This is not behavioural problems caused by drama but caused by a teacher having insufficient skills, knowledge and understanding of drama and, again, this is a CPD issue the school needs to address.

Behavioural problems can arise in drama if children feel insecure and are not sure what is expected of them, or are not listened to. So the drama contract (see pages 101 to 102) will benefit both teacher and children. If children know they need not feel concerned that they will be put on the spot against their will, they will relax more and contribute in role, within or hopefully just beyond their comfort zone. If they feel personally vulnerable and threatened by poor drama teaching, then they may just refuse to take part or clam up, or misbehave as a diversionary tactic, or they may just work at a very superficial and very safe level that does not challenge them. So teachers need to make sure children are helped to feel personally safe and respected in drama lessons and are respectful of the teacher, each other and the drama itself.

Enjoyment

> *'Can't we do drama all the time? It's much more fun!'*
>
> **Cathryn, Year 2 child** ∎

> *'The look of sheer delight when the children saw the drama symbol on the visual timetable!'*
>
> **Drama Subject Leader, Chapel Road Special School** ∎

> *'The children (aged 4 and 5 years) stayed on task and showed real enjoyment and concentration for a long time.'*
>
> **Teacher, Snettisham Primary School** ∎

> *'Parents have commented to me how much children are enjoying drama.'*
>
> **Year 4/5 teacher, Acle St Edmund Primary School** ∎

Children enjoy drama and so do teachers once they begin to feel more confident with it and see the impact on children. It is different from other lessons. It touches

14. Most children enjoy drama and are keen to work together in role.

the way that children played dramatically and enjoyably before they started school and it engages them once again in legitimized, imagined worlds, in ways that are important and relevant to them. Children enjoy and understand the idea of being active in imagined worlds. It lets them socially interact with each other in a unique way. It empowers them and makes anything possible. It uses their ideas and this gives them pleasure, so drama has a 'feel good factor'. The enjoyment and pleasures are multi-faceted, e.g. pleasure in being engaged, curious, using their imaginations, working creatively and socially together, using body, spirit and mind, focusing on what is of interest, having appreciative feedback, feeling part of the class, being able to express thoughts in many ways, being listened to and watched, and so on, as well as the excitement of not knowing what will happen next and the enjoyment of having some ownership of it.

The brain is able to pretend and it usually associates pretending with emotion and enjoyment. What the brain enjoys releases a chemical associated with pleasure and this increases the likelihood that what provides the pleasure will be repeated. The brain ensures young children pretend a lot because their brains need them to. There are neurological reasons for this that link to motivation, memory and learning. (Baldwin 2004, see reference 13.)

> 'When I asked the children what surprised them about drama ... replies included: 'It helps me remember things' ... I have noticed that one or two children who normally have problems retaining information have improved and can remember things we did a term ago.'
>
> A teacher action researcher (D4LC) (Reference 4)

Drama as pedagogy in schools recognizes, uses and develops this ability to actively imagine and pretend, whereas so many teaching approaches and styles ignore it.

Team work and co-operation

> *'It seemed like half the class were being really difficult and challenging for the first half of the morning in the classroom but they began to co-operate when we got into the hall for drama.'*
>
> **Key Stage 3, Special School teacher** ■

> *'Children were helping each other during the drama.'*
>
> **Teacher, Hall Special School** ■

Whole class drama only works when all the children work co-operatively together.

> *'It was not a big surprise to me that a year one child instantly volunteered. The biggest surprise was that when dressed up and looking like a fox this became too much for her. This normally confident child turned into an introverted little girl who was now very nervous. I quickly asked her if she had any friends that would come and join her. It was not long before she was supported by two friends who quickly became sister foxes.'*
>
> **A teacher action researcher (D4LC) (Reference 4)** ■

> *'My best friends looked after me when I was shy.'*
>
> **A pupil's voice (Year I child) (Reference 4)** ■

It involves, at different times, working alone, in pairs or small groups and with the whole class. It enables and requires children to fluidly and flexibly work in task orientated groups that are likely to be outside the usual friendship and/or ability groups. They may be working with different people several times during most lessons on a range of tasks. The drama itself often dictates that they interact and co-operate with children who normally they may have little to do with. They are motivated to do this as they want the drama to succeed and don't want to let their peers down and break the drama.

> *'Children have to work co-operatively in drama sessions. Some find this hard to achieve. I have allowed children to choose who they work with, specifying the approximate size of the group in order to allow flexibility. Some children are kind and will quickly volunteer if someone is left out. Now that their confidence is growing, I am trying to encourage them to work with people they did not join up with last time. This is also productive and is helping dynamics within the classroom.'*
>
> **A teacher action researcher (D4LC) (Reference 4)** ■

Once children have worked well together for a drama purpose there is every likelihood that the group dynamics between them will have changed and that they will be better able to interact together well in other contexts outside drama and also in the playground. The teacher is also part of the team in drama and again the dynamics of the relationship between child and teacher may be altered in, and then later beyond, the drama lesson.

Personal, Social and Emotional Learning/Personal Development

> *'Two children who are usually quite difficult to engage were particularly responsive to the drama approach. They showed increased motivation and interest and were empowered by the opportunity to talk and work in role. They had a stronger sense of self-esteem being addressed as police officers.'*
>
> Year 5 teacher, Acle St Edmund Primary School ■

> *'We have begun to use puppets and role-play in our Social and Emotional Behaviour curriculum and found that drama is an excellent medium for children to use when they are learning about their emotions and how to handle strong feelings.'*
>
> Headteacher, St Peter and St Paul C of E Voluntary Controlled School, Carbrooke ■

> *'One student who has a known history of being bullied, really shone through with some very strong ideas on body language and how to cope with the stresses of the situation.'*
>
> Year 9 Drama teacher, Attleborough High School ■

> *'The advantage of using drama was that it enabled the students to discuss drug, alcohol and sexual health issues in a safe environment without feeling judged.'*
>
> Year 10 Drama teacher, Attleborough High School ■

> *'I know of no other subject that could present, explore, explain and qualify the individual's understanding of Family Love as holistically and authentically as Drama.'*
>
> KS2/3 teacher of residential boys with Social, Emotional and Behavioural Statements at Eaton Hall Specialist College SEBD ■

Many schools are now using the National Strategy SEAL materials and drama can have very strong links with this and enhance the learning. The methodology of drama easily lends itself to support teachers using SEAL, and of course whole class drama by its nature is a social learning medium that can focus on social issues and

PART ONE

be used to provide opportunities for and to improve social interaction. Drama can help children to become self-aware and to manage their feelings and those of each other. The teacher as a co-participant can model desired attitudes and behaviours. When children are working in role they are able to engage emotionally with people, situations and content and possibly resolve imaginary issues and conflicts, which will be of support to them when facing real issues.

'You said in your questionnaire that you'd learnt that you should not boast about your new things. How did you learn that?'

'When we did it in drama we acted out what it was like if you boast. We did the two different endings and if you boast it doesn't feel very nice. It makes you feel upset because you haven't got something your mate has.'

'So what did you learn from the role-play?'

'I learnt that it didn't feel nice if someone boasts to you and you could lose friends if you boast.'

'Did the drama make you think?'

'Yes. I was thinking about the times I'd boasted and how it wasn't the right thing to do. It's difficult, but you shouldn't do it. I know what it feels like now.'

Teacher/pupil discussion (D4LC) (Reference 4) ■

The use of role also enables distancing for reflection, which supports emotional and affective learning. Drama allows children to safely engage emotionally in role and then to step back, observe and consider their feelings, opinions, attitudes, beliefs

15. Working in role offers opportunities for teachers to publically raise the status and maybe the self-esteem of specific children.

and those of other people, as well as the consequences of actions. Drama encourages empathy. In role they are actively considering things from the viewpoints of others. Through using drama strategies and conventions the teacher can help children to hold important moments still and can support reflection that may lead to real attitudinal and behavioural change, e.g. having empathized with a victim through a drama focused on bullying (Unit 5, The Bystander), a child may be more empathetic when faced with a similar situation in real life and be less likely to bully or to support a real bully.

Drama can also help to build the self-esteem of children. Within a drama the teacher can enable certain children in role to have elevated moments in the eyes of others. As already mentioned, success in imagined worlds has no limits and an imagined success in role can lead to a feeling of real success that helps raise self-esteem.

A sample of headteacher feedback after a year of regular 'whole class drama'

Staff are injecting drama into more of their lessons and talking about it together in the staff room. They are enjoying it and I am seeing it in their classrooms.

There is greater and broader understanding of creative drama and through feedback they are demonstrating greater subject knowledge. This has given them increased professional confidence and their enthusiasm for drama shines through! The children are showing a deeper understanding related to whatever the learning focus of the drama has been.

It has legitimized drama as a teaching approach without us wondering if someone will come along and question it. I have seen the difference in how the children have worked and how their writing is more imaginative when it is linked to the drama.

Having to commit to teaching drama at least once a week this year has meant that teachers are seeking new opportunities so that English did not always become drama-led. Once we saw its power it became obvious that we could use drama in any subject for learning, understanding and creativity. It appeals to many and seems as if it is the only way some children can develop their thinking. The children enjoy it and keep asking for more drama!

Drama has had a very motivating effect on reluctant writers. They enjoy writing more because they understand the context and the purpose of the writing.

'Next steps' headteachers identified at the end of the year

In the Autumn term we will be evaluating the impact of drama. In Spring we have organized a full day of INSET for all staff on drama. We have reviewed the curriculum this term and made sure drama is integrated as well as timetabled drama lessons from September. Monitoring of drama is now in place.

Drama now will have a prominent place in our action plan to improve writing.

We have set up a lead drama team who share ideas and encourage drama within all classes. I intend giving them release time to plan drama with less-confident teachers.

Drama has improved the quality of teaching. It is in our next School Improvement and Development Plan in its own right and with its own budget next year for the first time.

PART ONE

Leading and managing Drama

■ Leadership

Improvement in any area requires effective leadership. Leaders of Drama do not have to be the headteachers themselves (and are unlikely to be so in secondary schools or larger primary schools) but the headteacher needs to be involved and informed, needs to be clearly committed to Drama as a means of school improvement, and needs to give the consistent message that they are determined to facilitate and ensure Drama happens. Class teacher heads in smaller primary schools will need to involve themselves as both teacher and the headteacher in developing Drama.

In both primary and secondary schools the status of Drama as a subject will probably be reflected by the staffing provision. Not all schools have drama specialists and not all secondary schools have Drama departments. Drama being placed within English in secondary schools has led to many schools losing discrete Drama departments. In primary schools Drama was taken over by Literacy co-ordinators, most of whom were not drama specialists, and this remains the case. Obviously, this does not mean necessarily that good drama won't happen, but it is more likely to happen when trained drama specialists are in a position to lead the development of the subject.

> 'Where management of the subject was in the hands of a principal teacher or assistant principal teacher of drama, the quality of leadership was almost always good or very good. Features of strong leadership included professional competence, enthusiasm, energy, good relationships with staff and pupils, and the development of teamwork in constructing policies and courses. Effective principal teachers and assistant principal teachers gave a clear lead in curriculum development, organized aspects of administration and communication efficiently and provided clear and succinct course documentation.'
>
> *Effective Learning and Teaching in Scottish Secondary Schools: Drama, HMI (Scotland) (Reference 15)* ■

Interestingly, there is evidence to suggest that in primary schools in England now, the role of drama subject leader is gradually being reinstated in more schools. Ironically it is at a time when drama specialist initial teacher training places have been cut and so fully trained drama specialists are getting thinner on the ground, whereas the number of theatre educators working in schools more casually is burgeoning.

If a school is totally committed to developing drama well across the school, then it makes sense to ensure a trained drama specialist leads the whole school improvement in drama and receives the full support of senior management (preferably, actively including the headteacher). Very few headteachers are themselves drama specialists (Downing 2003, see reference 16). If the school does not have a trained drama specialist, then do ensure that whoever leads on drama has access to high quality

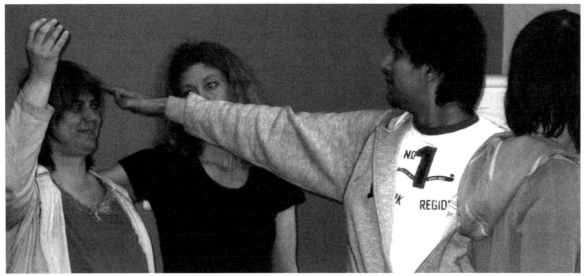

16. There is value in teachers experiencing drama as participants, in order to better understand it as learners and teachers.

drama training, advice and support. If you don't have a drama leader or aspiring drama leader in your school, then maybe the next appointment to the staff needs to include drama specialism within the job description. In the meantime, maybe some whole staff drama training and a call to the local authority for access to specialist advice and support will be a worthwhile step, or a partnership appeal could be made to your local specialist arts college.

■ Reviewing and developing drama provision

If a school wants to create improvement *through* drama it needs to ensure improvement *in* drama too. If you are going to use drama as a key tool for school improvement then you will want to make sure that all teachers' drama skills (and those of teaching assistants) are at least satisfactory and improving and that drama is actually being taught to all children across the school. For all teachers in a school to teach well through drama, all teachers will need to understand that drama matters, know what good drama looks like and have the necessary skills and the confidence to provide it.

> *'For change to be successful, there must be a compelling reason for it.'*
>
> **TDA, School Improvement Planning Framework (SIPF)**
> *(Reference 17)* ■

Change does not happen easily or well in classrooms until or unless teachers see the need for it. So initially some teachers will need to be helped to understand that drama is important. Just telling teachers to teach drama will not work unless thought is given to the fact that all teachers are at different stages of skills acquisition, knowledge and understanding in relation to drama in schools. Teachers need to feel led and supported through necessary change, to be helped to be confident in what they need to do and in time to see that the changes are leading to worthwhile outcomes.

PART ONE

So, time needs to be made available to really talk together about why drama is important and to have professional dialogue that gives a sense of shared understanding and ownership of the changes. It often helps to use an activity as a framework so as to focus staff discussion. The following active and interactive activities are designed to scaffold professional dialogue around drama as a means of school improvement.

Activity 1 Why is drama important?

The following four-part grid could be drawn onto flipchart paper or onto four pieces of paper to frame the discussion and feedback. Self-adhesive labels and felt pens could be used to record ideas that can then be stuck on, yet flexibly rearranged.

Ideally this activity should involve all staff and the full leadership team. The leadership team might be wise to hold back to enable staff to consider and contribute their ideas first.

Table 2 'Why drama is important' grid

Drama is important for learning because...	Drama is important for teaching because...
Drama is important as a whole school development because...	**Drama is important in the planned curriculum because...**

Activity 2 What do we want different 'stakeholders' to say about drama in this school in three years' time?

The next activity is an adaptation and extension of an activity contained in the Training and Development Agency, School Improvement Planning Framework (see reference 17). It has been adapted to help clarify the school's vision for drama by considering what different stakeholders would ideally be saying about drama in the school in three years' time. This activity can be carried out as a whole staff, or better still with everyone in pairs or groups, which then feed back to the whole staff.

You could ask each group to focus on one category of stakeholder (see the Stakeholder visioning grid below). Then, instead of just reporting back normally, they could carry out the feedback activity itself 'in role' with different stakeholder groups pretending to speak as children, governors, parents or teachers, etc. In role, they would speak as if it were in three years' time about how great the drama in the school is now ... with the shared vision achieved! By doing this they are voicing success criteria and speaking the vision.

Stakeholder visioning grid

Change the stakeholder e.g. teachers, support staff, parents, governors, community, local authority, SIP, Ofsted	In 3 years' time what do we want children to ... ?	
	Think about drama ...	Feel about drama ...
	Say about drama ...	Do about drama ...

Activity 3 What do we provide already?

Having agreed together that drama is important (Activity 1), you will want to start to look at what is going on in the school already. There is an unfortunate tendency to always look first at what is not being done in schools, rather than acknowledging and celebrating what is already happening and working well. So, what is the place the school is starting from drama-wise? Activity 2 leads you to think about what success might look like, but where are you starting from? You need to identify what you want to achieve drama-wise, find out what is happening already, decide where gaps exist and identify the areas for improvement in prioritized stages.

This could be a mapping exercise. You can adapt the grid below (Table 3) to fit your school classes or year groups and add other columns if you wish. Copy the grid onto a large piece of paper for the activity and then transfer it to a spreadsheet for future

PART ONE

reference and comparison. You could either ask teachers to tick and cross the grid for different year groups or you could make it more informative by inviting written comment and annotation. If you think this activity is best done individually and you then gather the information without making the activity so public, that is for you to decide.

Future discussion and action will be informed by where you find the gaps are. It may not be possible to aim to quickly fill gaps in provision until you have put professional development opportunities in place and/or reconsidered curriculum planning and/ or timetabling. The reasons why the gaps exist will need to be considered and some barriers to progress may need to be addressed. You may have good reasons to decide not to fill all gaps, e.g. maybe you won't want to take very young children to the theatre but would prefer to bring a theatre group in. The judgements should be made together for your school, with the focus on what is best and most necessary for the child.

Table 3 Basic provision grid

	Regular role-play opportunity	Drama approaches used in English regularly (at least weekly)	Drama approaches used in other subjects	Timetabled regular Drama lessons (at least fortnightly)	Opportunity to regularly access an out of school hours drama club	Visiting theatre or actor/s	Visit/s to theatre	Every child will perform in a class/school play
YR								
Y1								
Y2								
Y3								
Y4								
Y5								
Y6								
Y7								
Y8								
Y9								

It needs to be remembered that this is just a very basic grid to map provision. The quality of what is provided is a separate issue that will need to be addressed. Provision is important but it needs to be good quality provision.

■ Carrying out a drama audit and review

The provision grid is just a very basic starting point. You will find it more useful and illuminating also to carry out a more detailed drama audit (see the Drama Self Evaluation Framework (Drama SEF) pages 236–249).

Few schools have carried out a rigorous drama audit, except maybe as part of an arts audit undertaken when they apply to Arts Council England for an Artsmark. The Drama SEF is intended to support schools in carrying out a whole school review of drama together in a way that will guide the school towards the creation of a drama action plan. It is very unlikely that many schools will find that everything outlined in the audit is already fully in place and is of high quality. Even if it were, things change constantly in schools and review, improvement and development is an ongoing process and drama should be considered regularly as part of the whole school review and development cycle.

The Drama SEF is just a support, and how rigorously and well it is used will depend on how well the school leads and manages change and improvement. At the very least the audit process should get the leaders and managers, teachers, support staff and children talking about drama together. The process of self-review itself is arguably more valuable than the completed document.

You can't do school improvement *for* people or *to* people, you can only do it *with* people. The audit forms should not be taken away by a subject leader and filled in by them alone, without involving all relevant staff interactively in the process. The audit tool should stimulate discussion and should be given to staff to consider in advance of at least one whole staff meeting focused on drama (and preferably a series of staff meetings) or else a professional development day.

The Drama SEF provided in this book (see pages 236–249) is designed to engage all staff with what the 'big picture' for drama might look like. It may or may not be the 'big picture' you actually decide for your school but it is something concrete to work from and adapt. The completed audit form can provide part of the evidence base that will link to and support the school's Self Evaluation Form (SEF) for Ofsted.

The audit/review could:

- prompt the school to designate responsibility for drama to a key member of staff

- lead to the governors designating responsibility for monitoring drama to a named governor

- be used to guide a systematic and drama focused discussion at a staff meeting or series of meetings

- be helpful as a tool used at an appropriate time in a school's cycle of self-review as a way of gathering evidence that could contribute to the school's Self Evaluation Form

- lead to drama becoming a priority (or linked to a priority) in the School Improvement and Development Plan

- inform future appropriate CPD drama provision

- highlight the need to allocate part of the budget to support the development of drama, e.g. resources, courses, drama subject leader release time, etc.

- inform judgements about the quality of drama provision

- highlight whether or not all children are actually receiving drama

- lead schools towards planning in visits to theatres as a curriculum entitlement

- help schools to consider together why, where and how drama is happening across the school

- help schools to vision and agree what they want drama entitlement in their school to look like

- help schools to find and agree steps towards what they want to achieve in and through drama

- help schools consider partnership arrangements that could support drama for children and/or teachers, etc.

- result in the school considering drama subject association membership.

If drama is to become a tool for whole school improvement then it needs to be strategically embedded in school priorities and plans. Drama should have its own plan at some point. It might also appear as part of an arts plan or as part of the main school improvement and development plan or drama could be threaded through, as a way of supporting other priorities, e.g. raising standards in writing, improving speaking and listening, etc.

Activity 4 Which are the drama gaps we agree we need to fill?

There needs to be discussion and reflection about the implications for school improvement and development, arising from the completed grid and/or full drama audit. Look together at the completed grid or full audit. Where are the gaps you all agree need to be filled? Don't worry about 'how' to do it yet, or even 'when'. If you are the school leader then there may come a point when you have to direct that drama happens (as it is a statutory requirement from ages 5 to 14 years) but work collaboratively as far as possible to keep everyone on board and wanting to make drama happen. Keeping it focused on what children need rather than what the law dictates is a more palatable and constructive starting point for most teachers.

If you are a pupil or student passing from year to year through your school, what is the experience likely to be as far as your experience of drama goes? Does the drama in your school offer all children or students continuity and progression? Is it feast some years, followed by famine in others (dependent on an individual teacher's preferences)? Does the child get significant amounts of drama in one class and little or none in the next? You are looking at provision initially at this stage and then moving on to consider quality. Agree together where provision gaps exist that need to be filled before moving on together afterwards to considering how this will be achieved over time. Keep the 'where' and 'how' separate at this stage so as to avoid responses that put up barriers and blocks; for example, 'We can't do that yet because ...' should not get in the way of early visioning of what is ideally required.

Activity 5 What shall we focus on first?

Once you have decided on the gaps you want to fill, you will need to decide together which gaps need to be filled first. You can't achieve everything at once and so you need to prioritize. Your priorities will need to be decided by your school and there may be very good reasons in relation to other, non-drama, priorities why you need or prefer to tackle certain aspects of drama improvement first, e.g. Ofsted key issues that demand a different focus, staff changes pending, a whole curriculum review scheduled, change of leadership pending, staff well-being. Certain things are easy to put in place quickly, e.g. a designated governor with governor responsibility for drama (although you may need to then spend some time with the governor, agreeing what this role means in practice and how and when they might carry it out appropriately).

'Traffic lighting'

It could be helpful to make an enlarged photocopy of the completed Drama SEF and get three different colour highlighter pens to highlight the varying immediacy with which you need to tackle the gaps, i.e. where you put a P for 'partly in place', or an N for 'not in place'. If you have put F against a statement, i.e. indicating that something is 'fully in place', then no immediate action is likely to be required. If it is 'partly in place' or 'not in place' at all, then consider how urgent it is to start to take action on each area. It is better to prioritize well and put things in place gradually and strategically than try to do it all at once, overload everyone, and fail.

You might decide that the highest priority will be to ensure that all children/students are actually experiencing drama approaches in lessons other than drama (before moving on to all experiencing full drama lessons). There should be no child in the school who has no regular access at all to drama. If even the use of drama strategies in English is not fully in place across the school then you may decide to highlight it as an immediate priority (e.g. highlight it green for 'go' as an immediate 'act now' priority to be tackled within the first term). You may find that drama lessons in their own right do not exist in all classes but decide that a whole staff professional development day for drama will be necessary first or that this development should wait until the start of a new term or school year (so you might highlight this in amber or 'move very soon', indicating that this will be in place within the first year). Then you might consider what you want to achieve from the list within the first three years (possibly highlighting this in pink). You may decide that there are areas revealed by the audit you will miss out of your initial plan (maybe highlighted red on the audit) at this stage. You have to keep the plan manageable and achievable. You will be agreeing together which are the high, medium and low priorities for drama and balancing these with what can realistically be achieved within each time frame and within the context of other school priorities.

The highlighted plan gives you a basic drama development timeline that you can build from. You could highlight two copies and cut one up, putting all the green, orange and pink highlighted sections together and then attach actions to them, start and finish dates, budget and time allocations, success criteria and arrangements for

PART ONE

monitoring and evaluation. The grid below does not display all the columns you might expect in a full development plan as it is an abbreviated action plan rather than a full development plan.

If you create a drama action plan then it is worth displaying it in the staff room as a 'living' document that can be highlighted and maybe annotated as actions are completed. It can become a public and visual reminder and record of progress against priorities.

Table 4 Drama Action Plan Grid

Timeline	Tasks	Person responsible	Start and finish date
Green (first term) Drama is an agenda item at SMT/governor meetings			
Orange (within first year) Drama is taught in its own right as a discrete subject			
Pink (within three years) External drama/ theatre partners work creatively alongside staff to help deliver the planned curriculum with a focus on learning outcomes and enabling children's creativity			

Activity 6 What are the perceived barriers to improving drama?

Ask teachers to consider what they perceive are the barriers to improving drama in the school. Barriers are better seen as problems to be overcome. The atmosphere needs to be positive, constructive and forward looking. This is not an invitation for laying blame or making excuses and blocking. This is an opportunity to professionally identify perceived barriers to progress that you will all work together to overcome with the support of the leadership team. When perceived barriers emerge they will be able to be categorized. You may find it helpful to ask for perceived barriers to be written onto self-adhesive labels. Then you might ask staff to negotiate and agree together how the labels might be placed visually to indicate the strength or significance of the barrier. For example, they might build them as a wall of bricks, or in a linear way, or radiating from a central barrier. The discussion that ensues during the process of negotiating and agreeing where to place the labels will be revealing and informative to the leaders of change and the participants themselves. The activity gives everyone a voice and lays the ground for everyone to be part of the solutions.

Without predetermining what barriers might end up being written on the labels, some are likely to relate to individual teachers, and some will be more general 'perceived barriers'. Some will be 'whole school' issues. Other barriers to progress may be more delicate: individual teacher personality, health or competence issues. These will not be written down by anyone but you will need to know this and keep them in mind anyway. Some may be timetabling or budgetary and resource issues. Some may be curriculum issues and some (that teachers may be hesitant to voice or record in front of school leaders) may be leadership and management issues.

Diagram 1: Some teachers' responses to drama

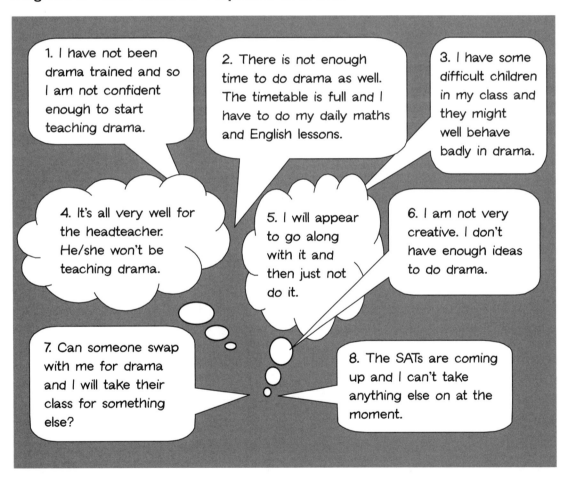

There may be some issues that arise that are 'whole school' issues and some that relate to individual teachers. It will be important to tease out which are which in order to understand and effectively resolve them. Some 'barriers' can be resolved quickly and more easily, e.g. providing teacher resource books and courses for drama. Others may take longer, e.g. shifting the attitudes to drama of certain teachers who might be avoiding change and/or avoiding drama.

PART **ONE**

Table 5 Interpreting teachers' responses to drama (See Diagram 1, page 63)

Comment/ thought	Possible interpretations	Possible implications for headteacher/ Drama leader
1	Genuine insecurity and lack of subject knowledge and skills.	Need to arrange Continuing Professional Development in drama. Maybe arrange peer support from more confident colleague or Advanced Skills Teacher. Maybe enable visit to observe AST.
2	May not realize the possibilities of developing drama approaches in English and other subject areas.	Ensure that the teacher is sufficiently using drama approaches in English and Maths (planning and monitoring). Maybe offer time for colleague planning support with Drama subject leader. Enable flexibility in planning. Ensure teacher has access to/knowledge of the National Strategy resources that use drama approaches. Find out how much drama is being done already (if any) and set a target for more but make sure the teacher has support if required. Make sure there are resources available and used.
3	May genuinely be concerned about drama being 'free' compared with other lessons and concerned it could enable poor behaviour.	This teacher is likely to have genuine concerns about behaviour management. Ensure that there are sufficient support staff available in Drama lessons. Encourage the teacher to increase the use of drama approaches as a precursor to starting Drama lessons. Consider whether the teacher is positively managing behaviour in positive ways that are not restrictive if he/she is avoiding freer situations. Be sure of the reasons for behavioural difficulties in this class, i.e. is pupil boredom or restraint a contributory factor?
4	Headteachers and subject leaders need credibility.	If you are a teaching head then involve yourself directly in teaching drama too. If it is to be a pedagogy it will be part of every teacher's toolbox (including the headteacher's). Your commitment to drama and determination that the whole school addresses it with you is important.

Comment/ thought	Possible interpretations	Possible implications for headteacher/ Drama leader
5	It may be that not everyone behind closed doors will actually carry out what has been agreed.	This is a matter of making expectations clear (e.g. all teachers will plan and carry out drama approaches in literacy lessons at least weekly and do a Drama lesson fortnightly) and then monitoring to ensure that what has been agreed actually happens. If not, then you will need to talk to the teacher about this and hold them to account clearly and in a staged way. You do need to be sure that you have done all that is necessary to give them confidence, subject knowledge and skills, and be sure that your expectations of them are reasonable and fair. Once a whole school approach has been agreed, non-compliance is not acceptable as it is denying the children drama and self-hampering the teacher's own professional development. However, if you are the leader you will need to make an informed judgement about how far to push this and in what way.
6	Teachers sometimes have acquired a view of themselves as not creative and don't think they are able to have the ideas required.	Maybe pair this teacher with someone more confident to support shared planning and maybe a bit of team teaching. This teacher would also benefit from CPD opportunities and access to a range of lesson resources. Be very positive and praise what is achieved to help realign this teacher's view of their own creativity, confidence and competence.
7	Teachers often enjoy most teaching only or mainly to their strengths and avoiding areas they feel less sure of.	Sometimes it makes sense to arrange teaching in ways where everyone is teaching mainly or only to their strengths. However, if you view drama as a pedagogical tool for all teachers and you want all staff to take it on board and improve these skills, then enabling a teacher to opt out won't be helpful in developing that teacher. You may decide to use a compromise approach by asking the teacher to attend training, use more drama approaches in lessons and evaluate their impact but maybe let another teacher take the regular Drama lesson. Or you could say, 'Try it for a term and we will evaluate together how it is going half termly'.

PART ONE

Comment/ thought	Possible interpretations	Possible implications for headteacher/ Drama leader
8	Teachers often feel very pressured and single-minded in the build-up to the SATs.	This could be viewed as a temporary situation and you might decide to let the teacher wait to take on board more teaching in and through drama but agree when they will start doing so, post-SATs. However, drama can be used to raise standards if it is used well, e.g. improving creative writing by using drama to generate vivid characters, settings and plots first. Also, preparing for SATs can be done in enjoyable ways and drama could be one.

Activity 7 Is drama making a difference?

The impact of whole school drama, when done well, can be far-reaching. It is important to identify some of the key impacts of using drama as pedagogy as well as what progress children are making in drama itself.

The outcomes you may be looking for are likely to vary from school to school. The outcomes may be drama outcomes or else might be outcomes in other areas that are achieved *through* drama. It may be that the whole school is focusing on similar areas, e.g. drama as a way of improving writing, or it may be that different teachers will need to take a different focus, e.g. in Class 1 the focus might be to use drama to support improvement in speaking and listening. In Class 2 drama might be used to promote creative thinking outcomes. In Class 3 the focus might be drama as a way of improving group interaction. However it is best to have at least some shared areas of focus.

Table 6a Impact of teaching through drama

What are you trying to achieve **through** drama? (By when?)	Have you achieved it? (When?)	How do you know you've achieved it? (Evidence?)
1. 2. 3.		

Table 6b Impact of teaching in drama

What are you trying to achieve **in** drama? (By when?)	Have you achieved it? (When?)	How do you know you've achieved it? (Evidence?)
1. 2. 3.		

The outcomes may be qualitative as well as quantitative. It helps schools to be able to share measured outcomes with children, parents, Ofsted and the local authority, but much of value can be achieved and celebrated that does not lend itself to being easily measured. 'Improvement in writing' may be more easily measurable than 'improved attitudes to learning', for example.

Also when gathering the evidence there are many ways, including parental and pupil comments, e.g.

> *'James is really enjoying the drama you are doing this term. He always talks about it when he gets home.'*
>
> *Parent of Year 4 child* ■

> *'Can we do drama every day? It's fun.'*
>
> *Year 2 pupil* ■

Building and improving your curriculum through Drama

'The job is to develop a modern, world-class curriculum that will inspire and challenge all learners and prepare them for the future.'

Mick Waters, Director of Curriculum, Qualifications and Curriculum Authority speaking at the School Improvement Through Drama Conference, 200 (Reference 18)

■ What do we mean by drama?

Before we consider how a school curriculum might look with drama well placed as part of it, we need first to decide what we mean by drama. Drama in schools can be defined narrowly or broadly. Drama in schools should not just be limited to the Christmas play and a few opportunities during a child's school life to stand up at school assembly and speak a few lines in a short performance. It's not just about taking part in a piece of theatre for an audience once a year or less, or only reading playscripts in English. It's not just about responding positively when children say, 'We have made up a play, can we show it to you?' It's not just about trying out a few drama strategies in English lessons but never attempting a Drama lesson. A child's experience of drama in schools may happily include all of these things but it needs to be much more holistic and planned into a child's education. Being taught drama is an entitlement for every child in Key Stages 1–3 and needs to happen on a regular basis if there is to be continuity and progression. There may be children and young people who might choose to develop a career linked to drama and theatre but if they do not encounter it sufficiently and in a planned way this opportunity might never present itself. How many potentially great artists, actors, dancers, musicians, etc., have passed through schools where they never found their talent?

Drama in schools might include:

- indoor and outdoor dramatic role-play/drama/theatre opportunities

- regular drama lessons that enable children to focus on learning practically about drama and how it works

- using drama to teach and learn in other subjects, e.g. History, PSE, Geography, RE

- using drama to link teaching and learning thematically across subject boundaries

- using whole class drama to encourage empathy and explore human issues and motives

- using drama to develop thinking skills, to generate ideas, create and problem solve together

Children and young people who are particularly talented at drama will benefit from being able to work with each other.

- providing opportunities to make, perform and respond to performances (their own, their peers' and professional theatre performances)

- visiting theatres (front of house and behind the scenes) and having theatre educators visit to work with children

- providing opportunities for children to work creatively with actors, playwrights and directors

- providing opportunities for children and young people to manage the business aspects of running a theatre.

It is surprising that there seems to be a willingness in many schools to embrace the idea of children learning through drama but without seeing that this means putting in place Drama lessons that enable children to learn about and get better at drama itself. To learn effectively through drama, children and teachers first need a knowledge and an understanding of drama, along with skills of drama. Nobody would realistically expect ICT to be embedded across a curriculum with no ICT training available but all too often there is an unreasonable expectation that drama will just happen without significant Continuing Professional Development for staff and a strategic approach.

If drama is valued in a school and there is a serious intention to use it as pedagogy then it needs to be part of every teacher's professional toolbox but it also needs to appear in the planned curriculum in a clearly identifiable way. It needs a timetabled slot that is regular throughout the school to ensure continuity and progression and it needs to clearly appear in curriculum plans and lesson plans for every year group.

PART ONE

■ The National Curriculum

The National Curriculum is statutory. It has to be delivered in full but how it is delivered is increasingly up to schools to decide. There is a new secondary curriculum in place (launched in July 2007) that is intended to provide a more flexible framework than previously and which should enable schools to tailor the curriculum more to meet their school's needs and those of individual students. The new Key Stage 3 curriculum is intended to provide a foundation for post-14 (Key Stage 4). Schools are now being encouraged to take more creative approaches to curriculum planning and teaching. The National Curriculum in secondary schools is still presented primarily as a subject-based curriculum within which Drama at Key Stage 3 is part of English. As a pedagogical approach at Key Stage 3, drama has enormous potential, although what the National Curriculum defines as statutory for Drama within English is rather minimal. There is now great opportunity and potential for secondary drama specialists to work in closer partnership with colleagues with other subject specialisms in order to strengthen and spread drama as pedagogy and to work more in a cross-curricular way at Key Stage 3. Some secondary schools are using this cross-curriculum studies approach on an experimental basis for a day per week or fortnight in the first instance.

Secondary teachers will find that many good Primary Schools are already experienced at working in a cross-curricular way and it might be that there is potential in working at some cross-phase planning with feeder schools. Secondary drama teachers can bring strong subject expertise into primary schools and good primary teachers can bring their professional experience of cross-curricular studies and planning to the partnership.

The D4LC initiative 'Drama for Learning and Creativity' (www.d4lc.org) is cross-phase and partly involves secondary and primary teachers working together, actively participating in drama CPD together and planning some lessons together. This has proved to be one of its significant strengths.

> *'I am the assistant headteacher of a High School and a trained drama teacher. I have written and team taught a scheme of work for a cross-curricular History/Drama project that was delivered by history specialists. We are planning to run a CPD session exploring drama strategies for the KS4 History curriculum. I line manage ASTs and have also arranged that a Drama AST leads an INSET day with MFL teachers. Our own AST for English has attended a local authority course on developing creative writing through drama. My commitment to using drama across the curriculum has extended to partner schools and I have established a very productive working relationship with a Special School now. Most of the staff attended a twilight CPD session on using drama with pupils with special educational needs. I am keen to develop drama as a learning tool across a wide range of disciplines.'*
>
> **Assistant headteacher, Wymondham High School** ■

> *'We are looking to expand creative curriculum opportunities through drama. We want to explore the use of drama strategies in the teaching and learning of the core subjects, within the context of the National Curriculum and National Strategies.'*
>
> *Arts Director, Sprowston High School, Specialist Performing Arts College*

> *'Drama is only taught as a separate subject in Year 8 and we wish to encourage Drama to be taught through other creative subjects, such as English. We want to promote the use of Drama strategies as a cross-curricular tool and this would be achievable through the school's Learning Groups project.'*
>
> *Drama teacher, Thorpe St Andrew High School*

The Secondary Curriculum is in place and the next Primary National Curriculum is under review and will start being taught in schools from 2011. The next Primary National Curriculum will need to continue to develop the core skills of literacy, numeracy and ICT but will also need to integrate personal development more clearly. It will also need to allow for flexibility and local ownership.

■ The Independent Review of the Primary Curriculum interim report

This report is downloadable from http://publications.teachernet.gov.uk

The new primary curriculum is intended to be less prescriptive and more flexible and has six draft proposed areas of learning:

- Understanding of English, communication and languages
- Mathematical understanding
- Science and technological understanding
- Human, social and environmental understanding
- Understanding physical health and well-being
- Understanding arts and design

These areas of learning are intended to 'dovetail' (reference 1) with both the early years foundation stage framework and the new secondary curriculum. As well as learning in and across these areas, the interim review (reference 1) indicates that discrete subjects should still be taught as well as cross-curricular studies. Literacy, numeracy and ICT retain their strong emphasis in their own right and across the new areas of learning. Early indications are that the value of drama will still be recognized within English but also as part of the arts, as well as across all areas of learning.

PART ONE

'When taught well drama is hugely appealing to children in its own right, before, throughout and beyond the primary years. However drama is particularly valuable for primary schools because of the unique contributions it makes to virtually all aspects of children's language development.'

Paragraph 2.13 of The Independent Review of the Primary Curriculum: Interim report (Reference 1) ■

'Attention should be given to realizing the potential of the visual and performing arts, especially in role-play and drama, for young children's language development.'

Recommendation 7 of The Independent Review of the Primary Curriculum: Interim report (Reference 1) ■

'... the potential of role-play and drama for young children learning a modern language.'

Recommendation 16 of The Independent Review of the Primary Curriculum: Interim report (Reference 1) ■

Secondary schools have been very focused on reorganizing the delivery of their new curriculum and many primary schools also are already well down the path of reorganizing their current curriculum (since feeling empowered to do so since *Excellence and Enjoyment* (reference 7). However, primary schools will now need to adapt and reorganize their curriculum again to take on board the requirements of the next Primary Curriculum from September 2011. Schools that are already using drama as pedagogy as an integral part of their curriculum will already be well placed to carry on doing so from 2011, especially as children's personal development will be a central aspect of the Primary Curriculum. The Primary Review remit calls for

'a simpler and more coherent structure of personal skills to be at the heart of the primary curriculum.'

Drama has a great deal to offer in all aspects of personal development, including those listed in the interim report:

■ teamwork skills and conflict resolution

■ empathy and tolerance

■ respect for others and the environment

■ self-respect and confidence.

The SEAL materials (see reference 19) offer some of the support required as a framework for personal development but it is recognized in the interim report of the Primary National Curriculum that they are not sufficient. It may well be that as SEAL will be adapted and extended in the new curriculum, drama could have a stronger role to play in bringing the SEAL materials to life and offering more active engagement (see Unit 5, The Bystander). Drama approaches are already used in

SEAL but a teacher with good drama skills can extend and enhance what is already suggested.

With the personal development of children at the heart of the next curriculum, schools will be aiming to help children to become creative thinkers, independent enquirers, reflective learners, self-confident and aware, able to manage and understand their feelings and those of others, self-motivated, effective participators and team workers.

Diagram 2: Personal development through Drama

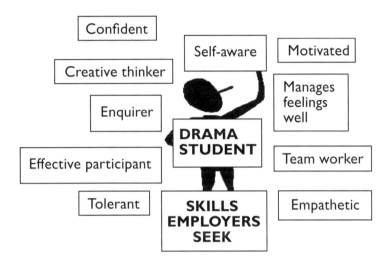

These personal qualities are important for learners, are developed in drama and match the skills and attitudes much valued in the workplace by employers.

> 'Our school is currently remodelling the curriculum to focus on promoting key skills and thinking skills. Learning to learn is a key priority, as is developing a more creative approach to teaching and planning. We are aiming for a structure to replace current practice based on giving children transferable skills and quality experiences based in a context and an emotionally engaging experience which will be well supported by Drama.'
>
> *Drama specialist teacher and subject leader, Millfield Primary School* ■

■ Curriculum aims

The Qualifications and Curriculum Authority (www.http//curriculum.qca.org.uk) state that the curriculum aims for children and young people should be for them to become:

■ **successful learners** who enjoy learning, make progress and achieve

■ **confident individuals** who are able to live safe, healthy and fulfilling lives

■ **responsible citizens** who make a positive contribution to society.

PART ONE

These three key aims are broken down further by QCA and can each be easily supported in and through Drama.

Successful learners:

◼ **have the essential learning skill of literacy**

The cornerstone of literacy is speaking and listening. Drama provides inspiring contexts for speaking and listening with an infinite number of possible responsive audiences and for an infinite number of purposes for speaking and listening. In drama we can give endless opportunities for the children to speak and listen to each other, as anyone (in role) in any situation, for any purpose, at any imagined time and in any imagined place.

◼ **are creative, resourceful and able to identify and solve problems**

Drama invites, uses and brings to life, the children's own ideas. Creativity is stimulated, enabled and required in order to make drama. It involves sponta-neity and improvization. The definition of creativity in All Our Futures *is synonymous with drama, i.e. 'Imaginative activity that is fashioned so as to produce outcomes that are original and of value.' Drama involves a great deal of problem solving when working with others to create a piece of drama or theatre. Also whole class drama lessons are a powerful and flexible context for engaging with problem solving. Dramas often involve characters and communities having to face and solve fictional problems but in doing so the drama participants are using and developing their real problem-solving skills.*

◼ **have enquiring minds and think for themselves to process infor-mation, reason, question and evaluate**

Creating drama often gives rise to enquiry. The enquiry may arise in role as we speak to characters and find out more about them, their motives and perspectives, e.g. through hot-seating characters and those who know them. Drama also inspires enquiry outside the drama itself, e.g. an historically based drama may well give rise to the children carrying out research at other times to inform the drama and help them feel, achieve and be convincing in role. When children take on the Mantle of the Expert, e.g. actually investigate and then carry out tasks in role 'as if' they are archaeologists, scientists, film-makers, etc., they become necessarily involved in enquiry-based learning to succeed.

Reasoning is among the range of thinking skills required and developed through drama. Again, this reasoning may be in role, where the children reason as characters and reason with characters. Or, the reasoning might relate to the making of the drama itself. For example, when working on a piece of performance as a group for presentation to others, the children may well reason with each other why a scene should be played one way rather than another. As different children will have different ideas about how to communicate and perform the piece, they will need to reason with each other, question each other and justify in relation to effect and impact. Performance will require evaluation and the children are required by the National Curriculum drama component to evaluate their own performances and those of others.

■ **communicate well in a range of ways**

Drama is about communication. It involves making and communicating meanings to others (and in the process increasing personal knowledge and understanding). It does not rely solely on communicating through speaking. It involves an understanding of both verbal and non-verbal communication. Drama communicates through juxtapositioning the visual, verbal and kinaesthetic aspects of the art form. Speech, sound, space, lighting, costume, objects, gesture, eye contact, setting, etc., all take on an interconnected, interactive and collective significance that communicates meaning to others. Drama is always going to have content and is always about something. Therefore it also communicates narrative, ideas, viewpoints, cultural knowledge and norms, etc.

■ **understand how they learn and learn from their mistakes**

It may be best to avoid the idea of failure or mistakes in drama and settle for agreeing that some drama works well and some works less well. It is important to consider with the class (and enable them to consider themselves) why some drama works better. Drama is dynamic, experiential and experimental. When they know what works best they can recall this and use and build on it in future dramas. Some drama is however weaker, less developed, less well communicated and may therefore be less effective.

■ **are able to learn independently and with others**

In drama children are likely to be operating and responding individually, in pairs, groups and also as whole classes. What is being learned in and through drama is being learned individually and with others. Good whole class drama utilizes and moves with the children's ideas and areas of interest. When improvising and creating a whole class drama the individual's contributions are valued and contribute to the whole. Drama requires children to work independently and together in order for it to succeed.

■ **know about big ideas and events that shape our world**

Drama is a type of virtual world that we create and interact within and is an excellent forum for exploring big ideas and events. Drama and theatre enable the creation and re-creation of imagined experience so that we can engage safely but emotionally with our inner selves and with other people, situations, times and places. In drama we can create images of how life has been, is now and how it might be. We can consider reality and ideals, fantasies and real possibilities. We can engage with big human ideas and issues through drama in safe and flexible ways that enable both engagement and distancing at appropriate moments. We are drawn emotionally into drama as audience and also of course through participants in role but we can step out of role, discuss and reflect. We can step in and out of role to try out different courses of action and take on different points of view and actively reveal different possible outcomes in relation to our different behaviours and responses. An excellent example of this is Forum Theatre (Boal 1992, see reference 20).

■ **enjoy learning and are motivated to achieve the best they can now and in the future**

Drama is enjoyable and highly motivating. Research (Harland et al. 2000, reference 14) suggests that drama in secondary schools is the most motivational of all subjects. When children are asked about drama, most will say they enjoy it. When adults are asked about their childhood dramatic play and drama experiences, most will smile and recall a range of positive emotions, with 'enjoyment' scoring most highly (Baldwin 2004, reference 13).

Confident individuals:

■ **have a sense of self-worth and personal identity**

Drama values the contributions of all participants and this helps build and sustain a sense of self-worth. In Drama, children and students are helped to get a better sense of who they are (ironically through taking on roles). Through working in role children and young people get a greater sense of the similarities and differences between themselves and other people and their personal identities and overlaps become clearer.

■ **relate well to others and form good relationships**

Drama relies on children and students working co-operatively and supportively together, otherwise it can't work. In drama they are working together towards the same goal (often under time pressure) and relying on each other for collaborative success, in which every child has a personal and shared stake. Creating, devising and performing together supports the formation and development of good relationships.

■ **are self-aware and deal well with their emotions**

Drama invites and evokes emotional engagement, yet gives safe distancing and opportunity for reflection through role. Children can genuinely respond emotionally to the drama and yet at the same time personally disassociate themselves through role from the emotions of the character they are portraying. Ironically, it is sometimes through imagining that we are someone else that we become more in touch with our own thoughts and feelings.

■ **have secure values and beliefs, and have principles to distinguish right from wrong**

As participants we bring our own values and beliefs to the lesson but also are invited to actively and cognitively engage with the values and beliefs of each other and of fictitious characters. We consider the motives and actions of other people and the outcomes arising from our own actions and those of others. This can make us clearer about our own personal values and beliefs. In drama we can play out the consequences of behaving with different attitudes and belief systems and values and replay things differently after individual and shared reflection. Drama often involves us in considering individually and together whether the actions and beliefs of characters are 'right' or 'wrong' and this gives us some insight into our own moral attitudes, behaviours and beliefs.

■ **become increasingly independent, are able to take the initiative and organize themselves**

In good drama, children and young people are the decision makers and are given opportunities to work individually and together and to take ownership of significant elements of the drama. Participants spontaneously improvise and create original drama, often in short periods of time that require them to organize themselves quickly and effectively as groups. Particularly if drama is being presented/performed, the participants need to be highly organized. In constantly changing working groups, improvisation in drama requires children to show initiative, to respond and to organize themselves and their thoughts quickly towards a shared goal.

make healthy lifestyle choices

The content of drama can easily be focused on healthy lifestyle choices and consequences. It can enable children to rehearse successfully making desirable healthy choices and having the confidence and ability to say 'no' to unhealthy choices.

are physically competent

Drama uses the body. It is a physical activity as well as a cognitive and affective activity. Some aspects of drama demand and develop significant physical control, e.g. mime, physical theatre. In drama, time is given to considering movement and gesture and the signals it gives and the impact on the responses of others. Through gaining a greater understanding of what the body is capable of and what signals it gives, children and young people can be helped through Drama to become more physically confident and competent.

take managed risks and stay safe

Drama can actively and reflectively enable children to rehearse dealing with and managing real-life risks safely. In role they can encounter and consider risk and safe choices with the support of others. Forum Theatre (see reference 20) can be a very effective way of empowering children to manage risky situations and actively consider the consequences of behaving and responding in various less safe ways.

recognize their talents and have ambitions

Drama clearly enables children with drama talent to come to the fore but it also provides a way of identifying a range of talents associated with drama (see reference 21). For example, some children may be multi-talented at drama performance whereas others will show talent at directing or managing perform-ances, etc.

In some drama situations children take on the role and imagined capabilities and talents associated with a possible future job or ambition, e.g. when children accept the Mantle of the Expert and are treated in the drama as talented archaeologists, museum curators, film-makers, company directors, etc. In drama (as in dramatic play) children can pretend to be talented in some way and try out what it feels like. They bring the aspiration one step nearer through imagining and practising.

are willing to try new things and make the most of opportunities

Drama involves having new ideas and then actively trying them out. The children are creating, using their own ideas and improvising, therefore much is new to them. Drama is risk taking and unpredictable and requires a willingness to be adventurous and exploratory in a co-operative way. Improvisation provides unique, transitory opportunities at a particular moment in time for children to respond and react to. Drama is a perfect forum for trying things out as it is a mutually supportive activity and the participant is protected by being in role.

■ **are open to the excitement and inspiration offered by the natural world and human achievements**
Drama can be about the natural world and can deal with issues linked to it, e.g. environmental sustainability. In dramatic play the outdoors inspires building dens, tracking, pretending to survive in primitive ways, hunting, being part of a tribe, etc. This links to Howard Gardner's 'Naturalistic Intelligence'. Sometimes teachers use outdoors and interesting natural environments to inspire and contextualize the drama, e.g. an island drama on a beach, a rainforest drama in a wood, etc. Theatre performances can also often be enhanced by natural settings. (See reference 22.)

Responsible citizens:

■ **are well prepared for life and work**
As Diagram 2 (see page 73) shows, many of the personal skills developed by drama are those also sought by employers. Children doing drama are being given opportunity to communicate well, understand body language, co-operate, negotiate, persevere with a team towards a common goal, empathize, listen, work successfully in a team, be resilient, problem solve, etc.

The roles children take within drama are most often those of adults and, frequently, adults with particular tasks to do (sometimes occupation related) and there are problems to solve (usually collaboratively).

■ **are enterprising**
Drama requires children to be enterprising in order to sustain the drama. Also, where schools are using Mantle of the Expert as a curriculum approach, children are working in role to set up and operate imaginary companies and enterprises and working for external clients.

■ **are able to work co-operatively with others**
Drama relies on co-operation with others to succeed. It gives opportunity for children to practise working co-operatively towards rewarding outcomes. Children co-operate because they want the drama to keep going and to work. Non-co-operative behaviours are often dealt with by peer pressure because most children want the drama to work and so, together, they demand the co-operation of each other.

■ **respect others and act with integrity**
Respect for each other's contributions is part of the drama contract. Children will need to listen to each other in drama and respectfully take account of each other's ideas. If they don't, then the drama will be difficult to establish or will fall apart. The roles within a drama often demand respect from others in order to work, e.g. a child pretending to be an official in a drama needs to be respectfully treated as an official by his/her peers.

■ **understand their own and others' cultures and traditions, within the context of British heritage, and have a strong sense of their own place in the world**
Drama is culturally rooted and an inspired experience. When children create drama they bring their own current cultural knowledge and understanding to the process. These may be culturally different from those of other participants in the group or class. The differences and similarities help children to gain insight into their own cultural identity, as well as learn, appreciate, understand and tolerate the cultures of others. In different cultures there are different theatre and performance traditions that can be brought to and infuse the whole class drama-making process.

■ **appreciate the benefits of diversity**
Diversities of experiences, ideas and viewpoints that are brought to the drama process by different participants benefit the drama and are a rich source from which to create together and gain understanding and appreciation of what each other brings. Drama enables diverse ideas to be shared, explored and given artistic form, as part of the creative process.

■ **challenge injustice, are committed to human rights and strive to live peaceably with others**
Drama provides a fictitious forum through which injustices that arise in real life can be explored and considered in a distanced way through working in role. It enables children to empathize with other humans and gives the possibility of conflict resolution in fictional contexts that nonetheless develop the real skills and attitudes associated with it, e.g. Unit 5, The Bystander.

■ **sustain and improve the environment, locally and globally**
Through Drama children can be helped to consider the viewpoints of different stakeholders locally and globally through working in role as if they are those stakeholders and by presenting their attitudes. It helps them to become clearer about their own attitudes to current issues of environmental importance.

■ **take account of the needs of present and future generations in the choices they make**
Drama enables children to engage with issues that will affect future generations, consider and rehearse the arguments and positions of different stakeholders and consider the likely effect of present actions on future consequences within a meaningful fiction, e.g. Unit 6, The Island.

Drama can easily and flexibly enable fictional time shifts. It is possible to move backwards and forwards in time and to hold moments in time still in order to support reflection. This means that scenarios and incidents can be played in different ways, involving different decisions, and lead on to different outcomes. Or, we can go backwards to find out how we might have arrived at the present moment in the drama, e.g. Unit 4, Night Walker. We can listen to and interact with those in role who hold different viewpoints.

■ **can change things for the better**
Through drama (and particularly the use of Forum Theatre) children can experience and begin to understand how different actions and viewpoints can lead to different (and more desirable) outcomes and how they can empower themselves to influence change for the better, e.g. Unit 5, The Bystander. Although they are working in a fiction, the thinking and learning is real and the skills and insights being developed are also real and are transferable to real life.

> *'In Drama we can help children become different selves. We keep giving them alternatives of where they might go ... They can take that make-believe, that pretend, that fiction into real situations to see if they can make the outcome different.'*
>
> *Mick Waters, Director of Curriculum, QCA (Reference 18)* ■

The National Curriculum is just the statutory bare bones that all children must receive. The way that the National Curriculum is planned and taught is for schools to decide and Ofsted can judge curriculum planning and provision to be outstanding. The range of learning experiences a child receives is also likely to be more than the school and its teachers provide in school hours. Mick Waters, the Director of Curriculum at QCA (until March 2009) points out that the entire, planned learning experience of a child includes not just what is laid down to be taught but also events and routines in school and what use is made of extended school hours and clubs.

Secondary students may have part-time jobs through which they learn and experience in a workplace things that will have connections with aspects of their school curriculum subjects or areas of learning. Children may be involved in charity work, out of school organizations, churches, youth groups and movements, etc. It will not be only teachers in school who will be supporting their learning. In relation to drama there will be secondary students who choose to take Arts Awards (*www.artsaward. org.uk*) on and off school premises. This award is being made available to primary schools, too, from 2009. In both primary and secondary schools there may be children who are taking accredited speech and drama examinations, performing in bands and orchestras, attending theatre and musical theatre and dance schools, attending arts festivals and theatre performances, etc. The organization of schooling is changing and this will impact on drama in and out of school hours and the premises.

Children and students may be accessing drama provision, and theatre education and experience, from external providers, some of whom may be theatre outreach workers or freelancers. These providers are coming into school more often now, enabled by the workforce remodelling agenda and the extended school hours requirements.

■ Planning drama into your curriculum

It has already been stated that drama can be considered broadly or narrowly in relation to the planned curriculum. If we embrace what drama in schools might consist of (see pages 68 to 69), then curriculum planning will have drama appearing in a range of ways both within and outside the subject, 'Drama', and potentially across all areas of learning (reference 1).

Indoor and outdoor dramatic role-play/drama/theatre opportunities

Drama can happen out of doors as well as indoors. There is a growing emphasis now on children experiencing more learning outside the classroom. Some schools have placed outdoor learning at the heart of their planned curriculum throughout the school year and found imaginative ways of planning learning experiences across areas of learning and across subjects. Indeed, some schools have appointed teaching assistants who work almost completely outdoors, particularly with younger children and some have even planned around half of early years lessons to be outdoors.

Before children went to school they were learning through play outdoors. Dramatic role-play often is inspired by the outdoor environment, e.g. building dens in bushes and surviving there without adults, making and trading perfumes and potions made with found rose petals and leaves, building outlines of rooms with mown grass and playing within them, building snowmen and attempting igloos, etc. These are familiar and almost timeless multi-sensory scenarios that we probably recognize and still happily remember from our own childhood play.

18. Drama can creatively link and support learning across the curriculam.

The outdoor play environment at school has many possibilities for drama, particularly as outdoor learning environments are being better planned now. The pond, the wildlife area, the willow dome or tunnel, the climbing frame, the hedges and trees, all have role-play and drama potential. When children are playing outside they create their own scenarios but there is no reason why schools cannot also plan role-play scenarios and drama lessons that also use outdoors, e.g. finding and maybe tracking the footprints of an unknown creature that is getting nearer each night to our encampment, surviving after a shipwreck (or kite journey, i.e. Unit 1, Whatever Wanda Wanted) on an imaginary island, an imaginary archaeological dig or dramatic treasure trail with prearranged 'finds', an expedition in an unknown land, a visit outdoors to the bottom of Jack's beanstalk, a walk around the castle grounds to hunt for a missing person or treasure, an outdoor walk around 'magic land' where nothing is what it seems, a visit to the talking tree that will put story pictures in our minds, seeing the moving castle (Simpson 2004, see reference 4), meeting or becoming a rainforest tribe, becoming physically part of an imaginary landscape, etc.

Exemplar lesson: Grounds for a Myth (Years 1–4)

Searching for signs of myths: The children, working in role outdoors as 'Myth Finders' (Mantle of the Expert) explored the school grounds searching for signs of forgotten myths. Each of the unearthed signs, e.g. an apple tree, a grassy mound and a tree stump, was physically represented by one of the children as a 'myth finder' who spoke as the object (Talking Objects). The class asked questions of the object (hot-seating). Then one at a time the children placed themselves by the object they thought should be explored first.

The rumours spread: The tree stump was selected and the children began to spread rumours and gossip about it, e.g. 'I think it's Jack's beanstalk', 'It is all that is left of a big Christmas tree', 'It is a very old tree from Tudor times' etc.

Travelling back in time: The children create a spell to help them 'rediscover' past mythical images connected with this outdoor place. In groups they locate and create these images (still image) and photograph them, e.g. the climbing frame became the beanstalk, the grassy mound was where the giant's castle had stood. Some children became directors for their groups to help ensure the images were clear.

Variations of the myth: The teacher in role as a passing traveller saw the photographs and told them that she had heard that the story did not end with Jack slaying the giant and living happily ever after but she couldn't remember how it did end! The children, split into two groups, devised a short performance depicting an alternative ending for the myth. The merits of each ending were discussed.

The magic lives on: The children decided the stump still had magical properties and was still able to transform (for the better) anyone who stood on it. What did the children want to become better at by standing on the stump? The myth finders in turn stand on it and become 'as strong as a bear', 'as fast as a cheetah', 'as clever as an owl', 'as kind as a grandma'.

The myth is recorded for future generations: The myth was then collectively written down and has become the first of many imaginative myths the children have created around different features in the school grounds.

Lesson by Teresa English, a D4LC class teacher at Great Hockham Primary School, Norfolk (see www.d4lc.org.uk and reference 22)

Outdoors can also be the perfect setting for creating, hosting or attending theatre performances. The outdoors can be defined as a performance space for the students to devise a fitting performance, for example, on an environmental theme. There are also many plays and types of performance that lend themselves to being staged and performed outdoors, e.g. 'The Tempest' or 'A Midsummer Night's Dream'. The Globe Theatre of course is effectively an outdoor theatre (with the audience as groundlings) and taking children to the theatre in Regents Park or to a National Trust outdoor theatre performance can also offer them a memorable, outdoor theatre experience.

Regular drama lessons focusing on practical learning

It is important that there are regular drama lessons that enable children to focus on learning practically about drama and how it works – to understand what drama is, what it can achieve, how to do it and how to get better at it. It has already been said that children and young people clearly need to do drama regularly. To do it now and again or hardly ever is not conducive to becoming skilled at drama and making progress in it. Putting on an occasional play is a valid project but not if this is all the drama children will get and it is always performance rather than process driven. A planning framework for drama needs to be assembled and adhered to, and ensures all children get regular access to drama teaching and learning from Key Stages 1 to 3.

Drama in the UK curricula

Drama in relation to the National Curriculum in England has been outlined earlier in this chapter but it is interesting seeing how drama fits into the curriculum and is developed in other countries in the UK and worldwide. In Northern Ireland there is now a new statutory drama curriculum (since September 2007). In Scotland Drama is a statutory part of the Expressive Arts curriculum and part of the new Curriculum for Excellence. In Wales Drama is now more prominent within English. The subject orders for English in Wales were rewritten in 2008 to provide greater flexibility and the position of drama and references to it within Oracy particularly have been strengthened. Whether Drama ends up in Arts and Design, Expressive Arts, Performing Arts, in English, as a sole subject in its own right or elsewhere, it should be a regular curriculum entitlement for all children.

The position of Drama in the curriculum of all United Kingdom countries varies slightly and so does the curriculum material available online to support the teaching of drama. Each country's drama curriculum support materials are interesting and worth looking at. They can be found at:

England: www.standards.dfes.gov.uk
Northern Ireland: www.nicurriculum.org.uk
Wales: www.accac.org.uk
Scotland: www.curriculumforexcellencescotland.gov.uk

National Drama, the leading association of UK drama and theatre educators (www.nationaldrama.co.uk), has been commissioned by the Training and Development Agency to produce online Continuing Professional Development materials for drama in England. These will be made accessible to all teachers (whether or not they are members of National Drama).

Drama curricula worldwide

Even though the curriculum of other countries is not of statutory relevance to teachers worldwide, it can still be interesting and helpful to have a look at what is 'out there' and available online drama-wise. Internationally, it is worth looking at what Queensland has put in place for drama, and the Tasmanian website has some very detailed drama support materials. New Zealand, too, has drama in its Arts curriculum and has a comprehensive website with many drama exemplars and film clips of 'process drama' lessons as well as a matrix of progress indicators that support the assessment of drama in the New Zealand curriculum. Information can be found at:

Queensland: www.qsa.qld.edu.au
Tasmania: http://resources.education.tas.gov.au
New Zealand: www.tki.org.nz

In many other countries worldwide drama is missing or just emerging in the curriculum. In some countries drama as pedagogy is beginning to spread because of enthusiasts who have studied in the UK (e.g. in Poland and Greece), even though it is not formally in the curriculum. In countries such as Sweden drama in schools is taught by drama pedagogues, who are drama trained rather than trained as teachers (rather like the emerging theatre educators in England). In some countries, e.g. France, drama is not in the curriculum and is viewed almost exclusively as theatre, with little or no place as yet for process drama. In the USA different states have their own curriculum and so the place of drama varies greatly (as it does in Canada). In Japan there is a growing interest in drama for learning, as is also the case in the Philippines and Hong Kong. Worldwide the variations are enormous and too many to mention. For anyone with a particular interest in worldwide drama it is worth networking through IDEA, the International Drama, Theatre and Education Association (www.idea-org.net) or attending international drama conferences, such as those organized in the UK by National Drama (www.nationaldrama.co.uk). Also, the website www.d4lc.org has an international forum strand.

Using drama to teach and learn in other subjects

Drama is a pedagogy. Children can learn just about anything through imagined experience that is supported and structured for learning by a good drama teacher. They can imagine themselves to be anyone, anywhere in any time or place for any purpose and facing any problem or issue. This makes drama as a way of working of use to any teacher for any subject or theme.

Drama in schools should be supported by drama specialist teachers but should be part of every teacher's toolbox. In secondary schools the Drama department or drama specialists in English departments can be used as a very valuable professional resource for all teachers of any subject. There are some schools where drama teachers are working in partnership with colleagues in other departments to help plan drama approaches into their teaching. Sometimes they are able to work alongside each other in lessons and unite their subject and teaching expertise to the benefit of the students. This is particularly seen in specialist arts colleges where teaching *through* the arts is being valued and developed as well as teaching *in* the arts.

Imaginative school leaders who have an understanding of drama will realize the potential of good drama teachers to support and work with other colleagues to improve teaching and learning. Good and visionary leaders realize that schools need drama specialists and that their role in the school is potentially much greater than just being the teacher who gets the Drama exam results and takes responsibility for producing the school plays.

Using drama to link teaching and learning across subject boundaries (cross-curricular studies)

Many primary schools are returning to cross-curricular and thematic teaching for at least some subjects and this approach finds support from QCA (although the term 'cross-curricular studies' is currently being promoted). The interim review of the Primary curriculum (reference 1) states that there will be a need to teach subjects both in their own right (as part of the new areas of learning), as well as across the areas of learning, i.e. as cross-curricular studies. There is already a move within the new KS3 Secondary curriculum towards teaching more creatively and planning across the curriculum more. Key Stage 3 curriculum planning and teaching is beginning to emerge in ways that seem to share many characteristics with existing good cross-curricular primary practice. More curriculum connection between primary and secondary schools in the future seems both desirable, and likely (reference 1).

Exemplar, cross-curricular lessons that use drama can be accessed from UK curriculum online websites. The Drama for Learning and Creativity (D4LC) website www.d4lc.org also has many unedited cross-curricular drama lessons that can be downloaded free and adapted. The units of work in this book do of course exemplify this 'cross-curricular studies' approach in ways that range across curriculum areas of learning and support personal development.

Using whole class drama to encourage empathy and explore human issues and motives

Drama has much to offer the proposed new Primary National Curriculum area of learning, 'Human, social and environmental understanding'. Whole class drama focuses on human issues, interests and concerns and supports children to develop together as social human beings. Drama is happening for us all in the same moment and we are emotionally connected and often united by it. Learning in role is highly engaging. We respond emotionally together and focus together on issues and ideas that are important to us as people. We are invited to respond on two levels, both in role (as someone else) and as ourselves. The role is developed by our real selves responding 'as if' we are someone else. Working in role encourages and develops our understanding of other people's viewpoints and motives. It also enables the issues being considered to be reflected on as if they are happening now and yet also (as it is 'pretend'), at a safe distance.

Drama can move us imaginatively through time and place. We can imagine ourselves as various thinking and feeling people at different times (past, present, future) and in different places (geographically and environmentally real or entirely imagined). We can think and feel individually or collectively as a group or class.

If you consider the National Curriculum for any age group, you will find opportunity to pick up through drama on the issues associated with different subjects and/or areas of learning. Although we want children to have certain knowledge and develop certain skills, we want them to develop personal understanding and to develop positively as 'confident, caring, responsible citizens' (the National Curriculum aims) at the same time.

We could for example just teach about Evacuees by telling the children about them or asking them to watch a film about them or read about or research 'Evacuees' on the internet but in drama we will bring it alive for them because they will be invited to feel and think in role 'as if' they are evacuees at different key moments. Through in-role interaction, they will begin to understand some of the parents' and host families' motives and experience some of the difficulties. It is likely that the children will want to enquire further about evacuees after being in role as them, and may well feel the need to enquire and research between lessons.

Using drama to develop thinking skills, to generate ideas, create and problem solve together

Drama stimulates and invites ideas. It involves thinking in and out of role. It involves thinking alone and together. It involves thinking, understanding, communicating and presenting thoughts using visual, auditory, kinaesthetic and tactile drama forms, strategies and conventions. In drama we can think with and through our bodies as well as our minds.

Different drama strategies and conventions help us to hold moments still, build them up or to move them on or back. We can stay with moments to deepen our thinking, exploring them from different viewpoints. We can build them slowly and think through, enact and feel the unfolding consequences of different courses of action and evaluate the outcomes.

Exemplar lesson: (Years 1 and 2)

A Key Stage 1 class were doing a drama lesson based on a book, A Lovely Bunch of Coconuts, *by Colin Reeder (reference 23), about a rich and greedy king who wanted to take the coconuts of a happy man, who lived alone on a small island with just one coconut tree.*

In the drama the children became groups of palace workers who were asked by the obsessive king (teacher in role) to first spy on the happy man (eye witness), report back and then to come up with a plan to get the coconuts from him. In role they logged the happy man's daily actions (writing in role) and reported back. Groups planned ways to get the coconuts and recorded their ideas on big sheets of paper (in any way they chose) before presenting them in turn to the king. There was opportunity to question the designers of each plan. During this process the children were problem solving, justifying, reasoning, explaining, describing, negotiating, co-ordinating, sequencing, co-operating, etc.

Some children felt uneasy about stealing for the king but did not dare tell him so. Some said it was bullying but others said it was acceptable just to obey the king's orders. The class split into two groups (as the happy man or the king) and then the children spoke these two characters' thoughts aloud.

The plans were creative and varied, e.g. sending an attractive woman in advance to give the happy man drugged food, trying to barter for the coconuts first, offering him a holiday at the palace to leave the island unguarded, giving him one chance to hand over the coconuts peacefully and, if not, taking him prisoner, arriving by submarine, warning the man he is in danger and helping him leave before harm comes to him, etc.

The children were then informed by the king that time had passed and that all their plans had failed. They acted out their plans in groups, showing where and why their plan had failed. These failed plans eventually became the source of additional text and illustrations (executed in the style of the author and illustrator) that were created later in Art and English and added in to the original picture book. The teacher also linked the work to a

Geography topic on Islands and to personal, social and emotional learning about happiness and about bullying. Design and Technology was stimulated by the drama, e.g. one group designed a machine that would catapult the coconuts from the island to the mainland and another group designed a boat with a hidden storage space for coconuts.

Drama utilizes and develops different types of creative and critical thinking. Throughout the drama the children are constantly gathering and processing relevant information. They are making sense, both alone and together, of what information they receive and are responding to it cognitively and affectively. They use logical reasoning skills and in role may be informing or justifying their reasoning. Their curiosity is stimulated and they are motivated to ask questions, to find out more, to enquire in role (and maybe also after the lesson, when out of role). They are evaluating the drama in terms of content, form, effectiveness and authenticity. The drama should inspire, use and develop the children's own ideas, not just be about enacting the teacher's ideas. Their creative and critical thinking shapes the drama and the drama itself becomes their 'in role' thinking, meaning made visible and communicated in order to shift and influence the thinking and understanding of others. The process itself also often leads to shifts in their own thinking and understanding.

Providing opportunities to make, perform and respond to performances

It is important that pupils and students have opportunities to make, perform and respond to performances, whether their own, their peers or professional theatre performances. In whole class drama the children are involved in what some practitioners refer to as 'Process Drama', where the focus is on the drama process and the associated thinking and learning processes, rather than a focus on performance as the key outcome. Process Drama can involve the use of performance as part of the learning process but performance is not its main aim. In whole class drama the children are usually the makers and performers of, and responders to, each other's performances within the lesson. In Process Drama the performance is internal to the class and not intended for an external audience as theatre.

All children, however, should have the opportunity to take part in theatre performances that are created and intended for presentation to external audiences. The process of making theatre for others gives additional dimensions and purposes to drama work. Being able to evaluate the performances is important. What worked well and why? What was the intended and actual impact on participants and audience? It is worthwhile to evaluate performance *as* performers and also *with* fellow performers, as well as with an audience.

In creating performances for invited audiences there are many other skills required and tasks to be done, besides acting. Drama students should start to gain awareness and experience of a range of theatre associated skills, e.g. directing, set design and building, scripting, make-up, costume, technical aspects (lighting, sound), advertising, front of house, etc. Theatre is a creative industry and there are associated careers that may be of interest.

Theatre visits and visits by theatre educators

It is important to arrange visits to theatres (front of house and behind the scenes) and to have theatre educators visit to work with the children. Any space can become a theatre space but, even so, there is value to all children from visiting professional theatres.

19. All children and young people should have opportunity to take part in a theatre performance.

Good theatre is inspirational and emotionally moving, as well as educational. If children are to be taught drama and learn through drama then there is value in them attending amateur and professional performances and evaluating them afterwards together. Theatre is an important cultural medium. As an audience of live theatre, they get a first-hand sense and understanding of what engages and captivates them. They begin to experience and analyse how space, light, voice, gesture and tension are used effectively, how the same play can be staged and interpreted differently, how costumes, sets, sound, music and lighting link to and support the performance, etc. They will increase their personal knowledge and understanding of theatre, which can then be transferred, adapted and integrated into their own drama and theatre work. Even mediocre theatre experiences can have positive impacts as the students themselves may see what worked well and what did not and can analyse how it might have been improved.

Opportunities for children to work creatively with actors, playwrights and directors

You may find that your local theatre has an education officer and making contact with them can be worthwhile. Increasingly theatres receive funding towards providing a range of creative industry work placements. Theatres are also increasingly receiving funding to enable theatre workshops to happen at the theatre (for students and teachers) or sometimes in schools, e.g. Royal Shakespeare Company Learning Department (www.rsc.org.uk/learning). Workshops are also sometimes provided by the touring theatre companies themselves, linked to the play that they are performing. They may involve working with one or two of the actors themselves.

You may find there are local and regular Youth Theatre opportunities for older students or regular theatre classes out of school hours provided by local theatres. Additionally, there are professional theatre freelancers (sometimes ex- or 'resting' actors) making their services available to schools, often through commercial companies that provide drama clubs or cover while teachers have their planning, preparation and assessment time. Covering teachers and replacing them to deliver the drama is not helpful to teachers in schools enhancing their own drama-teaching skills and less easily supports the integration of drama across the curriculum. Also, in terms of sustainability, you may need to consider whether the person is just filling in between acting jobs and therefore unable to sustain a regular commitment, or whether they are teaching acting or enabling process drama. However, if external provision is of good quality and is not 'bolt-on' provision at the expense of integrated and embedded provision, then it is probably worth arranging, but schools cannot abdicate responsibility for monitoring the provision they have put in place and they should take steps to ensure quality control.

With workforce remodelling increasing, enabling the employment of staff regularly who are not qualified teachers, there is great potential for school leaders to think creatively about employing professional theatre educators or freelance theatre professionals on a regular or blocked-time basis as long as the quality is at least satisfactory. Conversely, there is also the possibility of deliberately setting out to employ teachers who are (or have been) working in professional theatre already, and maybe are playwrights. Those who have worked in both theatre and education and understand drama/theatre and learning have a very valuable contribution to make to drama in schools. You need to be clear whether you are seeking people who will educate *in and about* theatre or educate *in and through* theatre. Ideally you will enable the children and young people to learn *in, through and about* theatre.

Sustainable links with creative professionals and creative industries are being encouraged and established in some schools through the Creative Partnerships initiative. Schools will increasingly have the opportunity to engage with creative professionals (including theatre professionals) through Creative Partnerships, which is a flagship, government initiative to support schools in developing and sustaining creative learning. The website www.creative-partnerships.com offers free access to many project exemplars, many of which involve drama and/or theatre.

There is also a government initiative (launched May 2008), called 'Find Your Talent' that aims to ensure a minimum of five hours' cultural entitlement for all children and young people (http://www.culture.gov.uk). This will increase the amount of partnership activity offered to schools in England by creative and cultural organizations and providers such as theatres. The activity will take place in and outside school and it is stated that all young people will have opportunity to perform on stage and attend top quality performances. This is very welcome as part of a school's drama provision.

Obviously, when you are creating your long-term plan, you will not know what the available performance will be in the future, but if you have mapped in that a theatre visit will happen then you are more likely to proactively seek out something suitable, without maybe discounting the possibility that you will adjust the curriculum timings to accommodate an unexpected opportunity that comes along and should not be missed.

It might be that you plan into your curriculum a drama/theatre-linked visit with another school on an annual basis, e.g. High Schools might be able to establish planned links with a local Further Education institution or Specialist Arts College whereby they annually plan for students to attend a performance they are putting on. Or it may be that the drama specialist teacher at a neighbouring institution whose school your pupils feed into will be willing to give some time to contribute to your planned drama curriculum, e.g. after Secondary exams are over it may be that the drama specialist teacher from a High School could go to the feeder primary schools to do some drama lessons (with the learning focus agreed with the class teacher) with Year 6 pupils who will be transferring. Maybe the Year 6 pupils could go to the drama studio at the High School for some sessions (possibly working alongside Year 7 students) as part of their induction programme.

■ Case study

The BTEC students at a sixth form college needed (as part of their course) to devise and perform a play for a specific external audience. The drama teacher arranged a visit to a local village primary school. The class teacher agreed that the drama teacher and his students could come in and work with the children (aged 5–7 years) and do weekly drama workshops in school time, leading to the students devising a performance afterwards for the children to see.

The teacher said she was doing a topic on 'The Sea'. The students planned four drama workshops around this theme and worked with the children for one afternoon weekly for four weeks. The workshops with the students and children led to children dramatic playing and solving problems encountered in underwater adventures and stories they created together.

Between visits the class teacher used the drama to stimulate art work and writing inspired by the drama. The children made fish and sea creature masks (and some props and scenery). The items made by the children were then used by the students in the devised performance they then created to show the children. The students' play could have been performed at the primary school but it was decided that the children would be picked up in the High School minibus and taken to its small studio theatre. This gave the young children a theatre visit experience, which they drew pictures of and wrote about (evaluated) afterwards. The students later took the show on tour to other primary schools in rural locations, where young children might find it difficult to get to a theatre. This process is now part of the planned curriculum for the BTEC students, although the theme and primary school now change annually.

The sixth form college takes each new performance on tour annually. The students create posters, advertise the annual theatre tour, make tickets and deal with bookings, etc. They charge schools for the performance to cover costs and make a small profit for their drama department. The tour is advertised to schools free by the local authority and if oversubscribed then the selection of schools is informed by local authority recommendations based on identified school improvement needs.

Opportunities for children and young people to manage the business aspects of running a theatre

Some secondary schools set up their own semi-commercial youth theatres and open their performances to the paying public to bring in funding and give business experience to the students. This enables the students to effectively manage and run a small theatre business together, rather than just be involved in drama as performers. It provides a valuable, authentic commercial experience to be built meaningfully into the wider curriculum that is linked to and part of their drama work. Even in some primary schools children are taking on the more commercial aspects of performances and setting up imaginary or even real companies through Mantle of the Expert curriculum approaches that involve completing tasks for real or imagined external clients. This curriculum approach (rooted in role-play and drama) has evolved in such a way that it now has developed striking similarities with business studies in secondary schools. Planning into the curriculum entrepreneurial and business opportunities such as this will support children and young people to develop skills that help them to achieve economic well-being.

A professional theatre is a business. It is possible that some secondary students might be interested in working in a theatre, as actors, directors, managers, front of house, lighting technicians, etc. So there is value in enabling students particularly to access the business aspects of a theatre as well as the performance itself. There are Arts Awards schemes now that support students to make and sustain connections with theatres as part of a national award scheme for students involved in arts activity and management. Currently this award is for secondary students but it is likely to be extended to primary children (www.artsaward.org.uk).

■ Where is the drama?

The planned curriculum will need to ensure that all children receive their statutory drama entitlement but that does not clearly define expectations in relation to the amount of time spent on drama. There are no hard and fast rules but an hour lesson at least fortnightly would seem a reasonable minimum.

One would expect to see drama strategies and conventions being used within the teaching of English. The national strategy frameworks offer some basic resources and lessons to support this but the emphasis is on the English rather than the drama. The national strategy framework is not statutory and it may be that schools can strengthen the drama aspects using the framework and the materials to support the creation of a more drama-rich curriculum experience for children (http://nationalstrategies.standards.dcsf.gov.uk).

In the proposed areas of learning for the new primary National Curriculum drama is expected to happen within arts and not just for English.

> *Exemplar lesson (Reception and Year 1)*
>
> *After listening to the story of 'Lazy Jack', the teacher asked her class if there was anyone in the story that they would like to talk with. Her intention was to use hot-seating for the children to find out more about a character through questioning.*
>
> *The children decided they wanted first to talk to Jack. They asked him why he was so lazy and why he let his mother do all the work. The teacher took on the role of Jack, who could not see that he was lazy or unreasonable.*
>
> *The children then said they wanted to talk to the Princess (who had decided she wanted to marry Jack because he made her laugh). The teacher was about to take on the role of the Princess when a 5 year old asked to be the Princess, so the teacher sat on the mat with the children and the child took the hot-seat and then confidently started answering questions and confiding in her audience that she objected to her father telling her who she might or might not marry. She told them being a princess was not easy and that everyone had ideas about who she should marry and she just wanted them to mind their own business. An Indian girl in the class said to the Princess that her father would only choose someone for her that was nice because he loved her. The teacher decided to stop the scene there and complimented the child on her working in role.*

Clearly there might now be considerable potential from this lesson, to make previously unforeseen links with Religious Education (arranged marriages) and with Personal, Social and Emotional Education and Citizenship. There was also the possibility of retelling or rewriting the story differently, challenging stereotypes (about princesses), creating alternative endings, etc.

Drama might be planned into the teaching of other subjects on your curriculum map if you want to ensure that all classes use drama approaches, e.g. for aspects of History or Religious Education each term. It may be that you plan for particular subjects or units of work to have a stronger drama emphasis than others, e.g. Ancient Greece provides a drama-rich opportunity for mask work, Greek Theatre and exploring myths and legends through drama. The key is to get balance, continuity and progression at the same time as having enough flexibility to 'go with the moment' if it is a learning pathway worth following.

To teach the curriculum for much of the time through drama would demand high levels of drama skill on the part of teachers and would possibly not be practical or desirable. Not everything is best taught through drama and it would be very time consuming and difficult to ensure full curriculum coverage. Also, just as some children prefer to learn through drama, there may be those who do not, so selection and balance is the key.

Your curriculum needs to be structured, yet flexible. Make clear where and when Drama will be learned and taught in the curriculum in its own right and where else it will be used within other areas. If it is not mapped out within your planned curriculum at all, it is unlikely to be valued or taught sufficiently or well.

A curriculum needs to be agreed but does not need to be set in stone. If a lesson develops in a way that seems to call for drama then confident teachers should feel able to deviate from the plan and next time plan the drama in. Conversely, if drama is planned in as an approach but during a lesson is not really working, then try another (possibly non-drama) approach, but evaluate why it didn't work in that particular lesson.

Drama is often used well as an approach to learning and teaching personal, social and emotional education. The SEAL materials (see reference 19) use working in role frequently and drama often and these materials are being further developed. Many schools also have Circle Time supporting their personal, social and emotional work. Circle Time is derived from the work of Jacob Moreno, founder of socio-drama and psychodrama (reference 24) and adapted by Jenny Mosely for use in school settings (reference 25). If schools find themselves getting into a bit of a repetitive rut with Circle Time and want to enliven it, then taking it back to its drama roots and strengthening the use of role-play and drama within it makes perfect sense.

Exemplar lesson (Year 5)

In English the Year 5 children had been studying narrative poetry and had done some text-based drama work based on 'The Lady of Shalott' by Sir Alfred Lord Tennyson (see reference 26). They had created the scenes contained within the poem that were reflected in the Lady's mirror and in her weaving. The teacher then decided to use the drama as a way of introducing loneliness as a theme in Circle Time.

With the children seated in a circle on the floor, she asked them (with their eyes closed) to imagine they are the Lady of Shalott and to try to imagine and feel her loneliness. What does her loneliness feel like? Can they think silently of times when they have felt lonely? Can they think of a way of completing the sentence 'Loneliness is …'? The teacher then asked them to remember one sentence starting 'Loneliness is …' and to maybe share it.

The teacher had a large ball of string and explained she would roll it across the circle and the person catching it would have opportunity to say their sentence aloud and then roll it to someone else, to say theirs. The ball of string should end up being rolled to everyone and if anyone did not want to offer a sentence they would simply roll the string on and just say, 'Loneliness is …' (without completing the sentence). There was, therefore, opportunity to contribute, but not compulsion.

Soon a symbolic web of string lay across the inside of the circle. The teacher asked, 'If this web represents loneliness, why might that be?' 'The web is like loneliness because it has big spaces with nothing in', 'The web is like loneliness because it can just go on forever', 'The web is like loneliness because it can trap you', etc. Long periods of silence were accepted.

The teacher asked the children to think of ways that they might be able to help people who are lonely and ways that people who are lonely might be able to help themselves. They wrote their ideas on self-adhesive labels and placed them ritualistically in the web spaces, speaking them aloud as they placed them, e.g. 'Ask a lonely person if they want to play', 'Ask a lonely person if you can help them', etc. The string was then silently wound up so that the web unravelled and just the labels remained. Groups of children then created and re-enacted short 'scenes of hope' inspired by the labels.

This activity can also be done so that the web is suspended across the classroom with tied labels left hanging or by hanging labels on a web woven around and between branches (indoors or outdoors), e.g. 'What suggestions will we hang on the tree of happiness?'

Assemblies can be drama rich and provide an audience for learning and performance opportunities. Assemblies can also be a forum for celebrating a variety of achievements in and through drama.

> *Exemplar lesson (Years 4–6)*
>
> *In a KS2 history lesson on the Victorians, the children had used an etching of a Lancashire cotton mill as the starting point for looking at and discussing the dangers and the working conditions of children who were mill workers (reference 13).*
>
> *Through drama they had created the scene depicted in the etching and brought it to life with improvised dialogue. The teacher was in role as an undercover spy in the mill, secretly gathering evidence and information about the dangers for Lord Shaftesbury.*
>
> *After the lesson the children researched on the internet and in books to find documented examples of real mill accidents.*
>
> *In the next lesson they created group still images of the documented incidents and brought them alive in a sequence of episodes. The children then answered questions in role from their peers. This led to eyewitness reports as a writing activity in English.*
>
> *In order to share the cross-curricular History, Drama and English work they had been doing, the class presented their scenes in a 'Celebration of Achievement Assembly'. They projected the original etching as a backdrop to their drama. Continuously, each group in turn presented the scenes they had created in the drama lesson, as a series of real, documented episodes. Each scene was introduced by a still image that was accompanied by a child reading out the original text and each scene concluded with a 'freeze frame' from which a child stepped out of each scene and read their eyewitness account to the audience before stepping back into the 'freeze frame'.*
>
> *Afterwards, the children in the assembly audience were invited to ask questions of the characters in any of the scenes, who answered in role.*

In early years settings you would expect to see role-play areas planned in thematically to reflect and support learning, e.g. a Chinese restaurant linked to celebrating the Chinese New Year, a boat and maybe a beach shop linked to a topic on the sea, a travel agent linked to a geography or travel theme, etc.

> *Exemplar – role-play area*
>
> *The area was set up as a hospital. Various bottles of pretend medicine painted different colours (sorting and colour recognition) and of different sizes and shapes (size and shape) were available but had to be signed for (emergent writing). A receptionist area had a computer (ICT) and telephone (speaking and listening) with a notepad (emergent writing) for taking messages. Magazines and books (reading) were available in the waiting area. There were nurses' uniforms and white coats and stethoscopes available (role-play) and clipboards with forms on (reading and writing). Patients arriving (role-play) had to take a number (sequencing and ordering) and wait to be called to the doctor. Trays of bandages of different lengths and widths were available (length and measurement) and children bandaged each other (role-play). There was a small shop area (money) for visitors to the hospital. The children created their own dramatic play scenarios spontaneously for a while before the teacher decided to enter and challenge in role.*
>
> *Teacher in role*
> *The teacher entered the waiting room, took a number ticket and waited to see the doctor. Her problem was she had hurt her leg (which he bandaged) and banged her head and lost her memory. She did not know who she was or how to get home again. This led to*

problem solving, with some children offering her a hospital bed until she remembered, others saying they needed to get a 'head doctor', and others saying that she could come to their house and stay. Another offered a cup of tea and a hug.

The teacher said she was worried and upset and started looking for a tissue in her handbag. She emptied her handbag and said maybe there were clues in her handbag that would help them to find out who she was and where she came from. The children and she looked through and discovered items such as a driving licence, debit card, etc., and so the mystery was solved and the teacher started to recall now who she was and had quickly recovered due to their help.

There are also close links to be made between drama, film and media and it may be that you link some of your planned drama to the use of digital media and technologies, e.g. different types of cameras to create still and moving images linked to drama. Conversely, there are some film clips available via the National Strategy website (http://nationalstrategies.standards.dcsf.gov.uk) that can easily stimulate drama, e.g. *The Piano* by Aidan Gibbons (also available to view via You Tube).

Improving the learning and teaching of Drama across the school

■ What does good drama learning and teaching look like?

Good drama teaching does of course share many aspects with good teaching generally, whatever the subject, but the nature of the subject itself, being an arts subject and with a focus on creativity, will yield particular aspects to look for in a good Drama lesson. Good teaching should result in good learning and it is by looking at what the children are doing and seeing how they are engaged, responding and progressing, that we can judge the teaching. In Drama lessons we may be both judging the progress being made in drama learning as well as learning in other areas that are being taught through drama.

Learning intentions

Drama has to be about something and have a purpose. Drama can be enjoyable, exciting, fun, but in school we need it to have learning intentions/objectives. Good Drama lessons are for more than just enjoyment and teachers need to be able to articulate what they want the children to learn and get better at as a result of a lesson or series of lessons.

Teachers' planning varies greatly and schools make widely varying demands on teachers in relation to the type, detail and format of lesson planning. However, whatever system is being used, it is reasonable to expect that a teacher can tell you the purposes of the lesson in relation to learning and what they want the children (and different individuals or groups of children) to achieve in the lesson and as part of a longer-term plan. There should be drama learning objectives in a Drama lesson but there may also be one or two objectives for other subjects or areas of learning, e.g. history learning objectives or personal, social or emotional objectives. A Drama lesson should always have at least one drama objective. No exact number of objectives is correct but maybe up to three objectives overall will ensure the learning focus is not so widespread that it gets lost when the lesson is under way and ideas are flowing.

The skill of the drama teacher is to achieve the range of learning objectives (drama and non-drama) while using the children's ideas as they arise. This is skilled teaching, to give ownership to the children for the direction of the drama and yet not abandon intended learning outcomes. The learning outcomes need to be referred to at the start of the lesson and achieved dynamically (as the drama is unfolding 'live' and may take unexpected directions).

It is noteworthy that a disproportionately high percentage of teachers nominated for the national Teaching Awards seem to be drama teachers or else have had significant amounts of drama training at some time (reference 27). There seems to be a correlation between drama teaching and exceptionally high quality teaching. That is not of course to say that all drama teaching is good, but (in almost the words of a well known nursery rhyme), 'when it's good it's very, very good and when it's bad it's horrid!'

If the objectives are for learning in other curriculum areas the drama teacher needs to be sure that the drama delivers effective learning in the other subject area(s). A criticism of some cross-curricular Drama lessons is that they meet the drama objectives but do not always achieve enough in relation to the learning in the subjects that are being taught through drama, e.g. History or Maths. It is one reason why (particularly in secondary schools) subject specialists might benefit from working in closer partnership with the Drama department and maybe even try some team teaching to

20. The purpose and impact of the teacher being in role needs to be clear and evaluated.

ensure the learning is at least satisfactory in all subjects being taught in and through the Drama lesson.

Teachers have to stay 'on the ball' in a Drama lesson as the teacher is an active participant who needs to be able to operate both as teacher and as co-participant 'in role', alert to all that is happening at both levels (as teacher and as participant). The teacher needs to structure and support the dynamic and unpredictably evolving Drama lesson while keeping the focus of the children's learning clearly in mind. It is far too easy (and pleasurable), once a Drama lesson is under way, to have a very enjoyable Drama lesson but lose sight of the original intended learning. So teachers need to stay learning focused and be clear when they evaluate the lesson, what learning actually took place and what progress was made.

The learning intentions will focus and inform the teacher's 'in role' and 'out of role' interactions and teacher moves. However, a good drama teacher is also responsive to and directed by the ideas that the children offer and so drama teaching can be a challenging balancing act that changes direction. Teachers need to remain open to unexpected learning opportunities that arise and are worth following, without habitually losing sight of original learning intentions.

Observation of Drama lessons should be a part of any school's normal lesson observation schedule, particularly if teaching in and through drama is a stated development area. It can link in with other subject observations, e.g. a literacy lesson might give opportunity to also observe and comment on the effective use of drama strategies and conventions.

Drama lesson observation guidance

Do look at any Drama lesson planning (preferably in advance). Lesson plans don't need vast amounts of detail and are working documents but the learning intentions or objectives should be evident from the start, even if just accessed through pre-lesson conversation with the teacher. Try to talk with the teacher about the lesson in advance and maybe ask if there is one aspect the teacher would like you to focus on and feed back on (in addition to one or two you have in mind that link to school improvement priorities). Focus your observation and maybe track certain children or groups of children, e.g. higher, average, lower ability pupils (HAPs, AAPs, LAPs), Looked After Children (LAC), English as an Additional Language (EAL), Learning Difficulties and Disabilities (LDD), etc., during the lesson. Drama lessons can have a great deal going on at times and it is easy to become swamped if you aren't clear about the focus and purpose of your observation.

Where are the children starting from? Is this the first Drama lesson on this theme, or is it one of a series? The learning intentions in Drama lessons should be shared with the children (as with lessons in other subjects).

There should be verbal (and maybe visual) reference made to learning objectives during the lesson and clarity about what is required of the children when a task is set, e.g. 'Your scene will show one important moment that helps us understand why the man is leaving his home. You will all start with a still image and then come to life for no more than a minute. Your scene will finish with a freeze frame and each person in the group will say just one line during the scene.'

Look at the dynamics between the children in the different groupings during a lesson and the impact (positive and negative) that the group membership is having on the learning opportunities for different children. You may find it revealing to track one or two particular children and judge whether they are enabled or hindered learning and creativity wise by the groups they experience being part of. Are certain children consistently dominating and taking prime roles, or do all children have opportunities and have their ideas taken account of?

What is the teacher doing while groups are working? Is he/she supporting individuals and groups during the group work or standing back? Is he/she tuning into the learning and moving it forward through comment, questions, challenges?

Also one can expect that the teacher will find a way (maybe in drama mode) of helping the children reflect on what has happened in the drama and what they have learned. It is worth you talking also with two or three children after the lesson about what they think went well, what they have learned and what they became better at and think they need to do next.

Talk to the teacher after the lesson about the progress the children (or different groups of children and individuals) made. Don't start by saying, 'What did you think of your lesson?' If they say it was fantastic and you think not, it's a tricky starting point! Listen attentively to the teacher and question supportively to help deepen the teacher's evaluative response.

Can the teacher identify and explain what worked well and why and for which child or groups of children and what went less well and why?

Ask also how the next Drama lesson will be informed or adapted as a consequence of the one you have just seen. Tell the teacher what you thought went well and what he/she/the children achieved and then suggest/agree one or two areas to focus on for development/improvement.

You do not need to be a drama specialist to observe and judge various important aspects of learning in a Drama lesson. Learning and teaching will have generic aspects in common in any subject lesson. However, if you are observing a Drama lesson, it is important to recognize appropriate 'on task' behaviours that may well, to the untrained eye, seem unusual, and can even be noisy at times. The creative process is not always quiet and linear, and engagement at certain parts of the Drama lesson may well legitimately involve moments of fun and laughter (which can be part of a group bonding), closely followed by periods of intense and serious concentration. Avoid snap decisions about what you see when judging a Drama lesson (or any other lesson for that matter). The context is important to know. Moments of laughter in preparing drama scenes do not necessarily mean children are not committed or working seriously. Inappropriate laughter in the midst of an improvisation might mean just that.

It may be worth considering arranging drama specialist observation of your school's Drama lessons, for example by arranging for a drama adviser to carry out some paired observations with the drama leader. This would provide a valuable professional external perspective and at the same time help validate the lesson observation judgements of the drama leader.

Every Drama lesson is different but some factors that militate against a successful Drama lesson are as follows:

- certain individuals are allowed to dominate

- children feel vulnerable to being mocked or put down by peers

- children's ideas are not welcomed

- the drama itself is not interesting or relevant

- the tasks set are too difficult, stressful or unclear

- the tasks set are not demanding enough

- it is the teacher's drama and the children just enact the teacher's ideas

- the children are not listening to each other and not valuing each other's contributions

- the teacher is not inviting, listening to and responding to the children's ideas

- the teacher communicates personal embarrassment about working in role

- the teacher is 'tongue in cheek' and does not take the drama seriously

- the children are being given too long (or not long enough) to carry out the tasks.

■ The Drama Contract

Do the children know the expectations about how to behave in a Drama lesson? Are their attitudes and behaviours that they are exhibiting conducive to good drama?

Negotiating a Drama Contract with the class is a helpful and important first step for teachers embarking on drama. It enables everyone to agree positive, individual and group behaviours that the Drama lesson requires in order to work. Messing up make-believe is very easy but sustaining it requires everyone's effort and agreement. Children know what helps make-believe work (or stops it from working) because they understand very well how dramatic play works. The Drama Contract is a social contract designed to help keep their shared make-believe (the drama) going. The Drama Contract also helps children to feel secure in Drama lessons and helps them feel relaxed enough to contribute without fear of ridicule.

A Drama Contract is likely to be similar to any other behavioural contract your school already has. If so, you could use this as the basis of a Drama Contract or set one up from scratch but using the same principles. If you have a Circle Time contract in place you will probably find it is very similar to a whole class Drama Contract. However, you do need to be sure that teachers' behavioural expectations are consistent across the whole school in relation to Drama lessons.

Like any social and behavioural contract, the children should understand and be involved in the reasoning behind it and feel they have joint ownership of it. They should help to create it, and agree it, rather than have it imposed on them by the teacher as a set of rules.

Exemplar Drama Contract

- We all agree to *pretend* that what is happening in the drama is real.

- We will work in role seriously and treat others who are working in role seriously.

- We will all help to keep the make-believe going.

- If we are finding it is difficult to pretend then we can 'pass' and not contribute until we are ready (but we will stay in the class drama).

- If someone decides to 'pass' and not contribute, the rest of us (including the teacher) will accept this without comment.

- We will never do anything that deliberately spoils the drama and deliberately breaks the make-believe.

- If anyone says or does something 'in role', then what is said or done belongs to the character and not the person who is pretending to be that character.

- When the drama is over we leave the characters in the drama world behind and we stop pretending.

■ Engagement

Are the children clearly interested and fully engaged in the drama? The drama needs to hook the children in from the start by being about something that is of interest to them and then the lesson needs to progress in a way that keeps them interested and actively involved. The opening few minutes of the lesson are crucial. If a teacher spends a long time talking out of role about the drama instead of getting on with actually doing drama, then the children will soon get fidgety, bored and switch off. Drama is an active subject so we don't really expect to see children sitting for most or all of the lesson unless there are good reasons for this that help the drama. Non-specialist drama teachers in particular are sometimes reluctant to let children get actively 'up and on the move'. This may be partly due to drama being within English in secondary schools and often being taught in classrooms by English teachers who are not drama trained. Also, with drama being mostly seen as part of literacy lessons in primary schools, the same static approach can result, with children spending too much time sitting on mats and doing drama mostly in the head and not with the body too.

If a child is consistently having difficulty engaging in drama, there may be reasons for this that link to that child's emotional state or specific needs. The teacher will need to be sensitive as to why a child might not feel able to engage or work in role and should try to keep the child present and attentive in the drama, without putting them individually on the spot or letting them just sit out and watch. Children on the autistic spectrum often experience difficulty with imagining but can be very accomplished at imitation and mimicry. The teachers should make the whole class Drama lesson inclusive and adapt tasks if necessary for individuals or groups and provide support for children experiencing difficulty working in role, rather than exclude them.

PART ONE

21. Drama needs to stimulate and use the body, mind and emotions.

If teachers are not secure about drama and/or behaviour and discipline then they sometimes keep children repressed for fear of poor behaviour. Ironically, too much repression can lead to children breaking free and exhibiting poor behaviour. Paradoxically, a Drama lesson can be fully engaging and yet very static, or can be physically very active but with little real engagement, but if the Drama lessons are mostly static, or conversely never have moments of stillness, then this would suggest that children are not being given enough variety and balance of drama forms and approaches. Different points in the drama require different approaches.

The start of Drama lessons should not always be predictable. Starting Drama lessons in a range of ways will stimulate curiosity and support engagement. A teacher might start the lesson using music, or an object, a piece of text, or by going straight into 'teacher in role', or by using a photo, picture or painting. Whatever the teacher decides to do as an opening move, it is important that he/she has the full attention of the whole class before starting. Children need to be self-disciplined to do drama well and the tone is set at the start by the teacher. The children need to be able to focus and listen well and be sensitive to nuance, atmosphere and non-verbal signals. Drama involves high levels of co-operation and teamwork and good teachers will consistently make clear what their expectations of the children in Drama lessons are.

■ Dramatic tension

This links closely to high levels of engagement. When children are emotionally engaged with a drama then there are likely to be moments of dramatic tension arising or built in, that they fully engage with and care about. Good Drama lessons have moments that hold and focus us emotionally and which we can influence. Some Drama lessons are poor because they are full of empty, teacher-directed drama exercise activities that do not invite or inspire emotional engagement from the children. Drama exercises may have a purpose at times but lessons that consist of little else are very limited.

The way to make drama flourish is to keep children interested rather than under the thumb. Build in 'cliff-hangers', moments of great tension and importance that fire the imagination. Don't let the plot just skate on fast at a surface level. Decide the key moments and hang in there awhile, building the tension. Help the children to realize that quite often in drama 'less can be more', and that just a small gesture, a sound, a single word, can have immense significance to characters and to the plot.

Exemplar lesson (**see reference 28**)

In a drama about migration, Year 7 students were working in pairs as a husband and wife who have one small child. As a class, they had built up the adult characters together, from an image in Shaun Tan's graphic novel, The Arrival (reference 29), *in which a couple are stood at either side of the kitchen table, looking downwards and away from each other. The wives in the pairs were all then taken aside and told that they knew their husbands were considering leaving them to find work in another country but were desperately hoping they would decide not to go. The husbands were then taken aside and told they had decided to leave and now needed to tell their wives. They were instructed not to tell the wives until several minutes into the improvisation. The delay led to a build-up of dramatic tension that would have dissipated if they had decided to tell their wives immediately. They tried the scenes in different ways and watched each other's before a husband from one pair and a wife from another pair volunteered to improvise the scene together in front of the whole class. The dramatic tension was strong as the audience heard the wife tell her husband she was pregnant again in advance of him having to say he was leaving. The tension was built because the audience knew what the wife did not and everything she said had additional resonance and built tension because of this.*

■ The teacher's role

Teachers have the simultaneous roles of structuring the lesson to the advantage of both the learning and the drama and at the same time being an active co-participant in the whole class drama. The quality of the teaching and learning is directly related to the quality of the interactions between the teacher and children. Unsatisfactory lessons can result if the teacher dominates and takes too much personal ownership of the drama. The decisions within a drama should be arrived at by the children and their ideas should be carefully listened to and should help feed and shape the drama. The children are not supposed to be the teacher's puppets or awestruck audience and will soon get frustrated and lose interest if they are not given any authentic ownership and sufficient opportunities for interaction. Domination of the lesson by the teacher sometimes occurs with insecure teachers, who are too frightened of losing control of the children and so keep everything on a tight and prescriptive rein. Poor lessons can also result when teachers are frustrated thespians who are putting their own

PART ONE

enjoyment of acting before the children's needs as learners and those of the drama. An Ofsted report on Creativity, entitled 'Expecting the Unexpected' (reference 31), cites some very good examples of drama teaching but also cites an example of poor drama teaching where the teacher's acting performance simply overwhelmed the children so that they felt disempowered and unable to contribute.

It is possible but not desirable for teachers to do Drama lessons without taking on roles themselves. Teacher in role (TiR) is a key strategy in the drama teacher's toolbox and one would expect to see it used in Process Drama lessons. TiR links closely to the way that empathetic adults with learning agendas spontaneously play alongside young children (see Glossary).

It is important that children know when the teacher is in role and so it is important that the role is 'signed' clearly for the children. Teachers should not always take on high authority roles, e.g. the Lord of the Manor (Unit 2, The Green Children), the Billeting Officer (Unit 3, World War 2 (Evacuees)), etc. To always take on high status roles could indicate that the teacher is insecure, as such roles often appeal to insecure teachers who dare not risk not being clearly still in control. Of course, even if the teacher plays a low status role, e.g. a beggar throwing themselves on the mercy of the children as rich townsfolk, the teacher is still actually in control as he/she is only pretending to be a beggar. The teacher can drop the role and stop the drama at any time. It is through using a range of roles, however, that the teacher provides broader opportunities to the children to respond in a range of ways.

22. Teachers in role are highly engaging to children and present at the point of learning.

■ Observing teacher in role

You will want to consider what the teacher is actually doing throughout the lesson (when both in and out of role) and what the quality and impact of the teacher/pupil interactions are in relation to the learning and to the drama.

When observing Drama lessons, notice how much of the lesson is actually spent doing drama, rather than talking about doing drama or preparing to do it.

■ Are the teacher interactions and the teacher structuring moving the learning and drama on?

■ Are they encouraging and guiding individuals and groups, while not overstepping the 'directing' line?

■ Are they modelling communication and techniques for the students?

■ Is there balance between the time the teacher is interactively involved in and out of role?

■ Is the amount of time the teacher spends giving instructions and structuring the drama itself sufficient but not over-laboured, i.e. not taking too much time from being in drama mode?

■ Are they using teacher in role and if so what is their stated purpose for doing so … and was it effective?

■ Is the amount of time the teacher is spending in role necessary and sufficient and does it support or hinder the children's learning and creativity?

■ Over a series of lessons does the teacher take on a range of roles of varying status or does the teacher opt consistently for high status roles?

■ Groupings

Whole class drama involves the whole class in role together at the same time but it can also involve working in groups of different sizes and in pairs or individually within the same drama. Good drama teaching enables groups to be well matched to the learning/drama activities being demanded. High levels of group co-operation and teamwork can be required in Drama lessons and friendship groups will not always work to the advantage of all children. Sometimes friendship groups are fine but changing the group dynamics is important to shift responsibilities and give opportunity to all.

Drama demands real group work, not just working alongside each other in a group. For a piece of performance or presentation to work it needs the active involvement and full concentration and co-operation of every group member. One cannot assume that all children possess the skills necessary to take part successfully straight away in group drama work and it may well be necessary for the teacher to state clearly what good group work in drama consists of, e.g. everyone's ideas are valued and listened to, no one puts anyone else down, everyone has opportunity to contribute and be actively involved, no one person dominates, etc. The children themselves can be asked to define and record together the criteria of good group work to bring it to the fore.

Although drama should give opportunities to work in groups of varying sizes and constitutions, the structuring of the drama experience should be led by the learning.

PART ONE

Teachers should not try to use a recipe approach for lessons. They do not always have to provide individual, group and whole class sections to each lesson. However, over time it is best to offer balance.

Drama teachers often use activities and games to get children to mix up and to be with children they do not normally work with, just prior to setting group tasks. Rather than explicitly saying, 'James, change groups because I don't want you working with Ryan' (which is likely to antagonize James and probably also Ryan), the teacher might just number children apparently randomly but make sure that James and Ryan don't end up together with the same group number. Or the teacher might do a drama game or quick activity to mix children in an enjoyable way before starting.

> **Lesson activity for creating mixed groups**
>
> 'Get into groups of ...' The children are asked to move around the room in different directions until you call out a number. They should then get into groups of that number and sit down, while avoiding being the last group formed. This means that pragmatically they group with people near them rather than waste time hunting out their friends. *(When James and Ryan are in different groups, you can stop the activity.)*

■ Differentiation and challenge

Getting the right level of challenge in the Drama lesson is important, as the right level of challenge is motivating. Too little challenge and the children may get bored and not bother to strive, whereas too much challenge and they may become overwhelmed or stressed and fail. It is worth getting feedback from the children themselves about how challenging a drama task was and how they felt about it. Children can be good critical friends to teachers and can become co-planners who are able to structure the drama with the teacher, once they are used to drama.

Giving children specific drama vocabulary (see Glossary) is empowering and makes it easier for them to shape and structure the drama themselves and in partnership with the teacher. Once they know and understand drama-specific vocabulary the teacher does not need to spend as much time explaining and setting up drama activities, he/she can just say for example, 'You will present your scenes as a Performance Carousel', without having to explain what it is, and the children will know what this entails.

> Teacher: We have decided that we want to find out more about what the character is thinking before he makes his important decision, so maybe it would be the right moment to bring him in and 'hot-seat' him.
>
> Year 6 child: Can we do 'thought tracking' instead?
>
> Teacher: Why would you prefer to use thought tracking?
>
> Year 6 child: Because if we hot-seat him he might lie to us but if we use thought tracking, we will hear what he really thinks.
>
> Teacher: Let's try both strategies and see what difference it makes.

Drama is very flexible. You can revisit the same character or moment in different ways, and make the tasks increasingly challenging in order to go deeper and demand greater levels of drama skill.

It is of course worth differentiating some drama tasks for different groups, to enable all children to be challenged and achieve, regardless of their drama ability. Whole class drama is often inclusive in its demands and yet is differentiated by outcome but nonetheless there is opportunity to make differentiated demands of various children or groups of children, e.g. a less able group might be asked to make a realistic still image of a key moment, whereas a more able group might be asked to create a symbolic still image representing the character's emotions at that same key moment.

■ Pace

The pace of the lesson and of different parts of the Drama lesson is important. In education there has been a tendency in recent years to assume that lessons that are moving quite rapidly from activity to activity with the teacher imposing short and challenging time limits are what is required, and yet for emotional engagement and meaningful learning to occur speed is not always best. Teachers are worried about being seen to 'waste' time and this can militate against the slower periods of reflection necessary as part of problem solving, creativity and learning. There are parts of Drama lessons where fast pace is appropriate and fits the mood of the drama, and other parts of the lesson where it is best to let the mind linger and work intuitively, to carry out what Guy Claxton calls, 'slow thinking', where ambiguity is tolerated and people feel 'comfortable being "at sea" for a while' (reference 30). All activity and no stillness and reflection limits and inhibits the learning.

Drama is a medium that enables us to use and express our conscious, subconscious and unconscious intelligences and can deal actively and reflectively with all types of human predicament.

■ Homework

Most drama activity is by nature interactive but, nonetheless, homework linked to drama can support learning in a range of ways (and in secondary schools may be a requirement for coursework). But it would be unfortunate if children always associated drama with writing afterwards. Writing *in* drama is different from writing *about* drama. Homework more often ends up being reflective and about aspects of the drama, as of course it is done outside the lesson time and more likely to be done individually. Homework can be an opportunity for revisiting what has been learned or extending the children's knowledge linked to the drama. It can also give opportunity for the pursuance of personal interests in relation to the drama. Effective secondary drama departments will have developed a range of homework provision linked well to learning in and through drama.

Homework exemplars

I. A class of 7-year-old children had taken on the roles of wolf experts in a drama based around the book by Ann Turnbull, *The Last Wolf* (reference 32). The children wanted to be convincing as wolf experts and so for homework found out more about wolves before appearing in front of the king (teacher in role) in the next drama lesson. The king interviewed them for the post of 'humane wolf catcher'. The need to know about wolves for the interview in the next Drama lesson motivated the learners to do research. The teacher had given the children some hints as to the sorts of question that the king might ask them in order to help focus their research.

2. A class of 11-year-old children were doing a unit of drama work based on 'The Lady of Shalott' (see reference 26) and used Part One of the narrative poem to create a pictorial map for homework (after the first Drama lesson). They used only landscape references found in the poem. The challenge was to be sure that the finished map fitted only with the text of the poem, i.e. river flowing to Camelot, fields of barley and rye, tower, etc. This meant that when the drama resumed, they had a clearer visual image of the geographical landscape in which the drama was taking place. Of course, it also meant that they had to keep revisiting the text carefully for an imaginative purpose.

3. Secondary homework might involve maintaining individual drama log books in which students regularly record their progress and their personal contributions to the drama. This might involve self-assessment of progress towards targets they have set themselves. Homework might also include reading/researching on an aspect of the drama/theatre, or preparing an oral presentation.

■ The assessment of drama

The assessment of drama (as in any subject) has two main purposes. It is used summatively as a way of knowing a pupil's level of attainment at a particular point in time (as in end of term or year tests and exams for example) and it is used formatively (as in Assessment for Learning) to help children to improve at drama. Through assessing, we find out what children can do and this reveals the 'next steps' they need to take in order to make progress and this, in turn, informs the teacher's planning.

The assessment and levelling of drama has been problematic in England. Despite drama being part of a core subject (English), there has been a dearth of officially generated assessment guidance or support materials for drama, compared with other subjects. No official levels for drama have been forthcoming from QCA. This has been a blessing and a curse for drama. This lack of assessment prescription can be seen as enabling, but when headteachers (in secondary schools) insist on being given National Curriculum drama levels, drama teachers look around for help.

In the absence of any formal National Curriculum official levels for drama, Arts Council England published *Drama in Schools*, second edition, in October 2003 (reference 33), which offers an assessment framework with eight levels, to support continuity and progression in drama across all Key Stages. The levels are not statutory levels. These levels were drawn up by drama consultants employed by Arts Council England and have not been arrived at in the way that levels usually are through QCA processes. However, many teachers have found them useful in the planning and assessment of drama and some teachers have adapted them. (See www.artscouncil.org.uk/information)

Secondary teachers who are well organized in their assessment of drama can usually provide written and oral evaluations of each student's work over time and have individual records of pupil progress. These are likely to outline the strengths and areas for development for each pupil. Good pupil profiles will identify 'next steps', both skills-wise and knowledge-wise, for each pupil. Individual feedback is most effective and good assessment approaches are also likely to incorporate self- and peer-assessment. Realistically very few primary schools have as yet felt the need to produce such detailed drama assessment for children.

It is interesting to look at levels for drama that have been produced in New Zealand as part of 'The Arts in New Zealand Curriculum'. They set out how students might progress from Levels 1 to 5 and are available online (www.tki.org.nz/r/assessment/exemplars/arts/drama/index_e.php).

New Zealand has the key aspects of learning in drama as:

- Working in role
- Using dramatic structures
- Creating dramatic space
- Responding to Drama

There is of course a danger with levelling drama that teachers might be drawn into teaching to the levels, which could narrow the teaching and lower expectations. Teachers should teach what is appropriate to the children and what creates good drama and then, if necessary, level the worthwhile process and outcome.

In terms of planning drama, teachers may find assessment frameworks useful to ensure that they can plan for and find evidence of students' progress in drama subject knowledge, understanding and skills, but the assessments must be meaningful and child friendly and fit for purpose.

Assessing through drama

Drama itself has been much used as a way of assessing in other areas, particularly speaking and listening. Fictitious, flexible scenarios give a reason to speak in role to a range of audiences for a range of purposes, using different registers. Drama has also been used as a way of improving assessed writing, with schools sometimes practising for English SATs by approaching questions and tasks through drama (reference 26). A wide range of personal, social and emotional competencies and skills can also be assessed through drama activities and lessons.

■ Evaluating the drama

In Drama lessons the children are each other's audience and need to be made aware of what is expected of a good audience. They need from the very start to be encouraged to give any performance their full attention. This is basic good manners but clearly a poor audience can have a detrimental impact on performers. Drama is about communication and expression. It needs to be listened to and observed well.

PART ONE

It invites cognitive and affective response. Children need to be encouraged and given opportunity from an early age to evaluate both their own performances and those of others (whether it be their classmates' performance or professional theatre).

Clearly evaluation is a skill that can be developed in Drama lessons, and as children gain more understanding and experience of what works well in drama, and why, they become increasingly able to evaluate the quality and impact of the drama. They should be helped by drama teachers to become more aware of drama vocabulary (see Glossary) and of the criteria by which they can critically and constructively evaluate drama. They will become more practised at individual, peer and group evaluation. The teacher can co-evaluate the drama with the children, sometimes offering a model of perceptive evaluation, or holding back to enable the children to evaluate it first.

Pupil voice

> *'I liked the way that Becky talked posh when she was being the Queen because it was funny. I didn't know she could talk like that.'*
>
> *Pupil, age 6* ■

> *'I think the way that they all came in together and made a tableau to start with was good because it let us think about what was going to happen next before any of the characters spoke. But I think it might be better if they did the tableau for a bit longer because it was a bit quick and I hadn't finished looking at it properly.'*
>
> *Pupil, age 13* ■

Of course, the evaluation of drama can also be practised through responding to recorded performances, including recordings of their own drama as well as professional performances available through the media. Recorded performance can be easily revisited or replayed at any time.

■ Monitoring the quality of external drama providers

If you bring in an external provider to teach drama regularly then you will want to observe them working as part of your scheduled lesson observations, as they are contributing to the overall quality of teaching and learning in your school.

When using external providers and freelancers, you will need to choose carefully. You may find that some drama freelancers do mainly drama games with children, whereas another provider might only work on theatre skills and performance. Some negotiate carefully what you want from them learning-wise and how it can link well to what classroom teachers offer curriculum-wise.

Some external providers will be trained drama teachers, some are out of work actors, some are enthusiastically committed to working in schools, others are only doing it because they have to in order to qualify for funding. Be sure about what you want from an external drama provider coming in, and do some research. Ask the provider where else they have worked in the last term or two and then ring up that school and chat to the head or relevant teacher to find out more. If you want regular commitment and sustainability then you will need to be sure that the same person is in a position to keep working in your school regularly.

If you are committed to improving your school through drama then drama cannot be only a 'now and again' or a 'bolt-on' after school experience handed over to an external provider, however good they might be. External provision can be a desirable addition, one part of the overall drama experience children receive at your school, but it should not be the only experience. If drama is accepted as a powerful pedagogy and whole class drama provides engaging contexts for learning across the curriculum, then an optional after school club that only some children attend will be very limited in terms of school improvement. It is better to make drama provision part of the curriculum fabric of the school, to ensure all staff are trained to teach drama, and then additionally and selectively to bring in external providers for specific purposes. The teacher with lead responsibility for drama across the school would ideally be working in close partnership with any external provider or freelancer, particularly if they are employed on a regular basis.

Professional theatre workers and drama teachers working in close partnership have much to offer each other developmentally, as well as the children and young people they work with.

■ Health and safety

Children and students will need to be taught directly the aspects of drama that relate to health and safety, e.g. safe use of equipment and space, etc. Local authorities have published guidelines on Health and Safety in Drama that are usually accessible through local authority websites.

■ Safeguarding children and child protection in drama

In improvisation and theatre work (particularly that which involves touch) teachers may wish to consider carefully what constitutes 'safe touch'. Teachers who are interpreting and directing plays in secondary schools need particularly to assure themselves (and be able to assure others) that students are not being made to feel unreasonably or personally uncomfortable or vulnerable by the demands being made on them in the drama, e.g. close physical contact in love scenes. National Drama, the leading subject association for drama and theatre educators, has produced a position statement to help guide drama and theatre teachers (see the website www.nationaldrama.co.uk) and the Welsh Assembly has produced guidance for managers and drama practitioners (reference 34).

Remember that if you employ a drama or theatre worker you will need to be sure they have been police-checked and are able to work in your school.

PART ONE

Continuing Professional Development in Drama

■ Professional Development in Drama for all

Ideally drama as a methodology and pedagogy will be part of every teacher's professional toolkit. Also, ideally a drama specialist with good subject knowledge and good leadership and management skills (and the full, consistent support of senior management) will be able to lead the development of drama confidently and be supported to establish appropriate professional support and development in drama for each teacher.

You need to identify the individual and whole staff drama professional development needs and then ensure that they are met through school and individual professional development plans, some of which will be for individuals and also for whole staff. Once the drama development needs of teachers have been identified there are a myriad of ways you might set about meeting them and a multi-pronged approach rather than a 'one-off hit' will be best. A combination of approaches is more likely to be effective in the longer term, than, for example, just one staff INSET day and then no follow-up support. Some professional development options will be more expensive in terms of time and budget than others, but remember that drama can be a way of meeting other priorities, for example improving speaking and listening or writing. This might enable access to budgets that are not specifically for drama.

■ Case study

The drama subject leader at a local primary school had attended a local authority drama course on using drama as a creative teaching and learning medium. She fed back to all staff and agreed with the headteacher that this course would be of benefit to all staff. They decided to 'buy in' the local authority adviser who had led the course, as this would be cheaper than all staff attending the course and the course could be tailored specifically for the school. It was easily linked to the priority in the school improvement and development plan:

'to continue to raise standards in teaching (and increase the range of active learning methods used)'.

The adviser (course leader) discussed a programme of advice and support with the drama subject leader and headteacher and it was decided that:

- there would be a Professional Development Day at the end of the Summer Term (to inform teacher's Autumn planning and practice)

- the adviser would visit to work alongside the subject leader in drama, early in the Autumn Term

- the subject leader would then be released to work alongside class teachers from each year group during the Autumn and Spring terms

- the adviser would keep email and telephone contact with the subject leader

- the adviser would return at half term and at the end of term to lead staff meetings to evaluate progress, troubleshoot and help plan 'next steps' for improvement

- as the school has two form entry, the pairs of year group teachers would plan their drama together and discuss it with the drama subject leader

- the adviser would also put the subject leader in contact with other drama subject leaders for mutual support

- the adviser should be given the school improvement and development priorities to suggest ways that drama could link to them and to discuss ways that the impact of the drama could be monitored and evaluated within the school

- the headteacher would allocate additional funding for drama resources and the subject leader (in consultation with teachers) would purchase a range of drama teaching books with units of work to support teachers (as well as music and picture books particularly suitable for drama).

Professional development days

If your school is developing drama as a whole school priority then it is reasonable to assume there will be a staff development day or half day and/or whole staff meetings or series of meetings to focus on this. Often schools have more than one such development day or meeting and often they enlist external specialist support for them, e.g. a local authority drama specialist adviser or drama Advanced Skills specialist teacher or equivalent, or maybe an established freelance consultant. Professional development time is very precious (especially with whole staff) and you need to be sure of high quality input and facilitation that meets your school's needs.

The sessions do, of course, need a clear purpose. Often they are focused on increasing the subject knowledge of the staff (which may include teachers and other adults supporting learning, such as learning support assistants). Many teachers need to learn more about the range of drama strategies and conventions that are available to them in their teaching. Many teachers have only a working knowledge of a few basic strategies, e.g. hot-seating, freeze frame and maybe thought-tracking (see Glossary). Also it is often the case with non-drama specialists that these strategies are being used repeatedly and in isolation rather than together within whole class drama lessons. A staff meeting or development day gives opportunity to work through a range of strategies practically and to discuss how they link to enabling learning and creating drama. Actually doing drama practically is for some teachers the first main stumbling block they need to overcome, as they may feel shy, insecure or embarrassed to work in role alongside colleagues (and maybe children).

This is when it may be helpful to have an experienced drama INSET provider who is external to the school and used to working with whole staff. Local authority advisers are very experienced at leading professional development but not all local authorities have drama specialists. There may be good Advanced Skills Teachers (ASTs) or Leading Drama Teachers who can start to take on this role.

23. Teachers need to gain drama subject knowledge and learn how to use and apply it in their teaching.

The teachers need to be kept safe but challenged and the leader of the session needs to be sensitive to the comfort zone of individual teachers and able to subtly accommodate this. Working in an advisory capacity or as a facilitator requires some different and additional skills to those of good drama teaching and not all specialist drama teachers will necessarily be good at leading professional development days (although of course they will be cheaper). But it is worth enabling the drama subject leader to lead some staff development in drama as one of the key approaches and it will probably benefit them professionally as subject leaders. Also they are in the school on a daily basis to sustain the drama support. Some less secure teachers prefer to work with fellow teachers who are maybe just a few steps ahead of themselves drama-wise, rather than work with external experts. A combination is preferable.

A handful of local authorities employ peripatetic arts advisory teachers to work in schools. They may be bought in or may be centrally funded. Most authorities have music peripatetic teachers but not necessarily for other arts subjects. In Scotland there is a visiting teacher service provided in some authorities with drama specialist teachers who can regularly visit schools. Unfortunately they are increasingly used to cover the classes of teachers released for planning, preparation and assessment, which significantly hampers their potential effectiveness as contributors to the professional development of the teachers whose classes they work with.

Exemplar: Professional Development Day

9.00–9.20   How is drama being used in the school at the moment?

Each teacher was asked to introduce themselves and briefly state what drama they are doing at present (if any), e.g. strategies in some lessons or whole class lessons sometimes/regularly. They were each asked to say what they felt about drama (positive or negative) and what barriers to the teaching of drama they thought there were for them (if any). What did they want to have achieved professionally by the end of the day?

The course leader asked them to tell each other the names of any drama strategies and conventions they knew of. This helped the course leader assess the levels of current subject knowledge.

The course leader pointed them towards the 'Drama Strategies and Conventions' list in their course pack (see Glossary) and pointed out that there were many more available strategies and conventions they could use and that the practical sessions during the day would exemplify them in the context of whole class dramas. She clarified and agreed the aims for the day.

9.20–9.45   Why is drama important for learning?

The course leader briefly contextualized drama in relation to current learning theory and its place in the current curriculum, as well as the way it links to early learning through dramatic play. This meant that when the teachers were working practically the course leader could refer back to these links. It gave a meaningful context for the drama lessons to follow.

9.45–11.00   A practical Key Stage 1 drama lesson (literacy based)

Unit 1, Whatever Wanda Wanted

This used a picture book as a stimulus (which linked into one of the school's forthcoming curriculum themes, 'Islands'). The course leader worked practically alongside as a co-participant but also stepped out of role occasionally to share her 'teacher thinking' aloud and to make links with learning theory and suggest and gather possible cross-curricular links and possibilities as they arose. Possible linked writing opportunities were gathered and suggested and ways that the outdoor learning environment might be used for this drama (as outdoor learning was another area already identified by the school for development). The whole staff worked in role.

PART ONE

11.00–11.30   Break

11.30–13.30   A practical Key Stage 2 drama lesson (history based)

This lesson used a photograph of Victorian street urchins as its starting point and the course leader took the role of Dr Barnardo gathering information from them, as if they were the photographers, about what they had seen (flashback/still image) and what they knew. The teachers also worked in groups to speak as one child (collective role), telling their story when questioned (hot-seating). The drama created possible scenes (small group play making) that had led to the children now sleeping rough, explored some of the dangers and events of street life (improvisation) and considered (through image theatre) possible outcomes for these children. The session went on to look at modern Barnardo children's photographs and consider timeless similarities between them. The teachers were then asked to work together in groups to map possible cross-curricular learning opportunities other than History, e.g. English (Dickens and diaries), Geography/Global Citizenship (street children/child labour nowadays in various countries).

13.30–14.30   Lunch

14.30–15.00   Plenary

The course tutor reminded them of the list of Drama Strategies and Conventions and the teachers discussed briefly, in pairs, which strategies they had experienced in the two drama sessions. Any that had not been used were exemplified briefly.

The teachers each created a 'pledge' to the subject leader as to what the next manageable step/s they would take would be in their planning and with their classes. 'No action' was not an option. They also jotted down what support they needed next. This left the subject leader in a position to discuss and monitor their progress against their stated next steps and arrange appropriate support.

Evaluation: Evaluation forms were completed. All teachers had gained in confidence and skills. Most felt more motivated to do drama now. All stated that it would have an influence on their practice.

■ Other professional development support

Other professional development support might include the following.

■ Enabling the subject leader for drama to be released to work alongside other teachers with their own classes

It is best if the class teacher joins in as a co-participant with the drama subject leader, rather than just sits as an observer. The subject leader should not be doing the drama for the class teacher but supporting the class teacher to gradually take the lead (maybe over several lessons). It is about professional development, not substitution. It is always more effective for teachers to be involved in their own class achieving in drama rather than someone else's, as it is a more meaningful context for them and enables them to see drama working with their class, so they can't say it won't! Of course, the subject leader is modelling, but the class teacher also has a role in the lesson and is not just audience. If the class teacher were to be just an observer, this would also change the dynamic of the lesson for the children.

■ **Enabling other teachers to be released to observe/co-participate alongside the subject leader working with the subject leader's own class**

This can be a less useful approach (especially if used as a stand-alone approach) as it can make the inexperienced teacher feel that they just cannot do the drama as well as the subject leader and so they become less secure about teaching drama rather than more secure. It depends on teacher attitude (willingness or resistance). Working alongside the subject leader is slightly better.

■ **Enabling the subject leader to support the lesson planning with the class teachers**

The drama subject leader should know what is being taught across the school in drama and that it links in with any agreed medium- or long-term plans. Often teachers are willing to use drama in their teaching but need support to see the opportunities to incorporate it into existing plans or to create drama lessons. This activity, of course, could be in or out of school hours but formalizing the joint planning during planning, preparation and assessment time in school hours will give the drama planning the significance it deserves and ensure that it happens.

■ Case study

The drama subject leader of a large primary school (three form entry) was released weekly for half a day a week for four weeks to work her way through each year group at KS2 (a total of two days' release time).

She met with each set of year group teachers to help them link drama to their scheduled literacy work for the next term, e.g. the theme for Year 3 was Myths and Legends.

The teachers brought resources to the planning session that might be used and so did the drama subject leader. Over a morning they mapped out the term's drama work and talked through possible approaches and strategies, with the teachers taking notes and also offering suggestions.

Then each teacher agreed to take one myth or legend and plan how to approach it through drama and then give their lessons to each other (after sharing them first with the subject leader).

Each teacher ended up with a term's work in outline and at least three drama/literacy lessons in more detail, but the most significant support came from the process of planning together and the professional discussions around this. Also, it meant that the teachers were communicating and supporting each other, and might well continue to do so informally at other times.

The ideas were shared and discussed and suggestions made but the drama subject leader did not plan the lessons for the teachers and the teachers therefore retained ownership and responsibility.

The teachers agreed to log their evaluations of the lesson and meet again to share outcomes and observations together.

■ **Visiting other schools to observe, meet with and work alongside drama specialists**

It may be possible to arrange for the teacher leading drama in your school to visit a drama specialist teacher in another school to watch them teach drama or even teach alongside them and take on a role for parts of a lesson. This offers peer support between drama specialists (who might even meet additionally with others as a drama network).

■ Accessing the support of specialist drama teachers

There are a range of national initiatives and schemes that enable schools to gain access to drama specialists, although their availability may vary locally. Teachers with particular drama expertise may have applied to have their specialism formally recognized in various ways and may have made themselves available for outreach work in other schools. But remember that there may also be very good drama teachers who have not applied to be involved in these national schemes, so local knowledge can enable you to make your own alternative and equally suitable arrangements.

Advanced Skills Teachers of Drama – Most local authorities will have ASTs listed on their website and you can search for them and apply either to visit one or ask one to visit your school. There may be different procedures for accessing ASTs in different authorities. Drama ASTs are recognized as externally assessed teachers who have excellent practice and wish to remain as classroom teachers rather than become managers but can be released for 20% of their teaching time to support teachers, mostly in other schools. They receive extra salary payments to share their expertise and experience. Your local authority should be able to tell you whether there are any Drama ASTs available in your area and how to access them. An advantage of working with another teacher is that for some teachers it can seem less daunting than working with a local authority drama specialist adviser and is cheaper.

24. Specialist drama teachers can support each other as well as support inexperienced teachers of drama.

Leading Drama Teachers (LDTs) – The national strategy funds the establishment of Leading Teachers for various subjects and areas, e.g. behaviour, able, gifted and talented, literacy, numeracy. Some authorities have enabled other areas and subjects to have leading teachers, e.g. Leading Drama Teachers. The local authority is likely to monitor the quality of Leading Teachers. Their schools are remunerated for their supply time when out of the classroom supporting teachers in other schools. Sometimes the receiving schools are asked to meet the replacement supply costs of the visiting Leading Teachers. They will help teachers to develop drama skills and offer coaching and mentoring in relation to drama teaching as well as work alongside teachers with their classes.

Excellent Teachers (ETs) – This is a new opportunity, open to post-threshold teachers and members of the leadership group. As yet, the way that Excellent Teachers might work differently from ASTs is not fully evident in practice, as the scheme is new.

Specialist Arts College Drama teachers – Specialist Arts Colleges are committed to outreach work linked to their specialisms. It may be worth making contact with your local Specialist Arts College (or Further Education College Performing Arts department) to see if there is a drama teacher you can work in partnership with. If your local High School is applying for specialist arts status try to ensure that support for your drama curriculum ends up being built into their application. This should ensure it will happen if their bid for specialist status is successful.

■ Case study

A local sixth form college that specializes in the arts (and whose Performing Arts was judged outstanding by Ofsted) was putting on 'A Midsummer Night's Dream'. They invited the local primary children to come to the matinée performance.

In advance of them attending the performance, a drama teacher from the college who was directing the play (and also happened to be a playwright) offered to go into the schools and do an active Shakespeare drama workshop about the play with the children to help them become familiar with the play before seeing it.

Afterwards the children attended the performance. At the end of the performance the children had the opportunity to call back characters and ask them questions. The characters (played by 'A' level Theatre Studies students) answered the primary children's questions in role as the Shakespearean characters, which helped the students deepen their engagement with the roles and display their knowledge and understanding of the play in front of their drama teacher. The primary children also learned more about the play and were very engaged and likely to remember.

Local secondary school drama teachers – Even if your local High School is not a Specialist Arts College, you may find that the drama teacher can come to do some outreach work to support drama teaching in local feeder primary schools. After all, it is mostly with the same children they will receive in time, and it helps transition and good relationships between cluster schools. Or, you may find that they would welcome teacher visits to their drama department (and maybe a visiting class of Year 6 children). Maybe a transition drama activity or project could be devised for the Summer Term.

Freelance drama specialists – There are many drama freelancers now and what each one offers varies greatly in terms of content, range and quality. The quality control rests with the school. Mostly they would be too expensive to use working alongside teachers in a sustained way for CPD. Freelancers are more often employed to work with children through one-off workshops or out of school clubs. However, among freelancers are those who do have the background, skills and experience to offer high quality CPD linked to whole class drama, e.g. recently retired drama lecturers and drama specialist teachers.

■ Accessing drama courses and conferences

The types, range and quality of drama courses and conferences vary greatly depending on the area and school phase you work in. It may well be worth a subject leader for drama or head of drama department attending area and national conferences, as they will meet with other drama subject leaders, make contacts and learn a lot informally as well as during the course or conference sessions. Drama subject leaders need to stay up to date with their subject knowledge as well as new initiatives at a local, regional and national level, and this is helped by meeting and talking with others involved in teaching and leading drama.

Local authority drama courses and conferences

In the early 1990s many local authorities abandoned the provision of drama advisers and the courses they ran, when drama was not made a separate subject in the National Curriculum. Then the national strategies, with drama as part of English, led to some drama courses for teachers but with the main emphasis being very literacy focused, rather than on drama as an art form. For some years, Literacy, Numeracy and ICT were the main, and, in some cases, the only focus of some local authority courses. The literacy courses were focused on reading and writing (and only later, speaking and listening). A few local authorities kept their arts advisers who organized drama courses or had National Strategy advisers who were drama specialists and used all opportunities to develop drama fully, but for several years most teachers found local drama courses had vanished.

The situation has thankfully changed a little and it is once again worth visiting your local authority website first and seeing what is available. You might also find that you can attend neighbouring authority's courses if you apply, as if there are spaces they are often pleased to sell them externally. Provision is still uneven but there are more local authority drama courses happening now.

If you see a course that the local authority is running that would be of benefit to all your teachers, then it is often more viable economically to try to buy the course into your school or cluster of schools. For example, 'Teaching Thinking Through Drama', 'Drama across the Curriculum', or 'Improving Writing Through Drama' will all be very different courses and one of these might be able to help achieve another non-drama school priority in your school improvement and development plan.

Subject association drama conferences

Teachers in England are being encouraged by the Department for Children, Families and Schools to join subject associations. The main subject associations are receiving some government funding to work together and build their capacity to deliver and support subject-specific teaching in a range of ways (www.subjectassociation.org.uk).

Drama subject associations already provide drama courses and conferences (regional, national and international). The leading association for UK drama and theatre educators is National Drama (www.nationaldrama.co.uk). English subject associations also provide courses and conferences that often have a drama focus or element, e.g. The National Association for the Teaching of English (NATE) (www.nate.org.uk) and the United Kingdom Language Association (UKLA) (www.ukla.org).

Commercial course and conference providers

There are several commercial companies (easily found through an internet search) that set up courses and conferences for teachers regionally, and more often nationally. They usually use very experienced course leaders, many of whom are freelance consultants.

■ Freelance course leaders

There are many freelance drama consultants of widely differing quality. It is wise to research a little before booking a freelancer. Some are excellent and have recent teaching experience in classrooms and/or universities and significant drama subject knowledge. Others may have little school drama experience and may be out of work actors between jobs, with a focus on theatre skills rather than on process drama. You need to be very clear what you want from the course and whether the freelancer whose course you attend (or invite to your school to run a course) is well matched to what you and your school actually require. In advance of booking a freelancer, you could ask for the names of maybe three schools they have worked with over the last year and then give the school a ring to ask about quality.

■ Teacher networks

You might find that there are teacher networks in your area (online and meeting face to face) with a drama focus. They usually enable teachers to meet and share resources, lesson ideas, planning and to support each other. Sometimes these are informal networks that have arisen naturally. Sometimes they are formal and may be supported by the local authority but they are usually nonetheless run by teachers for teachers. They may be Primary Strategy Learning Networks that have decided to focus on drama as a way of raising standards in, for example, writing. Teacher networks, when they work well, are a good source of colleague support, and often friendship.

There are also regional networks of drama teachers being established, sometimes by subject associations. For example, National Drama is in the process of setting up more regional networks for its members (www.nationaldrama.co.uk).

■ Online forums and support

There are drama teachers keeping in touch and sharing resources and ideas through a growing and ever-changing array of online drama forums (both primary and secondary). These forums attract worldwide interest and contributions and are open to teachers who register. The following are some of the well-established forums.

PART ONE

D4LC (Drama for Learning and Creativity)

This forum was set up in 2005 initially for teachers involved in the D4LC initiative but any teacher worldwide can register free, read and contribute to the forum. Teachers may set up topics of interest and invite and gather comments that can be read while on the website. This is for both primary and secondary teachers but more primary teachers are involved in D4LC than secondary teachers. www.d4lc.org.uk

Drama UK

This e-group was set up in 1998 and has a large, free membership. It is peopled mainly by secondary teachers (but certainly not exclusively) and topics attract UK and international input (often from UK teachers of drama abroad). Much of the correspondence links to syllabuses, exam marking queries, and secondary teachers asking each other for play and lesson suggestions. Also, teachers often recommend good theatre visits and groups. It is a particularly useful site for secondary teachers. http://groups.yahoo.com/group/drama_uk

Dramatool

This is an international site that aims to bring together drama and theatre educators to publicize, share and create international drama and theatre possibilities. The website is supported by IDEA, the International Drama and Theatre Education Association. There is an online forum that you can register on free of charge and so contact many active drama teachers from around the world. www.dramatool.org

Mantle of the Expert

This site has a forum that attracts teachers who are particularly focusing on Mantle of the Expert as a curriculum approach. www.mantleoftheexpert.com

■ Future CPD online development

The Training and Development Agency has commissioned National Drama to set up a national online Continuing Professional Development site containing materials that will be accessible to all teachers. This important site is under construction. The training and development agency are also creating a database for CPD providers to register. This is likely to become an important route for accessing drama consultants.

PART TWO

Glossary of Drama strategies and conventions

Name of Drama strategy or convention	Brief description	Main purpose/s
Captioning	A scene or still image is given one sentence that encapsulates it. The caption might be presented verbally or written down (rather like a one-sentence plaque).	■ to synthesize in words the meaning portrayed in the scene or image
Choral speaking	More than one person speaking in unison for dramatic effect (rather like a choir of speech).	■ aural dramatic effect ■ to strengthen the spoken word through unity
Collective role **Collective voice**	More than one person simultaneously takes on one role and any one of them can speak as the character they are together portraying.	■ to share ownership of a role ■ to give a reason for careful, active listening
Conscience alley **Decision alley** **Thought tunnel**	The class splits into two lines facing each other (standing about a metre apart). A character passes between the lines at a moment of indecision or turmoil in the drama. As the character passes by each person, they can speak aloud their advice to the character. Each line persuasively offers conflicting advice to the character before he/she makes their decision.	■ to make explicit and public the pros and cons of a course of action ■ to give opportunity for everyone to influence a character's actions ■ to model balanced argument and support persuasive speech
Dance drama	Drama (or parts of a drama) expressed through movement, usually with music and/or sound.	■ to kinaesthetically understand, create and communicate meaning
Eavesdropping (overheard conversations)	Short scenes are enacted or just spoken (usually in pairs or small groups) and the teacher passes by as if he/she is someone eavesdropping on each scene. The class is still and listening until it is their turn to speak and be overheard. The conversations and scenes could be set up as improvisations or else preparation time given. You can ask the children to improvise first and afterwards set up 'eavesdropping' to replay what was said in the spontaneous improvisation.	■ to give every child the opportunity to actively contribute to the fiction and be listened to ■ to gather and share information about character and plot quickly ■ replay enables children to select from improvisation for a confident performance

Essence machine	This activity is usually done in a standing class circle. Each person in turn enters the circle and performs a very short and continuously repeating sound or word (or short phrase) *and* a gesture (or short movement) that links to and portrays some aspect or moment in the drama, e.g. in a drama about bullying a person might repeatedly shake a fist and say 'Get out of here!' and another person might repeatedly flinch and gasp. The sounds, words and movements build up as each person enters and may or may not directly connect with what is already being performed and repeated. They sum up the essence of the drama. The machine can be controlled by the teacher through signals that speed it up, slow it down, make it noisier and quieter, stop it, etc., for dramatic effect.	■ to encourage reflective and selective thought (synthesis) ■ to enable everyone to contribute to a shared and collective synthesis of the drama ■ to remember and communicate visually, auditorily and kinaesthetically
Eyewitness	An eyewitness can observe a scene without being noticed by those in the scene or the eyewitness might be a partial or impartial observer present within a scene as it is happening and able to report back afterwards on what they have seen and answer questions put to them about what they saw. You can set people up as eyewitnesses to stand outside scenes and observe with a purpose. You can deliberately give eyewitnesses a restricted view, e.g. looking through a tube so they only see part of the scene and so more easily misinterpret and may miss crucial information and see the scene differently from someone else with a different restricted view, e.g. watching a murder through a crack in the door from different vantage points.	■ to give dramatic purpose to being an active and accurate observer ■ to demonstrate that people can see and interpret the same scene differently depending on current knowledge, partiality and positioning
Forum Theatre	This involves a group creating a short scene (or scenes) that authentically portrays a social issue of importance to them and reflects their real-life experiences, e.g. gender stereotyping, bullying, split families, etc. The audience can then get actively involved in prescribed ways, when the scene is repeatedly replayed. The interactive audience are known as 'spectactors' and they operate interactively with the performers, by invitation of an intermediary, known as 'the joker'. ■ The scene is played once before an audience, who then watch it a second time (or several times) and at the invitation and with the support of 'the joker' can	■ to engage together with a social issue that matters to the participants and is within their experience ■ to support each other to problem solve ■ to demonstrate that people's differing words and actions can lead to differing consequences ■ to empower people to influence personal, social and emotional outcomes for the better

PART TWO

	advise characters on how to play the scene differently. The aim is to shape the scene towards a better outcome, e.g. 'Instead of running off in a temper when she shouts at you, just stay still next time and don't respond for at least a minute and then speak calmly.' The audience (spectators) may individually direct characters to speak or respond or act differently and discover any impact. The players then improvise when they replay the scene, within the constraints of the new directions. ■ Or, members of the audience may volunteer or be invited by 'the joker' to enter the scene and take over one of the roles and play it differently (substitution) for a better outcome. ■ A third possibility is for members of the audience to volunteer or be invited by 'the joker' to enter the scene and work with and alongside a character in the scene to strengthen them and maybe speak with or as them (as a collective role).	
Freeze frame	This is when action is halted and a moment in a scene is held perfectly still, i.e. 'as still as a photograph'. It provides a still image that can be reflected upon and commented on by the participants or by those watching. It may be that the teacher calls out 'freeze' to halt the scene or maybe the participants have agreed a moment they will all freeze the action. The 'freeze frame' can be recreated again later (or at the start of the next lesson) as a still image in order to get back to the same moment in the drama. Often freeze frame is used with other drama strategies and conventions, e.g. at this moment, what are the characters thinking (link with thought-tracking), what might the characters tell us at this moment if we ask (hot-seating)?	■ to hold a moment still in order to allow thinking time, e.g. for reflection ■ to clarify visually a key moment and help make it memorable and significant ■ to create a visual frame that may be recreated and returned to for further exploration and reflection later
Hot-seating	Usually a chair is designated as the 'hot-seat' and a character from the drama sits in it and is then open to being questioned and will answer in role. A variation of this would be to say that the seat belongs to the character and that anyone who sits in it will become that character and may speak as them (as in 'collective role').	■ to find out information from a character ■ to find out a character's viewpoint ■ to give opportunity to all to engage with a character

Image Theatre	This can involve creating two or more related images (often for developmental purposes). Image making is sometimes used therapeutically to effect change by helping people express the current reality as an image and then vision and visualize what the 'ideal' would look like as an image if it could be achieved. Then they are helped to reflect upon what steps they would need to take to start to move from the reality towards the ideal. In drama lessons image theatre might involve telling parts of the drama through a series of images or showing what a character is thinking and/or feeling through creating and presenting realistic or symbolic images. Images can be made individually or in groups. Sometimes an image is built up gradually by asking one person to create an image and then the next person comes in and adds themselves to it, e.g. the first person comes in and is asked to portray themselves as 'powerful' through a still image. The next person enters and positions themselves as 'more powerful'. The third person's challenge is to enter and appear 'even more powerful' and so on.	■ to clarify and synthesize current situations ■ to support reflective thinking and positive reframing ■ to enable the visualization of positive possibilities ■ to help participants take ownership of change in achievable steps ■ to support the analysis and interpretation of non-verbal communication
Improvisation	This involves speaking and acting spontaneously in role without rehearsal. To do this you need to know who you are pretending to be, where and what the drama moment or situation is and then you seriously engage with the scene, as if it is real, and just make it up 'in role' as you go along.	■ to spontaneously generate dramatic action and words ■ to encourage and develop quick thinking and response in role
Mantle of the Expert	Children are given the roles of experts and treated respectfully as experts (and treat each other 'as if' they are experts) but are not told directly that they are 'experts'. They are given real work-related tasks to do in role for a fictitious external client, e.g. make a real documentary film about Ancient Egypt for a client. The tasks require enquiry and expertise that they gradually acquire and/or develop as they are motivated to complete the task. Some schools use this established technique in a widespread way as an approach to much of their curriculum. The teacher is the enabler and mediator. It works best when	■ to raise self-esteem and self-image ■ to empower and challenge children to respond as adults ■ to imagine and rehearse professional success ■ to motivate and provide purpose for a work-related task ■ to encourage and support entrepreneurship

PART TWO

	used in combination with or supported by other drama strategies and conventions. It is possible to use Mantle of the Expert as a strategy within parts of a drama lesson, e.g. the children as police officers (investigation experts) interview someone who has witnessed an accident and gather notes for their police report. The children may then drop the police officer role and take on different roles for the next part of the drama.	
Mime and movement	Mime uses the body to act or interact with something or somebody that is not visible and is imagined. It may be carried out alone or with others. Mime and movement use the body to express and communicate emotion and meaning without words.	■ to create the impression that someone or something is present ■ to support and communicate kinaesthetic expression and understanding
Multi-sensory imagining (including Visualization)	Visualization is about specifically giving time to supporting children to see pictures in their minds. It helps to ask the children to close their eyes and then the teacher can guide the visualization, e.g. *'Now close your eyes … Imagine that you are a very special kite … have a really good look at yourself … I don't know what you look like but you do … I wonder what colour you are … I don't know, but you do … let your eyes travel all around yourself … look carefully at what you are made of … and how you are joined together … do you have a tail I wonder? … are you plain or patterned? … etc.'* This example leaves the children to create the kite visually in their minds as the teacher is prompting without telling. Sometimes a visualization might give visual information, e.g. at the start of a drama based on Tennyson's 'The Lady of Shalott' the teacher might say, *'Close your eyes and imagine you are sitting in a field at night … there is a bright moon tonight and everything is bathed in silver and the air is still … you are tired as you have been working all day in the fields, cutting down barley … it is harvest time and the smell of freshly mown barley and rye fills the still air … all is moonlit and the only other light is from her window … the window high up in the grey tower … look up at that window … look at that candlelight … and wonder …'.* This leads the children from imagining a scene based on visual references in the poem, towards	■ to deepen sensory engagement ■ to 'tag' the moment by accessing and evoking multi-sensory memories ■ to make the imaginary setting for the drama more vivid and real ■ to enable the children to access and imagine the setting through a range of senses ■ to support the children to focus on, tune in to and become sensitive to the sensory aspects of a place and/or moment ■ to give time and space for sensory reflection and imagining

	thinking about what they are imagining they see. This second example uses visualization but also calls on the children to imagine and maybe use other sensory memories too, i.e. the smell of mown barley, tiredness, still air. Visualization implies just evoking visual images but we can take this further and make the experience a virtual multi-sensory experience by asking children to imagine and contribute suggestions as to the sights, sounds, tactile experience, smells and tastes that also can be associated with the drama and can be summoned up in their imaginations at a particular moment. The teacher can guide the visualization or multi-sensory imaginings but also can invite the children to contribute their imaginings to support each other in building this shared, imaginary environment. A way of setting this up is to ask children to close their eyes, to imagine themselves in a specific setting in the drama, e.g. a deserted beach on an island, and then to invite the children to offer multi-sensory imaginings, that all start with either, 'I can see ...' or 'I can hear ...' or 'I can smell ...', etc. You may decide that you will only invite each sense in turn. The children (with eyes closed) should try not to talk at the same time. This can be extended by asking for a short bit of description, e.g. instead of 'I can see waves' they might be encouraged to elaborate a little, e.g. 'I can see dark grey waves, smashing into each other'. They can offer new imaginings or build on those other children have already offered, e.g. 'I can feel the spray from the waves smashing and my face tastes salty'. A rule is that what one child says is then accepted by all, so a second child could not now contradict and say, 'I can see a calm, turquoise sea like a mirror'. The teacher can join in these activities, model the language and offer some ideas as a co-participant.	
Occupational mime	This is a mime that involves the person acting out an occupation. They use their bodies to pretend they are involved in an occupation, e.g. fisherman, farmer, shopkeeper, servant, etc.	■ to support engagement with and development of a role

Passing thoughts	This is a type of thought tracking 'on the move'. A character stands in the middle of a class circle and anyone in the circle can pass them by and speak one of the character's thoughts aloud. Alternatively it could be done with those who pass by speaking their thought about the character. Only one person at a time should be on the move, so that the thoughts are heard singly. There may be times when no one is moving and that is fine. You may decide that people may only pass through the circle once with a thought or may do so repeatedly with the same or different thoughts.	■ to enable everyone to have the opportunity to engage with the thoughts of a character ■ to share ideas about the character's inner thoughts and ownership of them ■ to link physical movement and thought (kinaesthetically)
Performance Carousel **Performance Wave**	Groups each create a short piece of performance within the drama. They are then presented in turn seamlessly without interruption. The teacher numbers the groups and explains that everyone needs to sit still and silent until it is their group's turn to perform. Group 1 will perform first, Group 2 second, and so on. Group 1 will move first and in slow motion will move artistically into a still image that they will hold still for 5 seconds (counting in their heads). They will then bring the scene to life and perform. The scenes should last no more than a minute each. The group will have decided the exact moment that they will freeze to signal the end of their scene. They will then hold the 'freeze frame' still for 5 seconds (again, counted silently inside their heads) before melting back down to the ground in slow motion. When Group 1 is seated completely still this will be the signal for Group 2 to get up in slow motion (artistically) and so on until all groups have performed. Atmospheric music fitting the theme of the performance will help create one seamless class performance made up of several scenes. *Variations* ■ Each group can give their scene a title that someone in the group will call aloud before the action starts. ■ The scenes can be performed again but in a different sequence if a logical chronological reason emerges to do so.	■ to create quickly a whole class, themed performance ■ to enable everyone to contribute and take part in a whole class performance ■ to support class unity of purpose and cohesion ■ to build and sustain theatrical atmosphere ■ to give opportunity to focus on different aspects of the same scene or see it through different lenses

	■ The scenes can be replayed but we hear the characters' thoughts rather than their dialogue. ■ The scenes can be replayed and this time there is a designated storyteller who provides an accompanying narrative and the scene is just mimed. ■ There may be a reason to perform the scenes in a line (or other shape) rather than a circle, e.g. they depict different episodes on a long, linear journey or in a life (with old age at the end of the line).	
Physical Theatre	This involves using the body (or several people's bodies) to actively represent and portray not just people in a drama but objects, scenery, etc. For example, if a man is standing under a street light, two people might use their combined bodies to become the street light. You might ask groups to depict scenes and say that they can use people in the group to be scenery or objects as well as people.	■ to encourage creative thinking ■ to make the drama physically active ■ to break down physical barriers between participants
Active storytelling	Sometimes 'active storytelling' can be combined with physical theatre. The teacher might tell a story and as he/she tells it the children physically become anything they hear in the story and keep changing into something/somebody else when new people, objects, places are mentioned. This can be done individually or in pairs or small groups. With younger children it tends to be done individually.	■ to make a storyline memorable ■ to ensure everyone contributes ■ to encourage speedy response
Whoosh!	This is a type of active storytelling. The class sits in a circle. The teacher tells a story and signals to individuals, pairs or groups of children at different points, to get up, enter the circle and spontaneously represent and depict that part of the story. This can include becoming objects and scenery as well as people. The scene being narrated is spontaneously brought to life. The teacher carries on with the story and signals to others to come and illustrate what is being told. When the circle becomes too full of people, the teacher as storyteller, at any time, just says, 'Whoosh! Whoosh! Whoosh!' which is the signal for everyone to clear the acting space and go back to the circle but the	

PART TWO

	storytelling continues uninterrupted, with further groups signalled to enter, until the story is finished, with a final 'Whoosh!'. The teacher needs to know the story outline well. This 'Whoosh!' activity can be used as a way of recounting and remembering a story/drama at the end or can be a way of familiarizing children with an unknown story that could become the basis of a drama.	
Proxemics	Physical distance between characters carries meaning. This can be highlighted and made explicit, e.g. people can physically place themselves in relation to characters in a scene to show where their sympathies or loyalties lie, e.g. 'I am standing close to Macbeth at this moment because I feel he is being bullied by Lady Macbeth', or 'I am standing away from Macbeth but am standing further away from Lady Macbeth. This is because neither of them has my sympathy but I think she is more evil.' When a scene has been created in any drama the children can be asked to place themselves meaningfully in relation to the characters within it and be able to explain why. Also, when creating scenes they should consider that the space communicates meaning to the audience.	■ to emphasize that physical space carries meaning in drama ■ to encourage justification and reasoning and reflection
Ritual	Ritual involves established and usually repeated actions, sounds, movements, gestures, words, etc., that have an agreed and attributed meaning and significance for the participants in the drama. A drama might give opportunity to create ritual, e.g. an imaginary community the children create through drama might decide to agree a way of commemorating an important event. The teacher might ask the children to use ritual language or action, e.g. as in 'Speaking object' where only the holder of the object is entitled to speak.	■ to provide a secure structure for contributing ■ to deepen engagement and commitment ■ to help them understand that ritual carries shared and deep meaning
Role on the Wall	This involves drawing an outline of a character (either full body or head and shoulders) and writing information about the character in and around the outline. This is best done using self-adhesive labels (which allow information about a character to be moved around or changed). The information can be categorized,	■ to focus and record what is known and felt about characters at different points in the drama ■ to generate discussion about characters

	e.g. what we know/think we know/want to know about the character. Or, for example, what the character says, does and feels. Or the placement of the information could be in relation to parts of the body, e.g. 'He walks every night' could be placed near his feet. 'He is frightened' might be placed near his heart, etc. Usually 'Role on the Wall' is done collectively and referred back to and maybe added to at different points in the drama. Alternatively, children can keep 'Role on the Wall' booklets individually to record information and their thoughts about characters.	■ to verify and agree information about a character ■ to support and encourage justification of opinions and viewpoints about characters
Rumours	The class, working in role, are given a short amount of time (2 or 3 minutes) to create, spread and gather rumours about a character or event in the drama. This works best if done in a confined space to create a 'hubbub'. The activity can be set somewhere connected to the drama, e.g. the market place, the pub, etc. The teacher can join in and feed in rumours useful to the drama. After a few minutes of listening to, making up and spreading rumours, the teacher can halt the activity and encourage the class to carry on gossiping, but all together, as a whole class in one conversation. They will start to connect rumours together and probably continue to elaborate on them collectively when they are gathered, heard and responded to together.	■ to generate and share many ideas quickly ■ to gather potential plot lines and character developments from the children ■ to give opportunity for connecting ideas creatively
Sculpting	This involves moulding people as if they are clay or some other sculpting material. The sculpting can link with the drama literally, e.g. one partner is a lump of clay and the other is a sculptor who has been commissioned by the king to create a statue portraying his power. The sculpting might involve just using safe touch to mould the person without using speech at all. Or the sculptor might give verbal instructions to the lump of clay who responds as instructed. Usually sculpting is done silently. This can be done as a group or whole class activity with several silent sculptors and the clay made up collectively of several people. Once a sculpture has been created it is worth spending time supporting children as an audience to interpret its meaning and evaluate its effectiveness. Sculptures can	■ to provide a tactile experience that breaks down physical barriers safely between children ■ to explore and make a meaningful 3D image ■ to support the interpretation of a 3D image ■ to give opportunity for verbally and aesthetically communicating artistic interpretations ■ to show that different interpretations of sculptures are possible and accepted

PART TWO

	be given plaques (written or spoken). They can be put together into imaginary sculpture parks and opened to the public within dramas, e.g. when the townspeople of Hamelin visit the sculpture park in their leisure time and see the Mayor's statue, what do they say and hear others say about him? The sculpting might be less literal and more ambiguous and symbolic, e.g. sculpt your partner into a shape that shows your character's inner thoughts. Sculptures should be looked at from a range of vantage points so children should be able to move in, amongst and around the sculptures and also the sculptors should look from different angles and levels.	
Sensory Journey	One way of doing this is for children to work in pairs. One child closes their eyes and the other creates a safe but stimulating sensory journey (connected to the drama) for their partner. The journey leader may need a few minutes' thinking and preparation time first. The journey leader leads the 'blind' traveller gently but firmly by the arm to various sensory stimuli and provides an imaginative, accompanying narrative for the traveller, e.g. the traveller might be led to touch a curtain but told it is the king's cloak that he wears on special feast days. He may be given a stone to hold and told that this stone is from a sacred cave and the king holds it every day and listens to it. The stone only speaks to kings, etc. A sensory journey can involve the class together creating a journey experience for some of them to pass through in turn. For example the class might create a sensory tunnel that children with their eyes closed pass through on a journey in the drama, e.g. the tunnel to another land or a journey through the whispering cave, etc. They can create sound and whispers and maybe use musical instruments and props such as scarves to give a safe tactile experience. They can blow air and dangle string and feathers, as people pass by, etc. Children should want to take the journey and no child should be made to close their eyes unwillingly or be made to take a sensory journey unless they want to.	■ to encourage close co-operation towards a common goal ■ to stimulate and heighten a multi-sensory, dramatic experience ■ to encourage creative and lateral thinking ■ to stimulate the imagination through deliberately stimulating senses

Slow motion	This is self-explanatory. It means slowing the action down. This is a theatrical device that is helpful in terms of demanding individual and group co-operation, concentration and physical self-control. There may be reasons within a drama why slow motion is appropriate, e.g. slow motion is useful as a safety device in a drama that depicts anything violent (a battle or fight). It is also a useful device for showing memories (flashbacks) or different states of consciousness (dreams). Scenes can be played at natural speed and then shift to slow motion at a key moment to focus the audience and give significance to the moment. It is also interesting to ask children to play a short scene twice, once at natural speed and a second time in slow motion and for an audience to feed back on the impact. A slow motion silent replaying of the scene can be accompanied by a narrative storytelling, so we hear the narrative told as well as see it.	■ to give a longer time for the audience to focus on key moments ■ to build in controlled movement for physical safety ■ to denote different states of a character's consciousness ■ to portray a character's memories or dreams
Small group playmaking	This involves a group of children making up a scene or short play (usually for performance). Usually the groups will present their short plays to each other and they will each elaborate and extend aspects of the whole class drama. They may be presented using a Performance Carousel or Performance Wave.	■ to enable every child to share ownership of the fiction being collectively built ■ to create and develop the plot
Sound Collage **Soundscape**	The children (usually in small groups) are asked to find, make and organize sounds using their bodies and anything available to them in the room, e.g. objects, furniture, radiators, doors, etc. The sounds (which will link to the drama) should be explored and then organized and performed to an audience who have their eyes closed. The performers will need to decide where the audience should best place themselves to listen for greatest effect and impact, e.g. clustered in a group with the sounds performed around them or sitting in a class circle with the sounds radiating from the centre, etc. The sounds could be a logical, chronological sequence of sounds that are almost a soundtrack for the drama, e.g. footsteps, a key in a lock, a door opening, etc., or they can be sounds that are more randomly presented and not naturalistically presented, e.g. overlapping, repeating, crescendo effects, etc.	■ to focus attention on the aural aspects of the drama ■ to explore ways of creating sound ■ to link sound to performance and its impact

PART TWO

Speaking object (ritual)	There are times when many children are all wanting to contribute verbally in a drama at the same time and so cut across each other, with some children dominating. An object can be used that empowers only the holder to speak. The object can be passed among everyone to give all the opportunity to speak. The type of object can be selected to link in some way to the drama, e.g. a seashell in a drama set on an island, a stick in a forest drama, etc.	■ to ensure all children have equal opportunity to contribute ■ to prevent a few children verbally dominating ■ to reinforce the theme by using a relevant object
Still Image	A freeze frame (where action is halted and frozen) is a type of still image. However still images can also be created or devised. For example, a group of children might be asked to create a still image of the moment that a stranger arrived in their isolated village. They would need to discuss who would be which character in the scene and where each character would stand, etc. This is more demanding than just freezing action that is under way (freeze frame). If you ask children to create a still image you need to insist that they keep it very still, 'as still as a photograph'. Sometimes they can be asked to make a series of still images and maybe move between each image in slow motion (a controlled, theatrical and stylized way of changing images and telling a narrative visually).	■ to hold a moment in the drama still for exploration and/or reflection ■ to encourage and support group negotiation and problem solving
Tableau	A tableau is a type of still image or still picture. It can involve the whole class and the tableau can be built up slowly (devised) by letting one or two people at a time enter and place themselves within the tableau. A series of tableaux can be one way of depicting a story (rather like a storyboard of sequenced still images). See also 'Freeze frame' for suggestions as to what may be done with a still image.	■ to give a reason for everyone observing, analysing and interpreting an image closely ■ to share ownership of a key image
Talking objects	Talking objects are objects in a drama that can talk! The objects might be within any setting and can belong to any character, e.g. children can enter one at a time and place themselves as objects in a character's room. The children become the objects (as in physical theatre) and once in place are able to tell a little about themselves, the person they belong to and	■ to raise awareness that objects can be imbued with significance ■ to deepen knowledge and understanding of characters, setting and plot

	may be open to answering questions, e.g. about the comings and goings in the room. Another way of presenting talking objects is to hold a real object, e.g. a photograph. Whoever holds the object is empowered to talk as if they *are* the object. The object can be passed around so that several people have the opportunity to talk as the object. They need to listen carefully to each other to ensure that the object comes across as consistent.	■ to encourage and require active listening and co-operation ■ to actively support their understanding of personification
Teacher as narrator **Teacher as storyteller**	The teacher can act as a narrator or storyteller for parts of the drama for various purposes. This may be as an introduction to set the scene, e.g. *'Many years ago, before the world had cars and machinery and telephones, on a small island far from anywhere ...'* The teacher may narrate during the drama to gather and feed back the ideas that have been generated in role by the children, e.g. *'And so the villagers argued among themselves about what they should do with the stranger. Some thought ...* (inserting the children's drama-generated ideas) *... and others thought ...* (inserting the children's drama-generated ideas) *... and eventually they decided to ...'* The narration can be used to move the drama forward, *'And things might have carried on as normal but one day something happened that changed everything ...'.* Narration can also be used to support reflection and to close a drama, *'And years later the villagers still remembered clearly the day they had banished the stranger forever and they still wondered what had become of him ... but he was never spoken of again.'.* All drama is story so using story to stimulate drama and using drama to create story is a fairly seamless two-way process.	■ to blend episodes of the drama into a whole ■ to move the plot forward in time ■ to model how drama can be told as a narrative ■ to show that children's ideas are listened to and inform and shape the drama narrative ■ to stimulate prediction about what might happen next ■ to support reflection on what has already happened in the drama
Teacher in role	This is potentially the most important and enabling strategy that drama teachers have at their disposal. The teacher is a co-participant in the drama and takes on a role (or several roles), interacting with the children in role. 1. The teacher who is using teacher in role with children for the first time should explain it to the children and then try out a short TiR to check the children understand the approach.	■ to give or gather information in the drama as an active and interactive co-participant ■ to be a mediator of the drama experience from within a role ■ to focus, facilitate and enable children working

PART TWO

	2. The teacher must make clear when he/she is in or out of role and may sign this, e.g. through use of a piece of costume or a prop, e.g. 'When I carry this stick, I will be in role as the old man and when I put the stick down, I will stop pretending to be him.' 3. The teacher must carry out the role with commitment and seriousness and not half-heartedly or flippantly. 4. TiR needs a clear purpose in the drama and should last only as long as is necessary to fulfil the purpose. Teachers should avoid hogging the drama. 5. Teachers should avoid sustained, stunning acting performances that can disempower children. 6. The TiR can be defined by its function, i.e. information giving (e.g. TiR as a resident villager who knows the village well and has information to share with the children) or information gathering (e.g. TiR as a visitor to the village who wants information the children have or will create). 7. The TiR can also be defined by its status, e.g. high (e.g. a powerful king), low (e.g. an immigrant seeking asylum in the kingdom) or intermediate (e.g. a messenger from the powerful king). 8. Teachers should avoid always being in high status information-giving roles (which is how children view teachers anyway).	in role, from a position within the drama ■ to model committed working in role ■ to move a drama on from within the drama ■ to set challenges and create a need for deeper and different types of thinking from within the drama
Thought-tracking	This is a way of finding out what characters are thinking at a particular moment in the drama. In theatre this would possibly be a soliloquy. Thought-tracking makes public and shares aloud the 'in role' thoughts of a character or characters. The signal to speak an 'in role' thought in a drama lesson is traditionally by being touched on the shoulder by the teacher. If teachers are avoiding touch then the drama can be 'frozen' and the teacher can tell the class that he/she will pass by each person in turn and they all have the opportunity to speak their own character's innermost thoughts when the teacher is standing closest to them.	■ to deepen the level of engagement ■ to engage with a character's thoughts ■ to deepen our knowledge and understanding of a character ■ to gather and share the possible thoughts of one character ■ to share responsibility for the development of a character

	Alternatively, the teacher might invite all the children to offer the innermost thoughts of one character at a particular moment, e.g. the moment that the slipper is seen to fit Cinderella everyone might speak Cinderella's innermost thoughts as if they are Cinderella. Thought tracking usually happens 'on the spot' at a moment in the drama when the action is frozen and the thinking relates to the moment. Sometimes if we hear a character's thoughts they may be at odds with what a character is saying in the drama. This leads to some interesting discussion about why people might think one thing but decide to say another.	■ to share ownership and ideas about a character
Visualization	See 'Multi-sensory imagining'.	
Voice Collage	See also 'Sound Collage' and 'Soundscape'. A Voice Collage is like a soundscape that just uses voices. It can use voice sounds as well as words or short phrases and full and part sentences. Maybe at some point in the drama, you want the children to reflect back on some significant things that have been said and heard so far and may be in a character's memory. You might ask the children in groups to create a voice collage that depicts the voices and/or voice sounds that are in the character's head. The groups would probably be asked to perform the voice collages once they have prepared and rehearsed them. They should experiment with voices for best effect, maybe overlap voices, change tone or sound levels, etc. The voice collages are best performed to an audience with their eyes closed. The performers should consider where best to place the audience for maximum effect, e.g. sitting individually in spaces for the voices to travel in and around them, or maybe sitting in the centre together with voices around the outside, etc. The positioning of the audience should be considered at the preparation and rehearsal stages and not just seconds before the performance. The voice collage can be taped and used later as a soundtrack elsewhere in the drama, e.g. to accompany movement, or one group might perform the voice collage live as the live soundtrack to another group's movement piece.	■ to reflect, seek and highlight significant words and dialogue from within the drama ■ to experiment with and explore the voice as an instrument individually and collaboratively ■ to use collaborative voices only as performance ■ to focus attention on the significance, power and impact of voices ■ to separate out the dramatic voice as worthy of separate consideration

PART TWO

Working in role	This is self-explanatory. It involves the children acting and interacting deliberately, 'as if' they are someone else. As with 'Teacher in role' it needs to be clear to everyone when children are in or out of role, so teachers need to help define this clearly within the drama lesson. Dramas with very young children may involve children operating in an imagined world and situation but as themselves. They are doing drama as they are acting and interacting within a fiction but it could be argued they are technically not in role.	■ to safely distance children to act and interact as if they are someone else ■ to enable children to think and feel themselves into 'another person's shoes' and situation ■ to experience acting and interacting in a sustained way, 'as if' they are another person and learn from the experience
Writing in role	While in role (individually or collectively), the children write for a purpose that connects with and is informed by the drama. The resultant writing ideally will have significance for the drama itself and further inform it, e.g. a stranger in the drama has a letter in his room that he has hidden. The children (maybe together) create and write all or part of that letter. The drama can then proceed with the contents of the letter known and this is likely to influence the next part of the drama. It is possible to introduce many meaningful reasons for writing within dramas. The writing in role should matter to the drama and ideally should usually be more than just a character writing about the drama. It is possible within a drama to build in a reason for any type or genre of writing, e.g. a poster declaring a public meeting, a list of the contents from a character's pockets, a police report following an interview with a character, a letter between characters, an anonymous note, a bully's school report and a victim's school report, etc. If the curriculum and timetabling allow, it is helpful to have the option of stopping and writing during the drama at the moment that the writing is needed, and then carrying on with the drama, rather than writing after a drama lesson. It is while the children are in role and engaged that the writing in role will be best and will more truly be 'writing in role'. It is helpful to have big and normal-sized paper and pens available during drama lessons so that writing can happen spontaneously 'in the moment' without organizational disruption.	■ to inform and shape the drama ■ to deepen engagement with role ■ to find out more about character and plot ■ to inspire and stimulate writing for an immediate and worthwhile purpose ■ to enable a written medium of expression within the drama ■ to provide meaningful and engaging contexts for writing individually and collaboratively ■ to enable the teacher to guide the writing in role (if required) as a co-participant with a drama purpose for making it effective

Whatever Wanda Wanted

KEY STAGE 1 (YEARS 1/2)

This drama uses a picture book as its stimulus. The lesson does not focus on simply re-enacting the existing story. It is an opportunity to engage with its significant themes and further creatively develop the characters and plot. It is preferable (but not necessary) to have access to the picture book. Do not read the story to the children in advance of doing the drama lesson, as it will influence and maybe limit their own ideas.

■ Story outline

Wanda's very busy parents always buy her anything she wants, to demonstrate that they care. Wanda has no friends at school as she is unkind to classmates, always having to outdo other children, whenever they own something. On a shopping trip with her mum she strays into a kite shop while her mum is getting her an ice cream and is angrily adamant that she wants the one kite that the shopkeeper says is not for sale. She grabs the magical kite (which can talk)

and is swept off by it, past her mum, up into the sky and deposited far away to survive on a desert island alone, with no possessions. She uses her initiative and survives, befriends a lonely dolphin and misses her parents. The dolphin (a good friend) takes her home on his back. Her parents have sold all they own to look for her and reunited they are happy without possessions, having realized now that there are more important things.

PART TWO

■ Cross-curricular study links

English

- ■ Additional story text generated by the drama
- ■ Labelling
- ■ Shop signs
- ■ Newspaper reports
- ■ Messages
- ■ Letters

Mathematics

- ■ Symmetry (kites)
- ■ Measurement (kites)
- ■ Scale and distance (island map)
- ■ 2D and 3D shapes (kites)

Geography

- ■ Islands
- ■ Bird's-eye views and maps
- ■ The Sea

History

- ■ Island settlements
- ■ Flotsam and jetsam (artefacts)

■ Personal development links

- ■ Managing feelings (greed, anger, love, loneliness, jealousy, rejection, fear)
- ■ Self-reliance and survival
- ■ Work/life balance
- ■ Friendship
- ■ Empathy
- ■ Families/parenting
- ■ Child protection
- ■ Personal growth and change

■ Areas of learning

- ■ Understanding English, communication and languages
- ■ Mathematical understanding
- ■ Scientific and technological understanding
- ■ Historical, geographical and social understanding
- ■ Understanding physical development, health and well-being
- ■ Understanding the arts

Science

■▬■▬■ Flight

Floating and Sinking

Water

Art and Design

■ Kites

Design and Technology

■▬■ Food and Healthy Eating

Kites

Environmental sustainability

■ Biodegradable/non-biodegradable flotsam and jetsam

■ Resources

■▬■ *Whatever Wanda Wanted* by Jude Wisdom, Publisher, Gallane Children's Books (2001), ISBN: 1-86233-300-9 (optional)

■ A life-sized outline of a child drawn on a large piece of paper and labelled 'Wanda' (see activity 16)

■▬■ Felt tip pens (see activity 16)

■▬■ Self-adhesive labels (optional for activity 16)

PART TWO

	Drama strategy	Purpose	Grouping	Teacher guidance and possible cross-curricular links
1	**Improvisation in pairs** Mime	■ To deepen engagement with the role and gift in order to increase the impact of the rejection ■ To give a context for descriptive speech and explanation	Class circle Talking partners	Tell the children you will pretend to be Wanda and her parents will buy her any toy she wants. Ask them each to think of a toy they own or wish they owned and imagine it's in front of them. They can pretend to play with it for a while and then show it to the child sitting next to them and explain why it is such a good toy.
2	**Teacher in role**	■ To encourage sustained dialogue in a make-believe situation ■ To consider the motives underlying people's behaviour	Class circle	In turn, as Wanda's mum or dad they come and give it to you as a present. Take the presents as Wanda and stack them up without much interest. Out of role ask them for their responses to Wanda's attitude and behaviour towards her parents and their gifts. What do the children think of Wanda's behaviour and why? Why might she behave as she does? Go back into role and give them opportunity to talk with and advise Wanda on her behaviour and attitude to her parents and their gifts.
3	**Improvisation**	■ To share ownership of the development and speech of a main character ■ To enable children's ideas to be shared and integrated into the drama	Pairs	Ask the children to make up a conversation in pairs that Wanda might have with another child in her class. The conversation will help us see why Wanda has no friends. Discuss possible scenarios first if necessary (some are in the book), e.g. she wanted other children's lunch boxes, she boasts about how her toys are better than theirs, etc. You can then either ask the children to tell you (in role) about some of the things that Wanda has done or said that make her unpopular (based on their scene) or else you could walk around the outside of the circle and whichever couple you are standing nearest to repeat a snippet of their dialogue until you move to the next couple. You only need snippets of dialogue, rather than complete scenes to be replayed (as full replays

			will take too long). You might wish to encourage discussion about what Wanda's behaviour makes them personally feel, e.g. upset, angry, hurt, etc., and help them reflect that our behaviour impacts on the feelings of others and what they then think about us.
	■ To consider behaviours that militate against friendship		
4	**Occupational mime**	Individually	Divide the class in half. One half of the children will be shopkeepers and the other half customers. The shopkeepers decide what their shops sell and then stand in a space (their shop) and begin to carry out shop tasks, e.g. pricing, stacking shelves, stocktaking, etc., as they wait for customers to arrive. The rest of the class (as customers) visit the shops in role.
	■ To actively engage with role		
	Improvisation	Whole class	
	■ To give the children the opportunity to interact in role with the main character		
	Teacher in role		You will move around in role as Wanda, entering shops with other customers. Behave rudely, selfishly and greedily.
	■ To model narrative storytelling using the children's ideas		
	Teacher as storyteller		When you have been around several shops, retell the shopping scenes as an eyewitness (in the third person as a narrative), e.g. 'Wanda went shopping. She went to a computer shop and found the most expensive computer. She didn't like it much but she knew it would make other children jealous, so she jumped the queue and bought it …'. Move the narrative on from what the children have just enacted towards what happens next (using either the book or your own words), e.g.
	■ To generate additional storyline/plot		
			'Wanda saw a shop she did not know and this surprised her as she thought she knew every shop. She decided to go inside and was amazed to discover that it was full of KITES!'

PART TWO

	Drama strategy	Purpose	Grouping	Teacher guidance and possible cross-curricular links
5	Visualization	■ To engage and create visually	Individually	Ask the children to spread themselves around the room and close their eyes and stand silently to listen and imagine 'a picture in your mind'. Say something along the lines of:
		■ To provide a context for using subject-specific (mathematical) vocabulary		*'Imagine you are a kite ... you are hanging on the ceiling of a shop that is full of wonderful kites ... look at yourself carefully ... I wonder what you are made of ... Maybe you are paper or material of some sort? ... What colour or colours are you? ... Are you plain or patterned? ... What shape are you? ... Are you a box shape (3D) or a flat kite of some sort (2D)? ... Do you have a tail? (if so, look at it carefully and know what it looks like) ... Is it long or short? ... rolled up or hanging down? ... You are a fantastic kite, an extraordinary kite ... You think you know what makes you so much better than all the other kites ... I wonder what that is?'*
6	Teacher in role	■ To practise verbal description, reasoning, justification and explanation	Pairs	Ask the children to get into pairs of kites. They will talk to each other as kites (both of whom think they are the best kite in the shop). Without touching each other they will explain to each other why they think they are the best kite and why the little girl who has just come into the shop (Wanda) will want them most of all.
		■ A context for using and practising persuasive speech	Whole class	Having rehearsed their argument, they will now try to sell themselves to Wanda as she passes among them in turn. You will be Wanda and don't want any of them. At the end of the scene you will focus excitedly on an imaginary kite that you do want. And shout (with great determination) 'I want *that* kite.' The kite referred to is not one that the children are representing.

| 7 | Collective role | To give a challenging context for problem solving in role

 To assess how different children try to achieve the task, i.e. get the kite

 To encourage and practise creative and critical thinking | Whole class | Tell the children you will now become the shopkeeper. They will now all pretend to be Wanda. They must try to buy the kite from you but you will not sell it. It will be interesting to see what approaches they try. Do they just get angry when you won't sell or do they think and act strategically? In role be closer to being persuaded when they are acting strategically rather than angrily. Out of role particularly praise strategic thinking approaches.

Can they suggest why the shopkeeper won't sell that particular kite, when he is prepared to sell any other kite? What might be special about it?

They (again, as Wanda) can then ask you as the shopkeeper why you won't sell it. You can decide what you tell them but the book suggests that the kite has magical qualities and is capable of doing 'horrid things' when it is flying. Out of role afterwards, ask the children to suggest what some of the 'horrid things' might be that the kite does. You can then incorporate some of their suggestions into the kite flight, which comes next. |
| | **Hot-seating**

Teacher in Role | | | |

	Drama strategy	Purpose	Grouping	Teacher guidance and possible cross-curricular links
8	**Mime and movement** **Teacher narrator**	■ To physically symbolize their collective role ■ To build dramatic tension before moving the drama on episodically	Whole class	Ask the children to get into a line and join hands. You get to the head of the line and be the kite. They are all together in role as Wanda. Narrate what happened next (using your own words or the book and building dramatic tension) when Wanda grabs the string and shouts 'GOT YOU KITE!' and the kite replies 'GOT YOU WANDA!' and flies off with her.
	Still image (pause)	■ To give a sense of the journey and considerable distance from home ■ To build up the detail of a shared, imagined setting ■ To make deliberate links to support map work		Take the children on an exciting (but controlled) kite flight around the room (or you could do this part of the lesson out of doors). You can incorporate ideas offered already about the 'horrid things' the kite might do. While you are pretending to be high in the air, you might pause from time to time to ask the children what they can see far below, e.g. Wanda's mum, her house, the fields, sea, etc. You might point out that this is a 'bird's-eye view' and looks like a map from so high up (and possibly link this moment later to map-making).
				Map-making opportunity They can individually, in groups or together, create a pictorial (bird's-eye view) map of what Wanda saw from high in the sky.
	Slow motion	■ To ensure the physical safety of the children		Eventually slow down the flight and take them down (as Wanda) to a controlled landing on a desert island. Depending on the excitability of the children (and physical obstacles), you may decide to do the flight and/or landing in slow motion.

9				
	Visualization and imagined soundscape	■ To encourage empathy ■ To pre-empt easy rescue solutions	Individually	Ask the children to get into a space alone, sit down or lie down and close their eyes. Ask them to imagine they are Wanda and have just landed after a very frightening journey and now the kite has abandoned them. Tell them there are no people on this island at all and there never have been. Wanda is the first human ever to set foot here. Ask them to imagine the scene around them in silence. What can they see ... hear ... feel on their skin ... smell ... as they stay still and use their senses in this place?
	Collective role **Thought-tracking**	■ To support multi-sensory engagement with a shared setting and make it more vivid and memorable	Individually	After some silent time for them to imagine alone, ask them to keep their eyes closed and explain that you will touch some of them on the shoulder and if you do they can say aloud one thing they can see, hear, feel (touch) or smell. They will say the sentence beginning with 'I can see ...,' or 'I can smell ...,' etc. Gradually and collectively the setting will unfold in an imagined, shared, multi-sensory way. You can also add sensory detail alongside the children.
		■ To encourage empathy ■ To share the development of a main character		Conclude this activity by saying something like, '_I wonder what you are feeling Wanda as you sit on this island all alone (long pause) ... and I wonder what you are thinking (long pause)? If I touch you on the shoulder you have the chance to say out loud what you are thinking as Wanda._' Don't insist every child speaks and just pass on if you get no response.

PART TWO

	Drama strategy	Purpose	Grouping	Teacher guidance and possible cross-curricular links
10	Improvisation	■ To identify and solve basic survival problems creatively and collaboratively	Whole class	From listening to Wanda's thoughts (activity 9) they may have already identified some problems, 'How will I get off this island?', 'I am hungry', 'There are no toilets here', 'I wonder if there are any dangerous animals?', etc. In or out of role you need to help the children to identify and then prioritize the problems and concerns of Wanda before taking action in groups to start to resolve some of them. It is likely that you will end up focusing on accessing food, water and shelter in the first instance and maybe protecting Wanda from wild animals.
		■ To encourage and give opportunity for successful team work ■ To enable active group problem solving	Small groups (up to 4 children in each group)	Divide the children into groups with tasks they have identified to complete, e.g. find the best site to build a shelter, seek shelter-making materials, make a rod or net and catch fish, find wood and build a fire, find and pick berries, etc. They will all be exploring the island next with their agreed group task in mind. Agree a sound signal that means 'Come back together into a circle', e.g. a distinctive drumbeat. Emphasize that they will not meet any islanders as they explore and do their tasks, as no one but Wanda is on the island (or ever has been). Then let the children have several minutes to explore and improvise carrying out the tasks together in groups. Join in or observe. Wanda is alone on the island and yet they are all working collaboratively as her but you will find they accept this.
		■ To give a context for reporting back accurately on events	Groups in a whole class circle	Recall them to the circle with the agreed signal and ask them to report back in role (as groups or with a group spokesperson) what they have been doing, what successes they have had and what new problems/ observations may have emerged.
	Teacher in role	■ To use role to introduce another key character from the book	Whole class	After a while tell them that you saw a dolphin swim right up to the beach and smile. Even more amazingly, the dolphin spoke, welcomed you and then swam away. Improvise the answers to any questions they ask you about this.

	Strategy	Purposes	Grouping	Description
	Visualization	■ To encourage reflection ■ To encourage empathy	Individual	To conclude this episode, ask them to settle in a circle around the fire to sleep (in a space, without touching each other) and try to picture again what they have done and seen today on the island. Then ask them to think about Wanda's mum and dad and imagine/picture what they might be doing.
	Image theatre (episodic)	■ To envisage, construct and join together additional episodes happening in an earlier setting		Tell them to keep their eyes closed. Say that you will pass by and may touch them on the head lightly. If touched, they have the opportunity to say aloud what they think/'see' Wanda's mother doing, e.g. 'She is crying', 'She is driving around looking for her', 'She is talking to the police', etc. Imagining it happening and then speaking in the present tense makes it more immediate.
11	**Teacher in role** **Mantle of the Expert** **Hot-seating**	■ To give a context for practising and refining questioning skills ■ To provide additional information in role ■ To encourage empathy and help them know and understand a character's feelings and viewpoint	Whole class	Ask the children to imagine that they are good newspaper reporters, who will be asking questions to Wanda's mum. You may need to talk a little with them about what newspaper reporters do and what they are good at, i.e. asking questions, listening, writing reports, etc. Ask them what questions the newspaper reporters might have asked her mum (gathering and rehearsing a few possible questions) before you go into role as the newspaper reporter and answer their questions informatively and emotionally. Wanda's mum saw her flying off hanging on to the kite (eye-witness account). Questions need to have value. They could first decide one question to ask with their partner. Don't answer too many questions or stay in role more than a few minutes and maybe limit the number of questions they may ask to encourage more thoughtful questioning. **Writing in role opportunity** Ask them to write a newspaper report or scribe their collective report using their ideas and suggested sentences.

PART TWO

	Drama strategy	Purpose	Grouping	Teacher guidance and possible cross-curricular links
12		■ To learn that objects have histories ■ To learn that objects can hold memories and meaning for people (symbolic)	Class circle	Tell the children that even though no one else lives on the island, the seashore has objects and rubbish on it (flotsam and jetsam) that have been washed up by the tide. When Wanda finds objects washed up on the beach, they often remind her of home, e.g. a plastic bottle, rope, etc. What might Wanda find? What does it make her miss/think about to do with home?
	Talking objects			Explain that each child in turn (going around the circle) has the opportunity to pretend to be an object that has been washed up on the island. They may enter the circle when it is their turn, place themselves as that object on the beach and say (as the object) what they are. You then pass between the objects as Wanda and children say 'I am a ... and Wanda remembers ...', e.g. 'I am a plastic bottle and Wanda remembers her favourite drink was in a plastic bottle', etc.
				Writing in role opportunity The children could now suggest or write a message that Wanda might throw into the sea in the plastic bottle.
13	Collective role Teacher in role Improvisation	■ To actively consider the behaviour and responses of good friends	Whole class	The children will now all be the dolphin sitting together in a group facing you but not touching each other. You sit sadly as Wanda. Wanda is homesick (and might talk about home and missing her mum and dad but she does not miss her possessions) and the dolphin will act and speak spontaneously, as her good friend. The children might naturally offer to take you home (on the back of the swimming dolphin) but if they don't suggest this, then end up asking them to.
				Writing/Art opportunity Wanda could leave a message in words (or pictorially) in case anyone else comes to the island. What would she want them to know and how might she communicate it?

14	Mime and movement Freeze frame	■ To indicate and mark time passing and change the setting ■ To support the children to consider what they might see at sea	Whole class	Either as one big dolphin (or else individually) the children will mime swimming back to Wanda's homeland. You might decide to make it a long journey punctuated by freezing the action sometimes and inviting children to say what they can see on each day of the journey, e.g. 'On the first day Wanda saw a pretty fish', action/freeze, 'On the second day Wanda saw ...', etc. Finish with her seeing her mum waving to her (if you can).
15	Collective role Speaking object	■ To give an opportunity for collective reporting ■ To assess how well and accurately they can recall and recount the drama story ■ To find out whether they realize that the character has learned and developed	Whole class	You now take on the role of her mum and the children will be Wanda (who has by now been landed safely by the dolphin). You ask Wanda where she has been and what happened to her, etc. The children will report back as Wanda. You may need to introduce and pass a 'speaking object' (that empowers the holder of it to be the only child speaking to her mum at that moment). As mum, let them know that you have sold every possession and given up your job to try to find Wanda. She is coming back to no toys and no money but is coming back to loving parents. The response of the children here will be very revealing. Do they realize Wanda has changed and now thinks people are more important than possessions?

	Drama strategy	Purpose	Grouping	Teacher guidance and possible cross-curricular links
16	**Role on the Wall**	■ To visually and collectively focus and organize the children's knowledge and thoughts about the main character ■ To stimulate discussion and debate about a character	■ Whole class	In advance of this activity, on a large piece of paper draw an outline (preferably life size) of Wanda. Ask the children what they know about Wanda now, e.g. 'She missed her mum', 'She has a dolphin friend', etc., and record this around the character's outline (directly on the paper or else on adhesive labels). Through out-of-role reflective discussion help them consider what Wanda has learned through her island experience and how this has changed her for the better. **Writing in role opportunity** Wanda or her mum could write to the dolphin (letter in a bottle) thanking him and updating him as to how things are turning out now that Wanda is home again.

The Green Children

This drama is based on an East Anglian folk tale from about seven hundred years ago. It has been recorded by two chroniclers (the abbot, Ralph of Coggeshall in Essex and William, the canon of Newburgh Priory in Yorkshire). The events take place at Woolpit in Suffolk, which gets its name from 'Wolf-pits', which is where the children, who were 'green in the whole body', were reportedly discovered by villagers during the reign of King Stephen (1135–1154).

■ Folk tale outline

A dazed and frightened green boy and girl were found lying outside the entrance to a cave near the wolf pits. They spoke an unknown language and did not understand the villagers' language. They were escorted by villagers to the castle of Sir Richard de Calne, for him to decide what should be done with them. The hungry children refused food but it transpired that if the food was green they would eat it. The boy however failed to thrive, seemed very homesick (and was often seen wandering, trying to find his way back to his homeland) and sadly died. The girl learned to speak the villagers' language (Anglo-Norman), started to eat the same food as them and gradually stopped being green. She was christened and eventually married a local boy. She told the villagers about her Christian homeland, 'St Martin's Land', where it was always twilight and there was no sun or moon. The whole country and its creatures were all green. She had been looking after sheep with her brother when they heard the sound of distant bells from within a cave, followed the sound and ended up in Woolpit in bright sunshine. They were terrified and unable to adjust to the light at first and so could not see to run away and were 'caught' by the villagers.

PART TWO

Personal development links

- Survival
- Personal identity
- Empathy
- Respecting and accepting intercultural differences
- Awareness of the needs of others
- Child care and protection
- Personal growth and change

Areas of learning

- Understanding English, communication and languages
- Scientific and technological understanding
- Historical, geographical and social understanding
- Understanding physical development, health and well-being
- Understanding the arts and design

Cross-curricular study links

English

- Additional story generated by the drama
- Reporting in a chronicle
- Newspaper reports (modernizing the event)
- Scriptwriting of dialogue

- Old English language
- A memorial plaque for where the green children were found

History

- Invaders and settlers (Norman England)
- Feudal system
- Castles

Geography

- Migration

Science

- Natural dyes
- Light and Dark (and its impact on the body)

Art and Design

- Storyboarding the plot or the dream sequence
- Using natural dyes for art
- Tapestry design to commemorate
- 3D sculpture to commemorate

Design and Technology

- Food and Healthy Eating

Resources

- A white sheet

PART TWO

■ Further resources (optional)

Atmospheric dream music

There are several accounts of this story and relevant images accessible via an internet search

The Green Children by Kevin Crossley-Holland and Alan Marks, ISBN: 0-19-279958-4

Maudie and the Green Children by Adrian Mitchell, ISBN: 1-896580-06-8

	Drama strategy	Purpose	Grouping	Teacher guidance and possible cross-curricular links
1	**Occupational mime**	■ To engage with role ■ To ensure they have sufficient understanding of the historical context	Class circle Individual	Tell the children that the drama is set in the countryside, about seven hundred years ago. You might spend a few minutes ensuring they realize there would be no electricity, telephone, engines, etc. Villagers did not travel far and tended to stay living in the villages they were born in. Ask them how the harvest would be gathered in, i.e. by hand with scythes, and
	Still image	■ To model narrative storytelling		bundled. Ask them to stand alone and still in a space, posed as if they are farm workers gathering the harvest, e.g. cutting the corn, bundling, lifting sheathes, etc., using scythes or pitchforks. Narrate an introduction to the
	Teacher as storyteller	■ To establish the shared setting ■ To give a controlled start to the drama ■ To build dramatic tension		scene and when you click your fingers, they will bring the scene to life, e.g. *'It was a hot summer's day in Suffolk and the villagers were hard at work, gathering the harvest in for their master, Sir Richard … They had been working hard since sunrise and were hot and tired … It was an ordinary summer's day like any other … they had no idea that something remarkable was about to happen!'*
2	**Teacher in role**	■ To stimulate curiosity ■ To present a moral dilemma to be solved in role	Whole class	Tell them that you will now be going into role, i.e. pretending to be a stranger who they will find as they are working in the fields of their master. Ask for a volunteer to be another stranger with you (maybe a teaching assistant). Tell them that, amazingly, you will both be green children. Resume the harvesting activity and then place yourself
	Freeze frame	■ To hold a key moment still for individual and shared reflection		somewhere as two frightened children and await discovery. Do not speak to them when they find you both. Let them struggle to communicate with you. After a while say, 'Freeze', to hold the scene still.
	Thought-tracking	■ To offer an alternative viewpoint ■ To encourage empathy		Now explain that they should keep still as villagers and as you pass by each person they have opportunity to speak aloud what they are thinking in role, e.g. 'Poor things look frightened', 'These children might not be human.'

		Whole class	
Teacher in role (soliloquy)	■ To challenge prejudicial assumptions ■ To summarize and focus thinking		Then go back into role as one of the green children and invite them to listen to the thoughts of the green children. e.g. 'I am frightened of these people. Their faces are not green. I wonder if they will hurt my brother and me. I wish my parents were here', etc. You could also invite them to add possible thoughts of the green children.
Teacher as storyteller			Then bring this scene to a close by narrating along the following lines (trying to weave in their spoken thoughts) e.g. 'The villagers were amazed. They had never seen anything like this before. Some felt sorry for the children and wanted to help them but others were suspicious and thought they might not be human. What should they do with these children?'
Improvisation	■ To encourage divergent thinking		Having heard each other's thoughts, ask them to talk with each other as villagers about what possible courses of action they might take (if any) and why. Will they take the children into their homes, leave them out of doors, lock them up, try to help them get home, etc? Don't add suggestions yourself unless they need support.
Teacher narrator	■ To summarize and then move the drama on into another scene		Conclude this scene by retelling their ideas as a narrative and then say, 'But in the end the villagers decided to take the green children to Sir Richard's castle and let him decide what to do with them.'

PART TWO

	Drama strategy	Purpose	Grouping	Teacher guidance and possible cross-curricular links
3	**Improvisation**	■ To build dramatic tension ■ To set the scene for the arrival of a main character	Whole class	Now tell them that they have arrived at the castle of Sir Richard and should place themselves in the room, nervously awaiting his arrival. The green children will not be among them at this moment and are outside being guarded/watched by some villagers. Ask for two volunteers to be the green children and ask them to sit out and watch for a few minutes. They then have opportunity to talk together in role as they wait for you to arrive but should be silent when you enter as the listening Sir Richard.
	Teacher in role	■ To deepen engagement and thought and build plot ■ To build up dramatic tension		Question them as Sir Richard, to elicit more detail. Where exactly did they find them? Can the green children who are outside waiting speak? Did they have any possessions with them? Are they sure this is not a trick?, etc. Encourage sustained answers, justification and reasoning. Ask them to bring the children in now and study them without comment for a while. Try to build up dramatic tension through close silent scrutiny of the children, thus making the villagers wonder what you are thinking.
	Conscience Alley	■ To invite engagement with and shared ownership of a main character at a key moment		Ask the children to get into two straight lines facing each other and about a metre apart. You will walk up the middle as Sir Richard, and they have opportunity to speak your private thoughts aloud as you pass by each of them. They in turn offer conflicting voices in your head as you try to reach a decision, e.g. 'Take them back where they were found', 'They are only children, look after them', 'I wonder if their parents will come?', etc. After you have walked slowly between the lines of voices, turn to them and say, *'I have decided that they will come and live in my castle. My servants will take care of them. They look hungry. I will send for some food.'*

#	Activity	Objectives	Grouping	Description
4	**Game (ritual)**	■ To build dramatic tension ■ To encourage logical reasoning ■ To find out more about the main characters	Class circle	Ask them to get into a circle and quietly brief the two volunteer green children (away from earshot of the others) that they will only eat food that is green when it is presented and will firmly reject food that is not green. Then ask the rest of the class to think of a piece of food they could offer and present to the children that they might like. In turn they can step forward and offer the food, e.g. 'Here is a delicious piece of roast chicken' (which they will reject) or 'Here is a lovely bowl of peas' (which they would accept and eat). After a while ask the children if there is any pattern to what they like. You may need to tell them if they do not guess the 'rule', that the green children only eat green food.
5	**Small group playmaking**	■ To build up a sense of time passing ■ To raise awareness of the contrast between the green boy's and girls' attitudes	Small groups	Divide the class into groups of about four. Half of the groups will be asked to create a short scene (of no more than a minute) that shows a moment of happiness in the green girl's new life as she starts to settle, e.g. she makes a friend, she laughs, she eats a new food, etc. One child in each group plays a green child. The other half of the groups will show the green boy in a very short scene depicting his inability to settle into the new life, e.g. won't eat, refuses friendship, looks for the way back to his real home, etc. Offer ideas if required but try to get the groups to think of their own.
	Performance Carousel	■ To introduce clear performance criteria		The scenes should: ■ Start with a still image ■ Bring the still image to life for up to a minute naturalistically (with speech) ■ Freeze frame the action

PART TWO

	Drama strategy	Purpose	Grouping	Teacher guidance and possible cross-curricular links
		■ To support a focused, well controlled performance and audience		The groups could move from floor level in slow motion into the first still image and after the freeze frame melt back down to floor level again. This way, all movement is theatrical and controlled and the dramatic effect is not broken.
				Give only a few minutes to prepare and practise the scene before seeing the scenes in uninterrupted sequence, thus creating a piece of continuous theatre. Insist that all groups are completely still and focused between scenes (as if they are on a stage but in the shadows, while one group is in a spotlight).
	Hot-seating	■ To deepen engagement with the roles		The images could be reformed or scenes replayed with opportunity for characters in the scenes to 'freeze' and answer questions in role.
6	Ritual	■ To deepen significance of a key moment through repeated ritual ■ To offer a moment for spiritual reflection	Class circle	**The green boy dies.** Place a bundled white sheet in the centre of the circle. Tell them that it represents the covered body of the green boy, who was homesick, sad and weak, and died. Each person has opportunity to walk across the circle in turn and, as they pass the sheet, to pause and say a sentence (rather like an epitaph) aloud. What is the one sentence they would inscribe on a gravestone about him? e.g. 'He could never settle here', 'Gone home again', etc.

7	Ritual	■ To deepen significance of a key moment through repeated ritual ■ To offer a moment for spiritual reflection	Whole class	**The green girl marries.** Pick up the white sheet and tell them it is now a wedding dress. Maybe hang it over something tall, e.g. a hatstand, or else you hold it up high yourself in the centre of the circle. They have opportunity to give a one-sentence wish or positive comment to the bride (represented by the sheet) as they pass by it in turn, e.g. 'It is good to see you happy at last.'
	Teacher in role			**The green girl learns their language.** The villagers can at last communicate with the girl and ask questions of her. They can now find out whatever they wish to know. What do they want to know? Before they ask their questions to the girl (teacher in role) ask them first to say aloud what they are wondering about her, e.g. 'I wonder how she got to this land', 'I wonder if she will ever get back to her own land again', etc. After a few 'wonderings', you go into role as the girl and answer the villagers' direct questions in role.
8	Mime and movement	■ To offer opportunity for reflection around linking key moments and images ■ To give opportunity for working symbolically	Groups of about 4	Suggest that even though the green girl has married a local boy and has settled, maybe she remembers her homeland vividly in her dreams sometimes. Dreams can be a strange mixture of past and present, of real and symbolic. Significant dreams are sometimes repeated. Ask the groups to create a short dream sequence for the green girl made up of two vivid still images that are repeated (as in a repetitive dream).
	Image theatre Performance Carousel	■ To create a whole class performance quickly ■ To conclude with a reflective performance		Then ask each group to perform in turn, repeating their dream sequence in a seamless group performance carousel that will join to make one long dream sequence. If you have suitable atmospheric background music this would be helpful, but is not essential.

World War 2 (Evacuees)

KEY STAGE 2 (YEAR 4)

This drama is intended to support children to learn more about and empathize with WW2 evacuees, their parents and the host families. Using some of the wealth of available primary historical sources, the drama will track children through the departure, arrival and the return of evacuees to London.

■ Background information

In the first four days of September 1939 nearly 3 million people (mostly schoolchildren, with 100,000 teachers) were transported from cities to the countryside, for fear of enemy bombing. Four million casualties were expected in London and government propaganda encouraged city mothers by radio, through posters and leaflets to send their children away from home and into the countryside. It was named 'Operation Pied Piper'. Many set off walking to the stations in groups of several hundred with teachers accompanying them on the 'holiday' adventure. They were labelled (in case they got lost), carried gas masks, food rations, and a change of clothing. They were ushered onto crowded steam trains to unknown destinations. On their arrival, some areas had insufficient host families waiting and the children were lined up by billeting officers (usually in village halls) and went through the potentially traumatic and humiliating experience of being (or not being) chosen. Some children were treated kindly by host families and others were ill treated (some seriously so). Nowadays, evacuees who are still alive recall their vivid and emotional experiences fondly, and others with lasting distress.

The storyline

The children will take on various roles throughout the drama. At the start, the children as parents are wrestling with whether or not to evacuate their children and then considering how to break the news to their children, before bidding them farewell at the station. As children they receive news of their evacuation and poignantly pack for departure, not sure if they will ever return home or see their parents again. When the evacuees arrive at their countryside destination, they meet the billeting officer and experience the public humiliation of being selected (or not) by adults who have a range of motives for taking them in to their homes. Some children have positive and others negative experiences as evacuees, depending mainly on which host families they are billeted with. Some consider whether or not to run away and find their own way back home. Many years later, as the elderly, the evacuees have the opportunity to share their vivid evacuation memories on a live chat show.

- Playscript generated by the drama
- Labelling (making their own evacuee labels)
- Posters and propaganda (studying and designing evacuee posters)
- Leaflets (reading government information leaflets and then creating their own)
- Newspaper reports (reading old wartime newspaper reports and creating their own)
- Diaries (keeping a personal diary as an evacuee)
- Letters (from parent to child and vice versa)
- Wartime recipes
- Writing to the imaginary chat show host (see drama activity 12)

Media/ICT

- Emailing the imaginary TV programme researcher on Evacuees for 'Tell it as it was!' (see drama activity 12)
- Really filming during drama activity 12
- Planning and creating a documentary film on Evacuees

Mathematics

- How far did the evacuees travel and how long would it take both then and now?

Geography

- Where did the evacuees leave and where did they arrive?

■ Personal development links

- Managing feelings (fear, love, loneliness, jealousy, rejection)
- Self-reliance and survival
- Friendship
- Empathy
- Bullying
- Families/parenting
- Child protection
- Responsibility and duty
- Personal growth and change

■ Areas of learning

- Understanding English, communication and languages
- Mathematical understanding
- Historical, geographical and social understanding
- Understanding physical development, health and well-being
- Understanding the arts and design

■ Cross-curricular study links

English

- Additional story text generated by the drama

PART TWO

History

- Transport (air, sea, road, rail)
- Evacuation now and then

Art and Design

- Portraits of faces of evacuees leaving (full size can be used as masks)
- Designing, making or changing government posters encouraging evacuation

Design and Technology

- Making a replica of a gas mask case

■ Resources required

You need at least one photograph of refugees leaving, which shows them with labels and luggage (including gas mask cases).

Ideally you will make accessible a series of photographs to support parts of this drama, e.g. evacuees walking to the station, on the platform, in the train, arriving at their destination station, being selected, settling in, at their new schools, helping out, etc. You could use a whiteboard to present photographs but enabling the children to handle photos together as they talk about them is preferable.

■ Online resources

Excellent primary source materials are plentiful online, e.g. war posters, leaflets, evacuee letters and accounts, photos, newspaper articles, podcasts, sound effects, wartime wireless broadcasts, etc.

www.bbc.co.uk/history/ww2children

www.bbc.co.uk/ww2peopleswar is an online archive of wartime memories contributed by members of the public and gathered by the BBC

www.learningcurve.gov.uk

www.iwm.org.uk

Historical association website

An internet search will yield many more sites linked to this theme, as well as sound effects and recordings of evacuees' memories many years later.

■ Other possible resources

Wartime songs recording (optional).

	Drama strategy	Purpose	Grouping	Teacher guidance and possible cross-curricular links
1	Improvisation	■ To engage with role ■ To encourage empathy ■ To introduce a moral dilemma ■ To begin to establish and justify different, authentic viewpoints	Pairs	**Deciding to evacuate the children** Ask the children to get into pairs. It is August 1939. Tell them that they are parents and have read (or heard) the contents of Public Information Leaflet Number 3 that was published last month. The government is suggesting they register their children for evacuation. Tell them that you will read parts of the leaflet aloud to them (Resource Sheet 1) and that when you stop (at an agreed signal) they will discuss together (in role) what they should do as wartime parents with differing viewpoints. Explain that one of them wants to evacuate their child or children and the other does not. They need to each try to persuade the other to change their viewpoint and they must reason. They may reach a decision together, or may not. You then read aloud Resource Sheet 1 in the voice of a government official as an introduction to them starting their 'talking partners-style' improvisation in pairs.
2	Eavesdropping Freeze frame	■ To raise awareness of different viewpoints (pros and cons) ■ To give everyone the opportunity to contribute and focus on ideas ■ To give opportunity for reasoned discussion	Pairs	Then tell them that you will now pass by each pair of parents and everyone will be able to hear what they are saying to each other. Only the pair of parents you are standing near should speak aloud at any one time and the other pairs should be very still (frozen) and listen until you reach them. As you move away from couples they will freeze and the next couple you meet will come to life and be heard. Encourage them to speak loudly enough to be heard by all. Don't stay long by each couple. You are just gathering a few sentences from each.

	Drama strategy	Purpose	Grouping	Teacher guidance and possible cross-curricular links
3	**Decision Alley**	■ To clarify the pros and cons of a course of action ■ To give opportunity for using persuasive speech ■ To enable children's ideas to be shared and integrated into the drama	Whole class	After spending some time supporting reflective discussion around the parents' moral dilemma ask the class to get into two straight lines facing each other. One line will represent voices of parents advocating evacuation, and the other the voices of those parents against it. Tell them that you will pass between the lines. The lines represent the conflicting voices in the parents' heads (the pros and cons of evacuation). Each person in one line will vocalize to you a reason why you should send your child to the country and those in the other line will each give a reason why you should not, e.g. *'You know your child will be safer away from here when the bombs come'* and *'You might never see your child again.'* At the end of the line tell them your decision as a parent. Say that the decision
	Teacher in role	■ To bring together the children's ideas into an extended narrative		is a hard one but you have reluctantly decided to register your child immediately. You can improvise a soliloquy to help them recall and reflect, e.g. you might say aloud, *'I love my children very much and will be very upset to be parted from them but I will never forgive myself if they stayed here and were killed or injured. I hope it won't be for long and I am sure I will be able to visit them and make sure they are well looked after. Anyway, this war will probably be all over by Christmas and they will be back home soon.'*
4	**Improvisation**	■ To give a context for practising ways of breaking news sensitively ■ To encourage empathy ■ To give opportunity for evaluative, critical, supportive feedback by peers	Pairs	**Breaking the news to the child** Ask the children to get into new pairs. One of them will now be a parent and the other their child. How will they break the news to their child that they will be evacuated within a few days? Ask them to consider how they prefer to receive bad news themselves. Explain that they will need to think very carefully about the best way to break the news to a child. Maybe allow those who will be in role as parents some thinking time to decide on their approach. They could both play each role in turn. Will they build up slowly to telling their child or come straight out with the decision? How will they convince a child it is best they go for their own safety and

		■ To focus on a key symbolic moment ■ To highlight that what we say and think are not always congruous		yet the parents will stay? Afterwards you may find it helpful to critically yet supportively gather and consider the different approaches. What did the children feel about the way they were told? Out of role they can let their partners know (as critical friends) how they handled it.
	Still image			Afterwards ask the pairs to re-create a still picture of a moment from the scene they have just improvised and to decide on their character's (parent's or child's) innermost thought at that moment. As you pass by each still pair they will speak their character's thought aloud for all to hear, e.g. Child: *'Maybe she doesn't love me any more.'* Parent: *'He will worry that I am being bombed while he is away.'*
	Thought-tracking	■ To build symbolism		Then ask the parents to silently and meaningfully tie an imaginary label to their child and speak just one sentence to them as they do so.
5	**Visualization**	■ To engage and create visually with an imaginary object ■ To use an authentic image as a stimulus to support engagement with role ■ To introduce a symbolic imaginary object as a reflective reference point ■ To give the imaginary object a physical form	Individually	**Leaving home** Ask the children to find a space and sit alone in their imaginary bedrooms. It is just before they leave their home to walk with their classmates to the station. They have packed a change of clothes and have some food in one small case or bundle and they have their gas masks (show photos of evacuees with their luggage) which they take everywhere. Ask them to sit by their bag and carry their imaginary gas mask case (which could be a 'real' one they have made in D and T). They have their labels attached to them (which could be imaginary or be 'real' ones they have written in English). Ask them to close their eyes and think of one small personal object that they will take with them and conceal in their luggage. It is something that is precious to them and which holds important memories or meaning, something that when they look at it and hold it, will remind them of home and happy family times maybe, e.g. teddy bear, photo of parents, favourite toy, a piece of jewellery, etc. Ask them to imagine a picture in their mind of the object and then mime privately putting it into

PART TWO

	Drama strategy	Purpose	Grouping	Teacher guidance and possible cross-curricular links
				their luggage or about their person before lining up in twos, ready for the walk with their class to the station.
		■ To move the drama on in time and place	Whole class	
		■ To link and tag the emotional memory with music		If you have learned any relevant wartime songs with the children then they could sing them now as they walk to the station in pairs behind an imaginary banner with their school name on. Tell them that they should follow you (the wartime teacher going with them). They could sing 'Wish me luck as you wave me goodbye!' or 'Run Rabbit Run' etc. Or you could play an atmospheric recording of a wartime song as they travel to the station, e.g. 'We'll meet again'.
6	Tableau	■ To focus on a significant moment	Whole class	**At the station** Then ask all the parents from activity 4 to get into a straight line as if they are on a railway platform facing the train that is about to leave. Ask all those who were their children to stand in groups opposite them (as if they are on the train and looking out of a carriage window). Evacuee Resource Sheet 2 (photo B) can be used as a stimulus. Alternatively the still picture can be built up gradually with one or two children entering the scene at a time and adding themselves to it.
				It may be possible to project an authentic photograph of children looking out of the train window before departure as a sort of scenic backdrop for the tableau which they enter and add to. Also, you could maybe use a recording of a steam train pulling out of a station to add authenticity and atmosphere.
	Essence machine			1. Think of the last sentence that the child and parent might have said to each other as the train pulled out.

	■ To offer shared ownership of the scene	2. Then ask them to think of a short action that can be performed repeatedly, e.g. a repeated wave or hankie to the eye, a nudge, a sniff, a hand to the mouth, etc.
	■ To recreate a key moment of emotional significance and tag it in the memory through sound, action and repetition	3. Then ask them to rehearse speaking the sentence and doing the action together repeatedly, e.g. putting the hankie to the eye and saying, 'I'll come and see you soon', enacted and spoken again and again, like a recurring, vivid dream moment 'stuck in the groove' or like the repeating rhythm of a steam train.
	■ To synthesize the moment and hold it still for reflection	4. Ask the children to start perfectly still (tableau) and then one end of the line comes to life and then gradually the line comes alive in sequence, with each pair in turn joining in until everyone in the line is repeating their sentences and actions together.
	■ To support the evaluation of performance	5. This can be replayed, starting the actions slowly until everyone is involved and then getting faster (like a steam train gathering speed). Evaluate the impact of this with the children. What effect does speeding up have on the scene, e.g. rising panic, accelerating train?
Performance Wave	■ To demonstrate that different techniques can be used and will have different effects and impact	6. It can also be replayed with the teacher 'conducting' so that the crescendo of sound builds up in a controlled way and then the action can be halted to provide a 'freeze frame'. Or the sound and action could become a 'performance wave' rippling along the line.

PART TWO

	Drama strategy	Purpose	Grouping	Teacher guidance and possible cross-curricular links
7	**Teacher in role**	■ To support engagement with role by using primary sources of evidence ■ To create and develop characters ■ To encourage empathy ■ To support appropriate interaction between the evacuees and hosts ■ To offer authentic information in role ■ To support and deepen engagement with role ■ To challenge from within the role ■ To make public the private thoughts and feelings of characters	Whole class and a small group Individual	**The arrival and selection** Ask for about six children to join you. Tell them that you are now the billeting officer and they are villagers about to select evacuees. These villagers have come early to get the first pick. Give them each role cards (Evacuee Resource Sheet 3) and tell them that everyone will be improvising, using the information on the role cards to help them. You could have more than six villagers and use multiple copies of the role cards or let children create their own roles. **Writing opportunity** They could write their own role cards based on the accounts of real evacuees and then introduce them into the drama. Conversely they can spontaneously improvise and create characters while in the drama and write role cards for them afterwards in English. While they are reading their cards and engaging with their character, you (as the billeting officer) ask the rest of the class to get into a line as evacuees ready to be chosen. Ask them first what they would be feeling and experiencing, e.g. frightened, homesick, hungry, ill, needing the toilet, crying, etc. You can improvise as the billeting officer but maybe you would say something like this to them: *'Now stand up straight and smile when these kind people come in, and stop scratching for goodness sake. They aren't going to want to choose snivelling and unhappy children with fleas are they? And remember to be polite if they talk to you. Good manners cost nothing. Don't worry if you end up living in a different house to your brothers or sisters because you will still see each other at school. Stop scratching and smile! Stop sucking your label or it will get lost!'*

	Freeze Frame **Thought Tracking**	■ To support reflection in order to deepen the learning ■ To help them make transferable learning links with their real lives		Once you are sure the evacuees are engaging emotionally with the impending selection moment, you (as the billeting officer) welcome and bring the children who are hosts into the scene one or two at a time. Be persuasive and if necessary bossy. You want all the children to be taken in. Maybe try to get the hosts to take more children than they want. You know you don't have enough homes yet for all these children. From time to time you can freeze the scene and ask for the thoughts of different children or hosts at that moment, e.g. the moment a particular child is chosen or rejected. You will have most of the children left over when the hosts have finished. Freeze the scene and pass by the children who are still waiting, quickly hearing their in-role thoughts aloud. It will be worth talking together out of role about what it felt like to be choosing, chosen or not chosen, to be selected or rejected in role. They may make connections with their own lives, e.g. team selection, inclusion or exclusion in events and activities, etc.
8	**Small group play making**	■ To establish an individual role identity and a dual identity as part of a group ■ To give opportunity to use primary historical sources to stimulate drama	Groups of three or four Individually	Each host has already selected one or two children. Ask them to find a space together as a 'household' group. The remaining evacuees who were not selected are now going to change roles. They will spread themselves among the 'household' groups as additional family characters in the households, e.g. another host parent, a son or daughter of the host parent. Make sure that everyone in the group is clear who they all are role-wise You might find Resource Sheets 4 and 5 useful to introduce here if you want groups to work from primary source material rather than make up scenes only from their own ideas. The choice is yours.

PART TWO

Drama strategy	Purpose	Grouping	Teacher guidance and possible cross-curricular links
Small group playmaking	■ To highlight the fact that all households were different and experiences for evacuees varied ■ To encourage empathy in relation to both positive and negative experiences ■ To encourage physically active planning and not mainly verbal planning		Ask the household groups (host family and evacuees) to create a short scene that will show an authentic or imaginary moment of kindness or unkindness to the evacuee. Try to ensure before they start that there will be a mixture of kind and unkind hosts among the groups (as the experiences of evacuees were a bit of a lottery). Maybe one person in the household is kind and another is not. Maybe all are kind or all are unkind. The scene they create should be no more than a minute long and everyone in the scene will speak. Give them time-limited rehearsal opportunity, e.g. 'You have just 5 minutes to create this scene and practise it ...' Limiting the time makes them get active quicker (rather than spending too long talking about it instead of getting active) and prevents some groups finishing and having to wait too long for others.
Performance Carousel	■ To heighten the focus and attention of the whole class on each other ■ To give a sense for all children of belonging to one performance ■ To give supported opportunity to evaluate their own and each other's performances		Once the scenes are ready, number the groups. Then give the following instructions. All groups will start by sitting on the floor. In slow motion, each group in turn (one at a time) will move into a still image that depicts the start of their scene. They will hold the image still for a few seconds (freeze frame). They will then all bring the scene to life at exactly the same moment and will agree together (in advance) the exact moment they will all freeze to depict the end of the short scene. In slow motion they will melt back down to a sitting position on the floor and remain still. The scenes will be shown without a break as one continuous class performance. Maybe evaluate the performances and ask what they have learned about evacuees and host families from these scenes.

	Writing in role	■ To transfer learning from imagined to real and current contexts ■ To give a reflective opportunity and provide written evidence of their engagement with role and level of knowledge and understanding		Links might cautiously and sensitively be made between looked-after children nowadays (and the safeguards now in place to protect them) and the random home lottery for evacuees. **Writing opportunity** They could write the child's first letter home. What will the child say about the family? You could ask for two versions of the letter, one that they know will be read first by the family and the other that will not. They can use what they know about the other children and family scenes as well as their own.
9	**Rumours**	■ To help the children to realize that the experiences of evacuees and hosts varied ■ To generate a lot of missing information and plot quickly	Whole class divided into four groups	It may help if they have read or heard some evacuee accounts of their experiences (e.g. Resource Sheets 4 and 5) and have an idea of some of the real best and worst moments evacuees have spoken or written of. They can gather real ones and imagine others, e.g. being slapped, bedwetting, ostracized at school, used as free labour, being pushed under water, given the worst food, scrubbed hard with a brush and carbolic soap, bullied, etc., or conversely being taken to church, discovering fields, eating apples from a tree, being taught a rural skill, making a friend, receiving a present, etc. **Divide the class into four groups** A: Hosts with positive things to say about the evacuees who are staying with them. B: Children of hosts with negative things to say about the evacuees who are staying with them. C: Evacuees who have good experiences to talk about. D: Evacuees who have negative experiences to talk about.

PART TWO

	Drama strategy	Purpose	Grouping	Teacher guidance and possible cross-curricular links
	Improvisation Rumours	■ To give confidence through establishing, rehearsing and affirming a character's viewpoint ■ To provide a context within which to challenge and defend viewpoints		Each group will separately move among themselves for a few minutes giving and gathering self-affirming gossip and opinion (i.e. four separate gossip groups, A, B, C, D). Then ask groups A and B to get together and groups C and D, so that hosts with different viewpoints are now in one big gossip group and evacuees with differing viewpoints are in another gossip group. Let them mingle and converse with differing viewpoints and stories to tell. Afterwards explain that the experience varied for all concerned. This may become a stimulus to further research later.
10	**Improvisation (telephone conversations)**	■ To deepen engagement with role ■ To give opportunity for recounting events and expressing thoughts and feelings	Pairs	**Contact with home** Ask the children to get back into the parent and child pairs from activity 4. Ask them to sit back-to-back in their pairs so that they can hear each other but not see each other. They are about to have their first parent/evacuee telephone conversation. In reality this would be very unlikely but for the purposes of the drama it has been included. Tell them that you will cut them off at some unexpected moment by calling out 'Cut!'
	Eavesdropping	■ To share characters' thoughts and feelings ■ To encourage empathy ■ To highlight emotional dilemmas	Pairs	After they have had a short phone call and been cut off, tell them that you will now pass by each pair and they will be able to hear a few seconds of the call. The pairs should be still and silent until you pass by and then we hear them. They fall still and silent again as you move away. Ask the children in their pairs to reflect and feed back to each other out of role what they felt and thought during the phone call.

	Improvisation	■ To raise awareness of the impact of non-verbal communication		The above telephone activity could instead be replaced by a first visit by the mother to the child. This would be a face-to-face rather than back-to-back conversation in pairs. It might be interesting to play it both ways and ask the children to evaluate the difference it makes to look at the person you are speaking with.
11	Conscience Alley	■ To make explicit conflicting thoughts linked to running away ■ To give form to inner turmoil ■ To encourage empathy ■ To evaluate the different impact on the audience of playing a scene in different ways	Whole class	**Running back home** Some evacuees ran away and tried to get back home. Many must have considered doing so. Ask the children to get into two lines facing each other about a metre apart. You will travel slowly between the lines as an evacuee who is contemplating running back home. As you pass by each person they have opportunity to speak your thoughts aloud (for all to hear). Ask one line to try to persuade you to run and the other line to try to persuade you not to. You can remain undecided. You can pass through the line a second time quickly (as if rushing) so that the voices as you pass by become a cacophony of sound. The children can evaluate the two methods as well as the different impact that each makes.

	Drama strategy	Purpose	Grouping	Teacher guidance and possible cross-curricular links
12	**Collective roles**	■ To give an opportunity to recount and reflect	Whole class	**Remembering many years later** It is 50 years later. Ask them to imagine that they have agreed to come onto a TV morning chat show and you will be the chat show host. Ask the class to divide into two groups and sit facing forward (as if seated in a TV studio audience). You can have a pretend microphone or a real one.
	Teacher in role **Mantle of the Expert** **Eyewitness**	■ To provide an imagined media-related experience ■ To raise confidence and self-esteem		One side of the audience is evacuees (now around 60 years old) and the other side are those who were country children who had evacuees billeted into their homes. Before the programme starts the chat show host (teacher in role) will tell the audience that they have all been selected by programme researchers as they all have clear memories of the evacuation and all feel strongly about what happened to them. They have been chosen because they have stories to tell and have strong opinions and are willing and able to speak out with confidence. They are the experts and eye-witnesses, as they were there.
	Improvisation	■ To gain confidence through rehearsing speech in pairs before speaking to whole class ■ To give opportunity for gathering information to inform the teacher's role	Pairs or small groups Whole class	Tell them that before filming begins they have the opportunity to let those sitting near them know what they will say to the camera if they get the chance. You move among them and listen to help you decide who to approach when filming supposedly starts. After they have 'rehearsed' what they might say, ask them to be silent for the countdown to the start of the show! You might start it off with:
	Teacher in role	■ To raise the dramatic tension and focus attention		*'Cameras rolling. 5, 4, 3, 2, 1, ... Welcome to 'Tell it as it was!', the show dedicated to finding the people who were part of our important historical events and times ... people who know what their truth is and will tell you their stories. This week's programme is about Evacuees. Was it a happy holiday in the country for poor city children or was it a miserable and scarey experience? Were they welcomed or were they rejected? Were they hit or hugged? Now, 50*

■ To give information and raise awareness of polarized viewpoints ■ To give opportunity for reflecting and recounting in role ■ To challenge their memories and viewpoints and thereby deepen engagement with role ■ To bring the drama to a close	*years on, is it a good memory or just a bad dream? Well in our studio audience today we have those people who can tell us ... we have WWII evacuees and the country children whom they lived among ... so, who among today's studio audience would like to be the first person today to 'Tell it as it was!'?* You will pass among them as the chat show host with the imaginary (or real) microphone acting out (or really) filming the show. You might try to spark controversy and if it needs taming take a commercial break. At any moment you can freeze the action or else bring the show to a close. *'And I am afraid we have run out of time here on the show but as you can see even 50 years on feelings are still running deep for some of these evacuees and the children whose lives they entered. And remember, if you have got anything you want to add, then email us via our website www.tellitasitwas.com So it's goodbye for now and do join us next week for another revealing episode of 'Tell it as it was!'.*
Writing in role ■ To set up a reason to write and an imagined audience ■ To give a meaningful context for writing in role using ICT ■ To set up an engaging opportunity to continue writing in role	**Writing in role opportunity** Ask them to write an email or letter to the show after first discussing why they might decide to write, e.g. additional information and stories, correcting misrepresentations, commenting on the inequality of opinions and stories represented, new show ideas, etc. If the children want to receive a real email reply purporting to be from the show then ask them to put the subject as, 'Tell it as it was' and send it to northseadrama@lineone.net The author of this lesson will send a real email reply to them in role as the programme researcher.

PART TWO

Night Walker

This drama uses an evocative picture (Resource Sheet 11) as its stimulus. The picture of a worried-looking man, walking through an empty, mysterious street at night is stimulating and ambiguous, arousing curiosity and raising many questions and possibilities. No story exists at the start of this drama other than one image from it. Through drama the children will be supported to create their own collective fiction and 'drama-story' using just a picture as the starting point. The style of this picture (by science fiction artist Chris Pepper) does not seem to be fixed in any particular time. The buildings seem both medieval and futuristic and the man's clothes seem rather medieval. The strategies and conventions used in this drama unit can be transferred to enable any picture to be used as a starting point for a story-drama.

The picture also works well as a combined drama stimulus with either of the following well-known poems:

- 'The Pied Piper of Hamelin' by Robert Browning

- 'Acquainted with the Night' by Robert Frost

■ Story outline

A man is walking down a paved street at night. He is well lit by a hanging street lantern and the bright night sky. He is holding a pouch in his hand and looking over his shoulder as he walks, with a serious and concerned expression on his face. The length of his stride suggests he is moving quickly and determinedly. Who is he? What is he doing? Where has he come from? Where is he going? Does he belong in this place? Is anyone watching him? If so, do they know him? What will happen next?

Personal development links

- Managing feelings
- Empathy

Areas of learning

- Understanding English, communication and languages
- Scientific and technological understanding
- Historical, geographical and social understanding
- Understanding the arts and design

Cross-curricular study links

English

- Telling and then writing the drama story/stories
- Writing the notice pinned on the wall
- Role on the wall (writing around an outline of the man, what is known about him)
- Pieces of writing found in the man's room

History

- Buildings
- Costume

Science

- Light and Dark

Art and Design

- Drawing another picture, in the style of Chris Pepper

Resources

- Resource Sheet 11
- Atmospheric, mysterious music (optional)

PART TWO

	Drama strategy	Purpose	Grouping	Teacher guidance and possible cross-curricular links
1	Ritual	■ To engage with the setting, character and plot ■ To stimulate curiosity ■ To support and encourage speculation ■ To use ritual to provide a structure and tension ■ To visually organize their thoughts ■ To prioritize what holds their interest most	Class circle Individually	**What does this picture tell us? What does it not tell us?** Show the children the picture and ask them to look at it in silence 'as picture detectives'. Ask them not only to look at the man in the picture but also to take time to let their eyes and minds wander around every part of the picture and pick up on detail. After a couple of minutes, ask them to 'wonder'. What questions does the picture stimulate? After some silent reflection time, say, 'I wonder what you wonder?' and invite them individually and aloud (one at a time) to complete the sentence, 'I wonder ...', e.g. 'I wonder who this man is?', 'I wonder where he is going?', 'I wonder if that is the moon?', 'I wonder what the notice says?', etc. Don't rush this activity as periods of silence may lead to deeper thought and wondering. They could write their wonderings on self-adhesive labels and move them around and categorize them in various ways, e.g. divide them into character, setting and plot wonderings. Is there overlap? Arrange them to prioritize their wonderings. What do they most want to know? This activity can be done in pairs or small groups.
2	Ritual	■ To enable and encourage multi-sensory access and response to the stimulus ■ To encourage the use of adjectives and adverbs	Class circle	Ask them to look at the picture again and, this time, to travel the picture with their ears! Ask them to imagine they are actually inside the picture and can hear the sounds there. Any one of them can speak aloud a sentence that begins, 'I can hear', e.g. 'I can hear the sound of the chain above the light creaking in the wind'. Encourage the children to offer some detailed description, e.g. rather than, 'I can hear footsteps in the street', it could be, 'I can hear the sound of fast and heavy footsteps in the empty street.' This activity can be done with eyes closed, which helps focus and builds atmosphere. They need to try to avoid interrupting each other. The sounds can be linked to what they can see in the picture but can also

School Improvement Through Drama

#	Technique	Objectives	Grouping	Description
		■ To encourage active listening ■ To offer shared ownership of the emerging fiction ■ To mutually support the creation of a shared, imaginary setting		be linked to what they imagine could be heard and yet can't be seen, e.g. the sound of people arguing in the distance or the sound of dogs barking, etc. This same activity can be carried out with different senses in turn, e.g. 'I can smell food cooking', 'I can smell old rubbish rotting', etc. You can ask them to imagine they can put their hands into the picture and touch, e.g. 'I can feel the cold, wet paving stones – the soft leather bag – the damp paper and the cold metal nail holding it to the wall', etc.
3	Teacher in role	■ To start to give some information to help build the drama	Class circle	**Who can tell us about this man and his night walk?** Explain that you will become 'teacher in role'. You are going to pretend to be a night watchman who has seen the man in the street. They will be able to ask you questions for only a short while. You can ask them for examples of some of the questions they might ask the watchman when he enters.
	Hot-seating	■ To 'sign' that the teacher is in role ■ To support dramatic tension ■ To deepen active engagement		Make it clear exactly when you start being in role as the night watchman. Maybe you will signal it by sitting in a designated chair or 'hot-seat' while they question you or maybe you will signal it with a piece of material as the night watchman's cloak. When you are wearing it, you will be the night watchman. If other people wear it they will become the night watchman! You can play the watchman in any way you wish and make up your own information when the children question you. The children should have to work at getting the information from you so you don't just speak a long monologue. One way that works well is to play him as a very experienced watchman who has done this job for years. You (the watchman) know

Drama strategy	Purpose	Grouping	Teacher guidance and possible cross-curricular links
	■ To provide information to move the drama on		most of the townsfolk in your area of the town. You hear a lot of information and gossip from people you meet and know.
			■ The man seen in the street is not from these parts. His clothes are different.
			■ People say he has lodgings at the other side of town but you don't know where.
			■ You have seen him only twice and both times it has been late at night.
			■ He has been alone both times you have seen him and seems to be in a hurry.
			■ You have tried to catch his eye but he hurries away.
			■ You don't know who he is or where he comes from yet but you will make sure he talks with you next time you see him.
	■ To stimulate and sustain curiosity ■ To stimulate further enquiry		Respond consistently in role to the children's questions but don't give them huge amounts of detail. Keep them curious by telling them some pieces of puzzling and tantalizing information. Just because you are in role it does not mean you need to know all the answers. The night watchman might not know much. Leave them wanting more information.
4	■ To choose and engage with their roles as townsfolk ■ To create episodes that offer every child some shared ownership of the story so far	Groups of four	**What have the townsfolk had to do with this man so far?** Ask the children to imagine that they are people who live in this town. The man in the picture has been seen at different times over the last few weeks by various groups of townspeople. Who might these groups of townspeople be and where might they have seen him? Get ideas first from the children and only add others such as those below if you need to, e.g. ■ a group of people in the inn having a drink see him through the window

Technique	Objectives	Description
	■ To build up the past through episodes ■ To ensure that they move to action quickly	■ a group of people on their way to church see him entering a house ■ at the local bakers he is at the front or else joins the rear of a queue ■ he walks through the market place on market day and passes a group of children.
Small group playmaking	■ To stimulate individual and group 'in role' response ■ To clarify and make explicit what is expected of an audience	Ask the groups to prepare a very short scene that the man from the picture can walk into or past. The scenes all take place prior to the moment depicted in the picture (Resource Sheet 11) and do not have the man in them yet.
Performance Carousel		Allow only a few minutes' preparation and rehearsal time and stick to your stated deadline. Once they have rehearsed their group scenes, tell them that each group will shortly be playing its scene in turn and you will let each scene run a while (about a minute) before you will arrive in it and they will then improvise from the moment of the man's (your) arrival in their scene. The groups that are not performing must give full and silent attention to the group that is.
Teacher in role **Improvisation** **Freeze frame**	■ To define the start and end of a scene ■ To stimulate improvisation	You now pass from one scene to another in turn. Each group scene should start from a still image, then the first group brings their scene to life and you will arrive in or near their scene (as the man) once their scene is under way. You decide when to enter or walk away or past each scene. When you look back over your shoulder at the group (as the man is depicted in the picture), that will be the signal for that group to 'freeze' and the signal for the next group scene to come to life. You wait until the next scene is under way before entering it … and so on, until you have moved in or past every group's scene.

	Drama strategy	Purpose	Grouping	Teacher guidance and possible cross-curricular links
5	Rumours	■ To stimulate many plot possibilities quickly ■ To encourage social interaction between a range of pairs and small groups within the class ■ To consolidate the shared ideas and give particular focus to some	Whole class	**What might people be saying about this man?** Imagine that there is rumour and gossip about the man. Effective rumours might be believed and sometimes have their basis in truth. Ask them to each make up a rumour that could be true and then to start spreading and gathering rumours about the man. Give only a couple of minutes for rumour spreading before gathering all together as townsfolk to chat about some of the rumours you have all heard. There is no way at this stage of knowing what might end up being true but many possibilities and ideas will have been generated and will have inspired further ideas.
6	Talking objects	■ To learn about a character from his home ■ To share ownership of the plot and setting ■ To provide a framework to model and practise personification ■ To offer a context and reason for writing ■ To share ownership and give opportunity for all to contribute actively	Class circle Individually	**How can we find out more about this man?** We can go and see the room where the man lives and sleeps. Tell them that he lives alone in this place and has been lodging here for just a few weeks. The landlady lives elsewhere in the house. Explain that they now have the opportunity to enter the circle (the inside of which now represents the man's room). One at a time they can enter as an inanimate object in the room, e.g. a bed, picture, chair, etc. You could model this first. You enter and say what object you are and give a little information about yourself, e.g. 'I am the man's bed. He doesn't sleep well and is very late in bed most nights', or 'I am a letter that he has hidden under the floor. He reads me sometimes.' You don't want one child creating too much storyline and dominating, so explain that no one should provide too much information but all who enter as objects will add a bit. Just a few children will become objects as the room will get too crowded and the activity would last too long.

| Teacher in role | ■ To provide an opportunity for the teacher to provide a learning focus from within the drama

■ To imbue and make explicit that objects can have great significance in relation to character, setting and plot

■ To create, extend and deepen our knowledge about a key character at a key moment

■ To enable the teacher in role to comment or challenge in order to deepen engagement and encourage response | Whole class | You could enter as the last object and provide an additional object that could support the drama and learning, e.g. a piece of writing (that provides a writing opportunity), a picture of someone he keeps hidden (to suggest an important missing character or piece of plot), a key (which might suggest that some object, person or place, might have been locked or unlocked already or might be in the future).

Once a few children have placed themselves as objects in the room, stop and reflect with the class about their significance.

■ What of significance have the objects told us?

■ What more do we know about the man from what the objects have told us?

■ What else might we want to ask the objects in order to find out more about the man and his attitudes and behaviours?

Ask the children who are being the objects to stay in the man's room a while longer. Explain that it is now the moment just before the man next leaves his room to go on his mysterious night walk. The objects have some knowledge of what the man is doing and where he is going. What single sentence might each object say aloud to the man as he passes by each object in turn, before going out on his night walk? Tell them that you will be the man and as you walk by each object they have opportunity to speak aloud to you. Whether you just listen or comment or interact for a short time with each object, is up to you. Bring the scene to a close by leaving and locking the room. |

PART TWO

	Drama strategy	Purpose	Grouping	Teacher guidance and possible cross-curricular links
	Thought-tracking	■ To gather eyewitness thoughts at a key moment		This can also be done with the objects speaking their innermost thoughts in role rather than speaking directly to the man. The children who have not become objects can stand in their class circle as the walls and they also can have opportunity to speak to or about the man.
	Teacher in role **Collective role**	■ To offer shared ownership and create together the thoughts of another character		The same activity could be carried out with the teacher as the landlady snooping around the room when the man is out. The objects can speak the landlady's thoughts as she passes by each object.
7	**Small group playmaking**	■ To consistently use a key character as a way of linking and providing continuity between scenes	Groups of about four	Quite a few episodes have been generated in various ways by this stage in the drama and may now need piecing together. Ask them to get into new groups of four. Each group will create a very short scene with the man in it (so one child in each group will need to take on the role of the man). This role could be signed in some way, e.g. one child in the group wears a sticker or band to differentiate themselves visually as the man.
	Performance Carousel	■ To provide chronological continuity and fill in gaps in the plot and character's development ■ To share ownership of a main character and the plot development		Each group has a slightly different task. Explain that the scenes will be in chronological order and will end up being performed as a sequence that will show something of different times in his life.

Group 1 (his very distant past): A scene that shows us something important that happened to the man when he was a child.

Group 2 (his distant past): A scene that shows us an important moment for the man as a teenager or young man.

Group 3 (his past): A scene that helps explains a little as to why the man has come to this town. Was it his choice? |

			Group 4 (the present): A scene that has the moment depicted in the picture (Resource Sheet 11) as part of it but will reveal more than the picture.
			Group 5 (his near future): A scene with the man in it, showing a moment in the near future, i.e. within a few hours of the moment in the picture (Resource Sheet 11).
			Group 6 (his more distant future): A scene that shows the man many years later. Where is he now? What became of him?
	■ To link episodes to create one continuous and shared fiction	Whole class	It is impossible to predict what the children will create and how it will fit together as one narrative but the challenge is now to see if their scenes can be linked to make one coherent narrative that fits with all they now know about the man and his life.
8	**Mime and movement**	Groups of three	**How do different characters tell the story many years later to different audiences?**
	Teacher narrator		A personalized version of the story many years later can be told from different characters' viewpoints, e.g. the man, the landlady, the night watchman. With the children in groups of three, each person takes on one role and the other two become a listening and questioning audience:
	■ To give an opportunity for recounting as storytelling		■ **the man** tells his story to two trusted friends many years later
	■ To give an opportunity for speaking to a range of audiences		■ **the landlady** tells her version of events to two new tenants renting the same room many years later
	■ To exemplify ways that the same story will be told by different characters		■ **the old night watchman** tells two new night watchman his version of the story many years later.

PART TWO

	Drama strategy	Purpose	Grouping	Teacher guidance and possible cross-curricular links
9	Still image (sculpting)	■ To reflect on the whole story and symbolize it physically ■ To synthesize meaning in one sentence through captioning ■ To interpret the meaning of a physical, artistic form of expression	Groups of 4	Ask them in groups of four to use their bodies to create one sculpture together that depicts the story and then to give it a caption (which can be spoken aloud or written nearby). You could release a group or two at a time to move around the other groups' sculptures and interpret their meaning together. Then swap over sculptures and audience so that all groups get a turn to interpret other groups' sculptures.

The Bystander

KEY STAGES 2/3 (YEARS 5 to 8)

> *Bullying is when someone is hurt, intimidated or harassed by one person (or by a group of people), on a regular basis. Bullying can be direct (either physical or verbal) or indirect, for example, ignoring someone or not talking to them. Bullying happens to children and students of all age groups and all abilities.*

This drama uses a pair of poems about bullying. The poems have been written specifically for exploration through drama. They start in the same way but the two versions (Resource Sheets 6 and 7) offer alternative endings, depending on whether or not the bystander watching a bullying incident decides to take action. The verses focus the class intentionally on vivid scenes, strong images, inner thoughts and possible 'bystander' courses of action that can lead to alternative outcomes. Version A of the poem (when the bystander takes no action) is used as the initial drama stimulus. Version B is used only towards the end of the drama, or after it. This enables the class to have more ownership of the decisions that shape the drama and not be guided into a specific action by Version B of the poem.

The drama uses role to bring alive a realistic fiction we can experiment with at a safe distance, a fiction from which we can derive real learning and through which we can experience real, manageable emotions. The possible interventions and actions of the 'bystander' are often critical to the incidence and outcomes of bullying. The bystander who is watching bullying in real life is a 'knowing' audience and (as in types of drama) an audience can be active and interactive, rather than just passive, and can influence actual outcomes. In the drama the children may decide on their own bystander action that is different from that offered in the poem.

The examples of bullying within the poems (Resource Sheet 6) are all taken from real schools and the poem's authenticity has been verified by the author through discussion with real victims of bullying and teachers. The role cards for 'New Pupils' (Resource Sheet 8) are optional. They too are fictional but based on children's authentic life stories and character-istics. The names of course have been changed. If you are dealing with generic bullying you may prefer to create a 'neutral' victim rather than use some of the characters on the role cards, e.g. a child of a split family, recent migrant, possibly homosexual boy, etc. The choice is the teacher's but a 'neutral' victim is simplest for inexperienced drama teachers to play and for dealing with the responses (and is less culturally laden).

PART TWO

■ Story/poem outline

A girl starts her first day at her new school. She merely arrives and is confronted by a group of bullies, who block her way, insult her and poke and push her, as well as take and mistreat her property. The scene is witnessed by another child who has also been the victim of bullying at the school (presumably by the same bullies). The bystander watches in emotional turmoil, remembering flashbacks of times she/he has been bullied also and thinks about what she/he might be able to do to help the victim.

Version A

Ashamedly (in Version A) the bystander does and says nothing and turns away. The new girl is not seen again and rumour has it she has left the school. The bystander reflects on the fact that the new girl might have become a friend had things gone differently but that it is now probably too late.

Version B

The bystander recognizes the personal risk involved but is moved to take action and gets a teacher. The bullies lie to the teacher and disperse. The bystander helps the new child to gather her possessions, offers support and it seems likely they will become friends.

These poems support and supplement the SEAL materials, 'Say no to bullying' (Theme 3).

■ Personal development links

■ ■ ■ ■ ■ ■ ■ ■

Anti-bullying
Managing feelings
Personal survival
Friendship
Empathy
Human Rights
Compassion
Responsibility

■ Areas of learning

■ ■ ■ ■ ■

Understanding English, communication and languages
Scientific and technological understanding
Historical, geographical and social understanding
Understanding physical health and well-being
Understanding the arts and design

Cross-curricular study links

English

- Comparing poems
- Poetry (writing alternative endings)
- Graffiti
- Scriptwriting

Art and Design

- Anti-bullying posters
- Storyboarding the still images

Citizenship

- ...d and individual responsibilities
- ...tures and sub-cultures

- Behaviour contracts
- Collective responsibility

Resources

- The two versions of 'The Bystander' poem (Resources Sheets 6 and 7)
- 'New pupil' Role Cards (Resource Sheet 8)
- Copies of Verse 1 (enough for one per group of four pupils)
- Pupil voices (Resource Sheet 9)
- A school bag and coat (preferably not recognizable as belonging to one of the class)
- Bully and Bystander prompt cards (Resource Sheet 10)

PART TWO

	Drama strategy	Purpose	Grouping	Teacher guidance and possible cross-curricular links
1	Visualization	■ To familiarize them with the poem aurally and visually	Individually in a space	**Getting to know the poem** Read version A of 'The Bystander' poem to the class (Resource Sheet 6). Ask them to close their eyes and try to imagine 'pictures in the mind' as they listen. Tell them the poem is a fiction but is based on true incidents in real schools. Invite comment about the poem and its themes but make sure you stay working in fiction and don't get drawn into talking at this time about actual bullying incidents in your school.
		■ To require negotiation, verbal reasoning and justification	Pairs in a space	Ask them to sit with a partner and give each pair of children a copy of the poem. Ask them to agree together which four of the words in the poem have the greatest impact on them and underline them, e.g. victory, kicked, pain, cruel. They need to be able to justify their choices.
	Choral speaking	■ To highlight differing and similar personal responses to specific words used in the poem		Read the poem aloud again and this time, when you read a word that they have selected, they join in saying the word with you. There is likely to be some consensus emerging as to the words that have the greatest impact (and this could be discussed). Why are some words more powerful? Maybe they evoke a stronger emotional response?
2	Image theatre	■ To deepen engagement with key words and shared understandings by creating and combining visual, kinaesthetic and aural modes of expression	Pairs in a space Groups of two pairs	Ask each pair of children to make together a sequence of four still images (one for each of their selected words) and communicate visually the meaning of the words. They should then rehearse moving between the four images in slow motion. Each still image can be accompanied by them speaking the word aloud.
	Performance			Each pair can show their image sequence to another pair, as it may take too long to go around and see every pair's sequence of images in turn.

	■ To share and evaluate performance ■ To establish plot through 'seeing' past events			The 'audience' pair can be invited to comment positively on aspects of the performance they see. What worked well and why? Ask the class to imagine the images they have created are from scenes that have actually taken place in the fictitious school and that have all been witnessed in the past by the bystander. This suggests a backdrop of ongoing bullying incidents prior to the one that is the focus of this drama.
3	**Teacher in role** **Hot-seating**	■ To give information about the new pupil ■ To encourage empathy ■ To give opportunity for the children to question in order to build a character	Whole class circle	**Getting to know the victim** Explain to the children that you will be taking the role of the new pupil. It is the evening before he/she starts at his/her new school, i.e. before the scene depicted in the poem. Ask them to think about what they might want to ask him/her, e.g. Why are you starting a new school? Do you know anyone in your new school? Have you been bullied in your old school?, etc. You then enter, sit as the new pupil and answer their questions in role, making up whatever information you need to. You could signal the role by carrying a school bag when you are in role if you wish. You can create the character yourself or else use a role card from Resource Sheet 8 to support your role (depending on what suits your class context best and your confidence level). The new pupil you play should not be a confrontational character and is naturally nervous but hopeful of making new friends and settling in. The new child is an innocent victim. The purpose of your role is to help the children engage with the forthcoming victim as a 'real' person with feelings and a personal history. Making the victim come to life first as a character prior to being bullied will help deepen the level of empathy for the victim.

	Drama strategy	Purpose	Grouping	Teacher guidance and possible cross-curricular links
4		■ To give opportunity for pupil voice and experience to inform the authenticity of the drama	Groups of no more than four	**Past incidents**
				Verse 3 refers to images of past bullying incidents that have happened to the bystander.
			Whole class	*The day they took my coat and threw it down the loo* *The day they stole my money and filled my hair with glue* *The day they locked me in a room and threw away the key*
				At this point you can:
				■ Either use the bullying incidents referred to in the poem as the basis of different group scenes for creation and enactment.
				■ And/or ask the children to suggest other incidents that might have happened in this school but were not mentioned in the poem.
				■ And/or use the sentences that real children have spoken that are on **Resource Sheet 9.**
				There is opportunity here to discuss and define what constitutes bullying.
	Small group playmaking	■ To ensure that they understand that bullying has many forms ■ To provide a theatre-shared experience for discussion, exploration and evaluation		Ensure each group has a different type of bullying incident to work on and ask them to create a very short scene (lasting no more than a minute) that depicts the scene naturalistically. Ask them to avoid actual physical fight scenes (or else they must take place in slow motion or stop at the moment just before the physical assault).
				Give tight time limits on preparing this scene. Try to get the children planning by physically moving as they plan, rather than planning just through talking.

School Improvement Through Drama

Performance Carousel	■ To keep children physically safe ■ To support greater focus through pace ■ To support thinking through physical action	Enable each group to perform their scene in turn. You can do this with no interruption between the scenes (through Performance Carousel, see page 130), or you might decide to see each scene in turn and invite comment or audience/actor interaction between watching scenes. Or you can see all scenes first in an uninterrupted way and then see them again a second time but enable discussion and follow-up activities for each scene, e.g.:
Thought-tracking and freeze frame	■ To share performance ■ To encourage interactive audience ■ To support evaluation of the performance (form and content) ■ To discover character's inner thoughts at a key moment	■ 'Freeze' each scene at a key moment and ask the actors to speak their characters' thoughts aloud. ■ Or freeze the scene and invite the audience to speak aloud the probable thoughts of the different characters in the scene in turn.
Mime and storytelling (narrative)	■ To encourage empathy ■ To show that a scene can be presented with narrative storytelling	■ Or ask them to re-enact their scene as a mime with one person giving a narrative commentary to accompany the action, e.g. 'They saw the boy coming and started to laugh … etc.'
Hot-seating	■ To find out more about character's actions and motives	■ Or invite the audience to question characters from the scene, who will then need to answer in role, e.g. 'Why did you pick on this girl?'

PART TWO

	Drama strategy	Purpose	Grouping	Teacher guidance and possible cross-curricular links
5		■ To focus attention on the 'action' words in the poem at a key moment	New groups of four	**The incident** Ask them to get into different groups of four. Make sure each group has access to a copy of Verse 1 of the poem and felt tips. *They saw the new girl <u>coming</u>* *So they <u>clustered</u> round the door* *<u>Blocked</u> her path and <u>threw</u> her insults* *<u>Kicked</u> her bag around the floor* *<u>Called</u> her names, said she was ugly* *What a weirdo! What a geek!* *<u>Pushed</u> and <u>poked</u> her as she <u>shook</u> there* *She did nothing, did not speak.*
	Dance/drama movement	■ To slow down a key moment and deepen engagement ■ To avoid enacting the bullying naturalistically, yet enable physical engagement with the actions		This verse is full of verbs linked to physical movements. Ask them in groups to underline any words (verbs) that link to or imply movement. Then ask them to create a stylized, group movement piece that uses the movement words from the poem as its stimulus. The movements should: ■ involve everyone in the group simultaneously ■ involve everyone in the group continuously ■ be exaggerated ■ be in slow motion ■ have no sound or speech.

	Performance carousel	■ To use music for atmosphere and to heighten emotional engagement ■ To tag the scene in the auditory memory		Explain that each group will seamlessly perform the movement piece twice in succession (as if it is a repetitive and silent nightmare). One person in each group can be the victim or you may decide that they can have an imaginary victim instead. Use a performance carousel to share the performances in a continuous way. If you have any suitable background music to use as a soundtrack then this will help link the group movement pieces and add atmosphere.
6	**Soundscape or Sound Collage**	■ To focus on the auditory aspects of text ■ To focus on an auditory performance of a key moment ■ To evaluate performance in relation to the intended impact on the audience	Groups of four	Ask them to stay in the same groups of four and look at Verse I again. This time ask them to discuss the sounds that are stated or implied or could be there and to decide possible sound effects, e.g. footsteps, shuffling feet, bag being kicked on floor, laughter, bell, school chairs being dragged, hissing, slapping sounds, etc. Do not include speech. Again, working stylistically (rather than naturalistically), ask the groups to create a sound effects collage of the incident, in a way that leads up to a climax of sound and then silence. Using their bodies and voices to create sound and using anything you will let them use from around the room, they can play with repeated sounds, overlapping sound, etc., to suggest the atmosphere and build-up of events through sound alone. Encourage them to work creatively for dramatic and emotional effect rather than just making a naturalistic sound story sequence. You can give them the option of deciding where their audience will need to be when they hear their soundscape for best effect, e.g.:

PART TWO

	Drama strategy	Purpose	Grouping	Teacher guidance and possible cross-curricular links
		■ To discover that when sound is received in different ways it can lead to different responses ■ To signal the end of a performance		**Performance options** (all with audience eyes closed) ■ they might decide to perform around the class, who could be seated in the centre and surrounded by the group sound performance ■ or a group could decide to advance slowly, physically on the class who have their eyes closed (but they may not touch anyone) ■ the group might place themselves standing among the seated 'blind' audience, etc. Ask the performing group to clap themselves at the end of their performance (to signal that they have finished to the audience who have their eyes closed).
7	Tableau	■ To give opportunity for all to engage with and enter the key moment ■ To encourage creative, individual responses ■ To avoid using a child as the 'in role' recipient of the class bullying	Whole class circle Whole class	Explain that you will be building up the scene from Verse I together now. Each person in turn has the opportunity to enter the centre of the circle in turn and place themselves in the scene as a character, saying who they are and giving one or two short pieces of information about themselves. You can use Resource Sheet 10 prompt cards to support or preferably the children can create their own characters and their own lines. Explain that the people in the scene are all different characters and may have different thoughts, reactions and viewpoints in relation to the bullying incident. They should try to avoid saying the same as someone else. Tell them that no one among them will become the character of the 'new girl' victim. You could place a school bag and coat on the floor or on a chair to represent the victim and they can then build up the scene around it.

		Whole class
Tableau	■ To give a visual focus for their attention ■ To enable inclusion and keep all children engaged and in role ■ To consolidate and present key information ■ To hold a key moment still	There should be a few seconds between each person entering the tableau. You may decide (depending on the size of class) to just let some of the class enter into the circle and the rest can stay standing around the circle as bystanders at a distance. When the scene has sufficient characters in it tell them that they should hold the still scene (tableau) 'as still as a photograph' and you will narrate the scene to life and then they will improvise the scene for a few minutes until you call 'Freeze' at which point they are perfectly still again. The victim at this stage will still be represented by just a bag and coat rather than a person.
Teacher as storyteller	■ To use narrative storytelling to recount the events and support reflection	Your narration could be Verse 1 of the poem and then you click your fingers to bring the scene to life, or you could create your own prose along the lines of: *She was a new girl, just walking along the corridor and minding her own business but they saw her coming. And you can guess what happened next. They picked on her, all ganged together and said terrible things to her and kicked her bag around. She didn't do anything. She didn't even say anything but they just kept going … (click fingers to start the action).*
Improvisation **Freeze frame**	■ To enable an in-role freeflow of action and speech ■ To support evaluation of dramatic intent and impact	Don't let the improvisation run for more than a minute or two and don't hesitate to 'freeze' the action early if it feels counterproductive to continue or there is a particularly powerful moment that should be held still to finish on. You may want to invite comments before continuing. Can they suggest why you might have frozen the action at a particular moment?

Drama strategy	Purpose	Grouping	Teacher guidance and possible cross-curricular links
Teacher in role	■ Using costume and a prop to 'sign' the role	Whole class	Once you have frozen the scene ask them to replay it but this time you will take on the role of the new girl. Carry the bag and maybe put the coat around your shoulders or carry it. Then ask them to recall what they know about the new girl (they hot-seated her in activity 3) before you join in the scene.
Thought-tracking	■ To stimulate and support the children's ideas and improvised responses ■ To synthesize individual emotional responses to the scene ■ To encourage logical reasoning ■ To meaningfully and visually organize and agree the range of feelings evoked by the drama		In role as the new girl say nothing to them and don't provoke or retaliate. Let the scene replay and freeze it at a moment you decide. Tell them that you will now pass among them and as you do so they have opportunity to speak aloud their inner feelings about this scene as single words, e.g. frightened, disgusted, ashamed, excited, etc. Acknowledge that some children will feel a mixture of feelings and will need to speak aloud only the dominant feeling. You may decide afterwards to spend some time discussing the range of responses and the possible reasons for them. The single 'emotion' words can be written onto word strips, moved around and categorized and organized in various visual ways by consensus agreement.
8		Whole class circle	Ask them to get back into a class circle with you and then read Verse 4 aloud: *And I felt ashamed just standing there* *Eye witness to her pain*

I wasn't joining in with them
But felt bad just the same
I thought how I might help her
I thought what I might say
But my tongue was stuck inside me
As I turned my face away

Then place the verse on the floor in the centre of the circle and give opportunity for them one at a time to enter out of role, i.e. as themselves, and place themselves physically in relation to the paper with the verse on it. This paper now physically represents the bystander's viewpoint as portrayed in the poem. If they identify personally with the feelings expressed by the bystander within the verse they stand close to the piece of paper, or they can place themselves relatively further away from the verse to correspond with their degree of empathy.

You can ask them each to justify their physical position in relation to the verse as they place themselves, e.g. *'I am standing very close to the bystander because I felt ashamed when I was watching that bullying', or 'I am standing away from the verse because I didn't feel anything for the victim'*, etc. Do not suggest that there is a 'right' or 'wrong' place to be standing but seek reasoning and justification from each of them as to why they are standing in their chosen position.

Proxemics

- To enable and encourage individual responses to a viewpoint
- To give space meaning

- To require verbal justification and reasoning
- To avoid direction in order to encourage authentic pupil response

Drama strategy	Purpose	Grouping	Teacher guidance and possible cross-curricular links
9			
	■ To encourage the children to consider the possibility of change	Whole class	*I thought how I might help her* *I thought what I might say* Talk out of role with them about how the scene might be changed in ways that could lead to the bullying being averted or stopped. How might the new girl be helped? What might be said or done by her or by others (gang members and bystanders) in the scene that might improve the situation?
Forum theatre	■ To empower children to act differently towards achieving different outcomes ■ To consider the possible impact of a range of possible actions		After a few suggestions have been made, say that the scene will now be re-created and replayed again but differently because this time it will be played using some of their suggestions towards an improved outcome. Try just one or two ideas out at a time to see if they make any difference to the improvised outcome. Be sure they know exactly which suggestions will be incorporated into each rerun of the scene, e.g. what happens in the scene if …? ■ someone or several people go and stand alongside the victim ■ someone gets a teacher at the start ■ one or more members of the 'gang' break ranks ■ the girl stands up to the bullies and tells them to stop.
	■ To ensure the learning is explicit and transferred ■ To help empower children to deal with bullying		You will need to be alert to the learning opportunities that the drama is making available and you need to highlight the links between different actions and different outcomes. Use this 'Forum theatre' as an opportunity to help the children in role to become and feel empowered in the scene and to see that change for the better in group dynamics can be effected by various means, e.g. the action of one or more bystanders and/or the gang not remaining united and/or the 'victim' behaving differently.

10	■ To engage with the outcome presented in the poem	Class in two large groups	Divide the class into two groups and ask them to sit with their group while you read aloud Verses 5 to 8 of the second version of the poem (Resource Sheet 7). Invite any comments or discussion about the content of these verses before asking them now to focus in the drama on Verse 8.

So I knelt and helped the new girl
Took her bag out of the bin
I told her I'd stay near her
Whilst she was settling in
And she gave a look of friendship
A look both soft and long
And I gave a look of friendship back
And we both thought, 'Bring it on!'

Collective role	■ To deepen engagement with the bystander who took action and with the victim ■ To explore and develop the relationship between the bystander and victim		Tell them that soon one whole group (half the class) will have opportunity to speak as the bystander who has just helped the girl and the other group will be able to speak as the girl who has just been bullied. Only one child at a time may speak in either group. If they need them, two separate 'speaking objects' could be introduced and passed around within each group to ensure everyone in either group has opportunity to speak (i.e. whoever holds the object in either group is the only one empowered to speak).
Role/s on the Wall	■ To recall, share and organize information visually to inform the collective role	Whole class	Recall with them what they already know about both characters. This could be recorded on a 'Role on the Wall' by writing information about the character around a drawn outline of the character (see pages 132–3).

PART TWO

Drama strategy	Purpose	Grouping	Teacher guidance and possible cross-curricular links
Collective role	■ To give a reason for active listening ■ To share responsibility for a main character's development	Class in two large groups	Explain that each of the two groups represents one of the main characters and only one person at a time in each group can speak as that character. They will need to listen to each other carefully to be continuously convincing as one character.
Teacher within a collective role	■ To enable the teacher to support and focus the development of both characters		Tell them that the dialogue between the characters will start from just after the last line of the poem, i.e. just after, **'And we both thought, "Bring it on!"'**. Tell them that you alone are allowed to move between the two character groups and join in as either character.
Role/s on the Wall	■ To agree and share important information about key characters	Whole class	Afterwards, ask the children what more they have discovered about the characters during this 'collective role' activity. New information could be added to the Role/s on the Wall.
Eavesdropping	■ To enable a greater amount and frequency of individual contribution ■ To ensure all children get opportunity to contribute publicly ■ To explore the relationships and interactions of other key characters	Pairs	The activity above could be done in pairs instead of two large groups and then snippets of each conversation listened into through 'Eavesdropping' (see page 124) where you travel past each talking pair and only the pair you are near to can be heard aloud in role (with the rest of the class still and silent until you stand near them). The above activities can also be carried out with different pairs of characters, e.g.: ■ the victim talks with her mother ■ the victim talks with a teacher ■ the teacher talks with the bully ■ two bystanders talk together, etc.

	■ To provide a meaningful stimulus and context for writing poetry or playscript		These dialogues can form the basis of an additional verse to be added to the poem or can form the basis of a short playscript.
11	**Passing thoughts (a type of thought-tracking)** **Teacher in role**	Class circle (standing) Individual	Tell them that you will once more become the victim. You might signal this by carrying the coat and bag. You will stand in the centre of the class circle and each person has the opportunity to walk past you (the victim) in turn and say something positive to you that might be helpful, e.g. *'You will soon find friends'*, and *'They probably won't bother you again'*, etc. The aim is to end on a hopeful and positive note. This activity can be done around the circle in sequence or just random order.
	■ To make public the emerging collective advice that supports those being bullied ■ To give opportunity for children to speak positively with hope		
	Teacher in role ■ To safely make public within a fiction what children would like to be able to say to bullies		This activity could be carried out with the children all having opportunity to make a statement to the bully (who would be best played by the teacher), e.g. they might say *'You are making people very unhappy'*, *'You have no right to hurt people like this'*, etc. This is a way of indirectly enabling the class to speak through the safe forum of a fiction and yet any real bully in the class will hear what is being said to the fictional bully. If you decide to carry out this activity, do it before making statements to support the victim (see above) as you want to end the lesson on a positive and hopeful note.

PART TWO

The Island

KEY STAGES 2/3 (YEARS 6 to 8)

This drama is based on a powerful and disturbing Australian, award-winning picture book. It is not necessary to have access to the book but it is preferable, as the images are evocative and dramatically stimulating. The opening sentence alone is laden with tension and dramatic possibility.

'One morning, the people of the island found a man on the beach, where fate and ocean currents had washed his raft ashore. When he saw them coming, he stood up. He wasn't like them.'

This drama unit explores the themes of migration, racial prejudice and oppression. It has universal and timeless relevance and teachers will wish to be sensitive to this in relation to the cultural origins and personal histories within the class. Through working in role the issues are being opened up and explored in a distanced way. The children in role will make and justify their individual and collective views and decisions about the fate of this speechless and peaceful migrant. The book should not be read in advance as the children need to be free to create different outcomes that will hopefully be more positive and empathetic than those depicted in the book. The lesson broadly follows the plot in the book but there are opportunities built in to improvise and change the ongoing plot and the ending.

■ Story outline

A stranger arriving by raft is washed ashore on an island. The islanders are an insular people and most are fearful of him and unwelcoming. Opinion is divided about their responsibilities towards him and what they should do with him. He is kept isolated outside the town in a goat pen and initially ignored. Hungry, he enters the town looking for food and the people take him back to the pen and thereafter guard him. The imprisoned stranger however still haunts their thoughts and dreams. Fear and rumours abound and the children are taught to be wary of him. Fear builds to fever pitch and despite the protestations of an empathetic fisherman, the angry and fearful mob put the stranger back on his raft and cast him adrift again on the sea to meet almost certain death. The islanders then turn on the fisherman, burn his boat and stop eating fish forever. They build a high wall with watchtowers around the entire island to keep further strangers and even birds out. This stranger had done nothing to harm them.

■ Cross-curricular study links

English

Scripting

Creating propaganda

Commemorative poetry

Captions and plaques

Graffiti

Geography

Islands

Invaders

Settlements

Seas and oceans

Winds

Geo-political boundaries

History

Human migrations

Refugees and asylum seekers

Great walls and other man-made defences

Sources and impact of propaganda

Genocide

■ Personal development links

Anti-bullying

Anti-racism

Human Rights

Xenophobia

Managing fear of the unknown

Personal and cultural identity

Cultural diversity and tolerance

Compassion

Empathy

Responsibility

■ Areas of learning

Understanding English, communication and languages

Scientific and technological understanding

Historical geographical and social understanding

Understanding physical development, health and well-being

Understanding the arts and design

PART TWO

Science

- Tides and currents
- Floating and sinking
- Water
- Materials (statues)

Art and Design

- Adding pictures to the book
- Designing and making statues

Design and Technology

- Raft building
- Shelter building

Citizenship

- Community decision making
- Why and how rules and laws are made
- Shared and individual responsibilities
- Cultures and sub-cultures
- Festivals and celebrations

■ Resources

- *The Island* by Armin Greder, Publisher, Allen and Unwin (2001), ISBN: 978-1-74175-266-3 (optional)

	Drama strategy	Purpose	Grouping	Teacher guidance and possible cross-curricular links
1	**Guided visualization**	■ To engage with the setting ■ To start to engage with their roles ■ To build and co-own a shared, imagined environment	Individually on the floor in a space (seated)	**Don't show the children any pictures of the villagers from the book yet as this is likely to influence their own emotional responses.** Start by asking the children to close their eyes and imagine a 'picture in their mind's eye'. They should keep their eyes closed as you guide them to imagine themselves as an isolated island people. Ensure that you pause from time to time to give space for lingering and imagining, e.g. *'I want you to imagine you are sitting on the beach on a faraway island … you live on this island and were born here … everyone who lives on this island was born here … you have never seen or met anyone from another place … it is a beautiful island … as you sit here alone on the beach, I wonder what you can see in your mind's eye … what you can hear … what smells there are in this warm and clear air … etc?'* You can invite responses as you mention each sense, i.e. children can when invited speak aloud (still with eyes closed), *'I can see …',* or *'I can hear …',* etc.
2	**Occupational mime** **Still image** **Teacher as storyteller**	■ To further engage with and develop their roles ■ To give a clear and controlled starting point for the action ■ To re-establish the setting, roles and plot	Individually in a space	Ask them to stand alone on the island now and to imagine that they are carrying out an everyday island task. It is a time before machinery and engines, so tasks are basic and carried out by hand. Ask for some suggestions, e.g. fetching water, gutting fish, chopping wood, sewing, feeding animals, etc. When they have decided what they will be doing, they should get into a still image depicting them carrying out the task. Tell them you will narrate (tell) the opening of the drama and when you click your fingers, the scene will come to life and they will carry on working at their task alone. Narrate along the lines of *'It was very early in the morning and the islanders were working at their tasks. It was a day like any other day'* (click fingers). After they have mimed a while you will call *'Freeze',* and they should

Drama strategy	Purpose	Grouping	Teacher guidance and possible cross-curricular links
Freeze frame	■ To hold a key moment still for reflection		hold the scene perfectly still for you to narrate, 'Yes, it seemed to be a morning like any other morning but as the islanders carried out their tasks they did not realize that something about today was going to be very different ....'
Teacher as storyteller	■ To build dramatic tension towards a key moment		Let them come out of their 'freeze frame' and then explain to them that they will restart their tasks in a minute but that this time you will also enter the scene in role. Tell them that you will be a stranger found on the beach. They have never seen a stranger before. You could use a couple of chairs and/or a sheet to represent your washed-up raft nearby. Tell them that they won't all rush over at once. One of them will discover you and then news of your arrival will spread until all the islanders will learn of your arrival, stop their tasks and make their way to you. They will then improvise. You can start this scene by using the opening three sentences from the book before clicking your fingers to signal the start of the action.
Teacher in role	■ To give key information and sign the teacher's role ■ To direct the action in steps		
Teacher in role	■ To use authentic text as a primary stimulus	Whole class	'One morning, the people of the island found a man on the beach, where fate and ocean currents had washed his raft ashore. When he saw them coming, he stood up. He wasn't like them.' (click fingers)
Improvisation	■ To share ownership of a key moment		When they arrive be neutral and non-threatening, reactive rather than proactive. You can't understand their language. Let the improvisation run for a few minutes and judge when to call 'Freeze' and narrate what has occurred back to them as a storyteller, e.g. 'News soon spread and the islanders gathered on the beach. They looked at the stranger and they wondered ... I wonder what they wondered?'
Freeze frame			
Teacher as storyteller			

	Technique	Objectives	Grouping	Description
	Thought-tracking	■ To accept and weave the children's ideas into the narrative ■ To gather and share in role thinking at a key moment and about a key character	Whole class	Invite the children to share their wondering in role out loud. They should try to do so without interrupting each other and also pausing between utterances. Ritualistically each person starts their sentence with, 'I wonder', e.g. 'I wonder where he has come from?', … 'I wonder if he is dangerous?', … 'I wonder what we will do with him?', etc.
3	**Collective role**	■ To symbolize unity through physical contact ■ To encourage empathy ■ To consider the situation from another viewpoint ■ To make public differing viewpoints ■ To highlight common and shared human feelings	Big class circle (standing)	Ask the children now to make a big class circle around the stranger, leaving enough distance for people to enter the circle in turn and walk to the stranger. This time you will get back into position in the centre (as the stranger). They now have the opportunity to enter the circle in turn and place themselves near you and become the stranger with you. You might ask them to create a point of physical contact with the collective stranger as they also become him (collective role) to indicate they are all one person. Ask them as they join the stranger to speak one of his thoughts aloud at this key moment, e.g. 'They don't like me', 'I wonder if they will harm me', 'I can't understand them', etc. You may decide to just let a few children join the stranger, as if everyone does, it could take too long. You could change the activity and let some of the class enter and speak the stranger's thoughts and the rest stay in the circle as islanders and speak their thoughts.
	Thought-tracking	■ To highlight that assumptions may not be truths		It may be worth spending some time discussing out of role what the similarities and differences are between the thoughts of the islanders and the stranger, e.g. they are probably both frightened of each other and neither can understand the other's language. Are any assumptions being made? Are the assumptions able to be justified and are they based on evidence or fear?

	Drama strategy	Purpose	Grouping	Teacher guidance and possible cross-curricular links
4	**Teacher in role**	■ To encourage justification of viewpoints and actions ■ To make explicit a range of viewpoints	Class circle or whole class group	Ask the children to gather for a meeting. Whether they sit or stand and how they group themselves is up to you, depending upon how formal you wish to make it. It can be just a mob meeting to decide the stranger's fate or else a formal village meeting. You in role as a fellow villager (a fisherman) ask them what should be done with this man. Let this improvisation run awhile and challenge so as to enable children to justify their opinions and suggested actions. Hold back on your opinion as it holds too much influence.
	Conscience Alley	■ To give a structured opportunity for all to use persuasive speech ■ To physically reinforce the polarity of the viewpoints	Two lines facing each other	Ask the children to get into two straight lines facing each other (about a metre apart). Tell them you will walk between the lines and as you walk past each islander in the line they have the opportunity in turn to try to persuade you to their point of view. They need to speak clearly and with enough volume to be heard by all. You pass along the line and at the end you say that you (the chief fisherman) do not want this stranger's death on your conscience and that the islanders should let him stay (the viewpoint of the fisherman character in the book).
	Teacher as storyteller	■ To resolve where the drama storyline goes next		In the book they take him to an uninhabited part of the island now and put him in a goat pen. You can follow this storyline or else 'house' him in whatever place the children decide. If they want to kill him or cast him out to sea again at this point in the drama, then freeze the action and after the Conscience Alley activity narrate along the lines of, *'There were those among them who wanted to kill him (or send him back out to sea) but at last the villagers decided they would let him stay and they took him to the place on the island where he would live and locked him in.'*

5	Talking objects		Whole class standing in a square	Tell them that the class square represents the walls of the place where the stranger will live away from the islanders. The children now are the walls. Explain that some of them can one at a time elect to enter the living space instead, as objects (who can speak) and who are awaiting the arrival of the stranger in this room (in the book his home is a goat pen). They should enter the space, place themselves as the object and then say aloud what they are and add a short piece of information, e.g. '*I am a sack filled with straw. He can sleep on me at nights*', or '*I am a dirty tin mug. He can tap on me to make sound when he is bored*', etc. Once six to eight objects have entered the room, freeze the scene and tell them that the stranger is about to enter this space for the first time. What might these objects say to the stranger if he could hear them? What might he say back to them?
	Physical theatre	■ To create a shared setting physically ■ To support an understanding of personification		
	Teacher in role	■ To give opportunity for dialogue with the key character who is alone	Small group (the objects)	Tell them that you will enter the space as the stranger and pass among the objects. As you pass by each object it has opportunity to speak to you. Whether or not you respond or just listen is for you to decide, e.g. '*I will be your bed. I am lumpy with straw and you won't sleep well on me*', '*I am so tired I will be able to sleep anywhere.*'
6	Small group playmaking	■ To recall, re-create and re-enact the story from a child's perspective	Groups of four	Ask them to get into groups of about four. The island children often act out the capture and/or imprisonment of the stranger in their dramatic play. Ask the groups to create a short dramatic play scene (lasting no more than a minute), that will be performed.
	Performance Carousel	■ To bring together all scenes as 'instant' episodic theatre		Now each group will perform their dramatic play scene in turn. You could do this stylistically, using a performance carousel, i.e. all groups are melted on the floor (still and silent). Each group is numbered in sequence. Only one group at a time may move. The first group in slow motion gets into a still image that is the start of their scene and holds it still for a few seconds, before bringing the short scene to life and all freezing together at

Drama strategy	Purpose	Grouping	Teacher guidance and possible cross-curricular links
	■ To enable the children to respond as both spectators and actors, i.e. spectactors		the end of it. The freeze frame is held still for a few seconds, before the group melts in slow motion back onto the floor. When the first group is still and finished, the second group starts moving, and so on.
7 Occupational mime Thought-tracking Eavesdropping	■ To establish time passing ■ To encourage silent and shared reflection ■ To make public where their interest lies at this point in the drama	Individually	The people go back to their everyday tasks as if the man they have locked up does not exist. But he still exists in their thoughts and they wonder about him. Ask the children to find a space in the room where they can be alone with their thoughts as a villager. They can decide if they are just stationary or doing an activity while thinking. What are they wondering about the man whom they have not seen for several days? Tell them that you will pass by each of them and when you stand near them they have the opportunity to speak aloud what they are wondering about him, e.g. *'I wonder what he is doing at the moment?', 'I wonder if he will die?', 'I wonder if he will escape?'*, etc. Children may remain silent and not contribute and then you will just pass on by (as if eavesdropping).
Rumours **Teacher in role**	■ To speedily share further plot possibilities ■ To exemplify the unreliable nature and danger of rumour and gossip	Whole class	Then ask them to start to move around and meet each other. They are moving around the village, talking and gossiping about the stranger. They should spread gossip and rumour among several islanders fairly swiftly rather than stay talking too long with the same people. Rumours grow as they spread and return to them exaggerated and embellished. You may wish to spend some time now or after the drama lesson looking at how unreliable, dangerous and inflammatory rumours and gossip can be in the drama and in real life, e.g. *'I heard he can do magic', 'He never sleeps so maybe he is not human', 'He has been heard talking in a strange language to someone'*, etc. You can join in and add inflammatory or sympathetic rumours if you wish, e.g. *'I've heard he is very lonely and cries', 'I think he is homesick and frightened', 'He has nightmares.'*

School Improvement Through Drama

Teacher in role	■ To consolidate key information ■ To sign teacher in role		Then in role as a fellow gossiping islander gather them together to share (in role) the main rumours heard. Then tell them that they will carry on gossiping together but that in a few minutes' time you will arrive as the stranger, who has broken out of his 'prison' home and entered their town.
Improvisation	■ To create tension and give opportunity for spontaneous in-role responses ■ To support emotional engagement ■ To reflect on in-role responses ■ To gather plot ideas		The children will respond through improvisation. You can leave the improvisation to run for as long as is useful to the drama. You (as the stranger) are hungry and non-confrontational. You have broken free to seek food. You don't speak their language so will need to communicate in other ways, e.g. mime. Don't give too short a time for the improvisation (as this won't allow them time to develop their thoughts and actions). Don't make it too long a time if it gets repetitive or interest wanes. Ideally halt it at a key moment with them all still fully engaged. Then, out of role, help them to pick up on and reflect on the way they responded in role to the stranger and ask them what *might* happen next.
8	**Teacher in role**	■ To create a dilemma for resolution ■ To consider and justify alternative courses of action ■ To consider collaboratively the possible consequences of various actions ■ To incite and support debate	Whole class circle or theatre style	Gather the class together as islanders, who are meeting to discuss the ongoing problem of the stranger. Tell them (as a fellow islander) that the stranger can obviously escape from his present 'home'. They need to consider possible 'next steps'. These might be positive or negative, e.g. 'Put him back with a guard and stronger locks', 'Let him try to live with us in the town', 'Put him back out onto the sea', etc. In role alongside the islanders as a fellow islander try to draw out the reasoning behind suggested actions and the possible consequences. Try to gather a wide range of possible next steps (which might be recorded or minuted in some way). Be 'devil's advocate' in role if necessary to spark debate. The children may or may not reach a decision at this point.
	Improvisation		

	Drama strategy	Purpose	Grouping	Teacher guidance and possible cross-curricular links
9	**Passing thoughts** (A type of 'thought-tracking')	■ To give opportunity for shared reflection ■ To establish that there may be different viewpoints	Whole class circle (standing) Teacher standing in centre	You stand in the centre of a standing class circle now and let the children have opportunity (as individual islanders) to pass by you randomly and individually and speak aloud their 'in role' thoughts now about 'the stranger'. Ask them to try to only have one person passing by you at any one time to allow the thoughts to be heard singly and to allow time for them to be absorbed and reflected on.
10	**Small group playmaking**	■ To bring alive some possible courses of action ■ To enable space and form to be given to the children's ideas ■ To ensure a range of options are made public and considered ■ To encourage co-operation towards the same goal	Groups of four	Either way, ask them now to get into groups of about four. Give each group the title of a 'next steps' scenario to create and enact. The scenario should last no longer than a minute and may be much shorter. Use the children's ideas to stimulate short scenarios; you only provide additional ideas if necessary, e.g. the stranger is: ■ given a job ■ given a better 'home' ■ locked up again with stronger security ■ locked up where all can see him ■ cast out to sea ■ taken into a home and looked after ■ taught the language of the islanders Don't give the groups more than 5 minutes to prepare the scenario and try to get them actively 'doing' early rather than spending too much time talking about what they might do. Give them a clear time limit for preparation and stick to it.

Performance Carousel	■ To offer performance opportunities for all ■ To encourage projection and prediction ■ To 'fast forward' plot		Once the scenes are ready, explain that they will 'Performance Carousel' them (as in activity 6), i.e. one group at a time in turn. Once all scenes have been seen, ask them to create a second short scene that will show the outcome of their actions sometime later, e.g. a week, a month, a year later, for example if scene one shows him being taken into a home, scene two will let us see if it is working out or not at a future point. They could play it two ways, i.e. enact a positive outcome and also a negative outcome. Ask the groups to then perform both scenes in an uninterrupted sequence.
Forum theatre	■ To enable direct interaction between characters and audience ■ To encourage and support the transference of learning		You could arrange for scenes to be seen again and this time, allow questioning/challenging by the audience of the characters within the scene. How much time you want to spend discussing and helping the children to reflect on the different groups' courses of actions and their consequences is up to you. You may wish to sensitively help the children to make direct and real-life links with similar modern-day situations locally, nationally and/ or across many parts of the world.
Improvization	■ To give a context for recounting events ■ To give a context for questioning	Pairs	Ask the children to get into pairs. Tell them it is many years later. One of them will pretend to be a child and the other will be a teacher. The teacher is teaching the child about this episode in the island's history. The child is asking questions about it. How will the teacher tell the story? They can then swap roles or else the pairs of children can take on the roles of other pairs of islanders talking retrospectively about it, e.g.:

PART TWO

Drama strategy	Purpose	Grouping	Teacher guidance and possible cross-curricular links
			■ parent and child
			■ two children talking about what they have heard about it at home and/or at school
			■ two adults who remember the stranger came when they were children.
Eavesdropping	■ To give opportunity for appropriately adapting speech for a range of audiences ■ To give opportunity for sharing selected dialogue		After the pairs have talked (and effectively rehearsed through improvisation) then you will eavesdrop on them, i.e. all pairs will need to keep still and silent until you pass by. Whichever pair you are standing nearest to will come to life and their conversation can then be listened to by all (until you move away from them and they 'freeze' silently again).
12 Still image	■ To use physical representation to enable and support reflection	Groups of four	Tell them that the people of the island in the book built a wall to keep all strangers out in the future. However, ask them to imagine that they built a statue as a way of always remembering this episode in their island's history.
Captioning	■ Synthesis to support reflection and make the learning memorable		You could now ask groups of four to create statues to depict and commemorate this piece of history. They could agree and write a one-sentence plaque and place it by their group statue. Half of the class at a time could step out and walk around the other groups' statues, talking about them in role as islanders many years later.
Tableau	■ To enable individual and whole class reflection at the same time	Whole class	Or you can conclude the drama at this point by creating one, whole class statue that depicts this historical episode for posterity. This could be done by combining group statues into one big commemorative statue park

| Ritual performance | ■ To make practical links with arts as a culturally familiar, generic and specific medium of commemoration | | (involving the whole class) or you could build the statue up by one child at a time entering an agreed space and adding themselves to one big statue. This lets them take account of whatever parts of the statue have already been created and respond to it.

Other ways of commemorating could be through the children creating a song, a dance, a festival, a pageant or short commemorative performance that is ritualistically performed every year, 'lest we forget'. |

PART TWO

PART THREE

■ Excerpts from 'Evacuation: Why and How?' Public Information Leaflet Number 3 (July 1939)

There are still a number of people who ask 'What is the need for all this business about evacuation? Surely if war comes it would be better for families to stick together and not go breaking up their homes?'

... although our defences are strong and are rapidly growing stronger, some bombers would undoubtedly get through ...

One of the first measures we can take ... is the removal of the children ... to safer places called 'reception' areas ... The scheme is entirely a voluntary one, but clearly the children will be much safer and happier away from the big cities where the dangers will be greatest.

There is room in the safer areas for these children; householders have volunteered to provide it. They have offered homes where the children will be made welcome. The children will have their schoolteachers and other helpers with them and their schooling will be continued. Do not hesitate to register your children under this scheme, particularly if you are living in a crowded area.

Of course it means heartache to be separated from your children, but you can be quite sure that they will be well looked after ... You cannot wish, if it is possible to evacuate them, to let your children experience the dangers and fears of air attack in crowded cities.

Children below school age must be accompanied by their mothers or some other responsible person. Mothers who wish to go away with such children should register with the Local Authority. Do not delay in making enquiries about this.

A number of mothers in certain areas have shown reluctance to register. Naturally, they are anxious to stay by their menfolk. Possibly they are thinking that they might as well wait and see; that it may not be so bad after all. Think this over carefully and think of your child or children in good time. Once air attacks have begun it might be very difficult to arrange to get away.

Full public information document at: http://www.bbc.co.uk/ww2peopleswar/
stories/38/a6177738.shtml

■ a) Walking to the station

Image Source: **myweb.tiscali.co.uk/hstchg/evacuees.htm**

■ b) Evacuees looking out of the train window

Image source: **http://www.johndclare.net/wwii4.htm**

■ Host family role cards (fictional)

Rebecca Seaton

Mrs Seaton is a kind lady and likes children. She has two children of her own and she lives in a very small house. She is having to put her two daughters in the same bed to make a bed available for an evacuee. She has not been feeling well recently and thinks she might be pregnant again. Her husband is now away in the army and she worries about him. She is willing to do her duty and intends to take care of two evacuee children but she hopes it won't be for too long. She would like a boy and a girl as they might be more likely then to get on with her own children.

Emma Pank

Emma works as the housekeeper at the Manor House and has been sent to find a strong girl, able to work in the kitchens. She has no children of her own and is not married. She is determined not to take a lazy or weak-looking girl and would like an older girl who looks clean. She also wants a polite girl who won't answer back. She is not keen to have an evacuee helping at the house but her mistress says they must do their duty and the girl must earn her keep.

Mary Thurston

Mary is married to a local farmer. She can't stand children complaining and crying and she used to smack her own children hard if they cried. She has three sons and her eldest, Billy, is a well-known thief and bully at school. She doesn't want to take in an evacuee at all but has been told she has to by the billeting officer. She thinks she will take a boy. She knows her sons are likely to gang up and give any evacuee a very hard time but her husband will take his belt to any of them if he has to and that will soon sort out any problems.

Jack Smith

Jack is disabled and thinks it will be helpful to have an evacuee to help around the house. Their house is very dirty. He and his wife Betty are happy together but are poor and often hungry. Jack thinks that it will be helpful to have the extra food ration for the evacuee as this will bring more food into the house and some extra money. They have no children of their own and always wanted a daughter. He thinks this will help them feel like a real family. He hopes the child will want to stay with them and not return home to London.

Tim Bailey

Tim is the local vicar and he has no wife or children yet. He thinks he must set an example to others and offer a home to evacuees. He has a housekeeper, Jane, who is not keen on the extra work this will involve and she does not like children but Tim believes all Christians must do their duty to help keep these poor cockney children safe. He knows Jane is strict and will want the children to pray often and be very clean. She often says, 'Cleanliness is next to Godliness'.

■ Evacuees' accounts of their experiences

> We marched to Waterloo Station behind our headteacher carrying a banner with our school's name on it. We all thought it was a holiday, but the only thing we couldn't work out was why the women and girls were crying.
>
> *James Roffey, founder of the Evacuees Reunion Association*

> We were even given flannels and toothbrushes. We'd never cleaned our teeth up till then. And hot water came from the tap. And there was a lavatory upstairs. And carpets. And something called an eiderdown. And clean sheets. This was all very odd. And rather scaring.
>
> *From Bernard Kops' autobiography* The World is a Wedding *(1963)*

> Many of the mothers and children were bed-wetters and were not in the habit of doing anything else. The appalling apathy of the mothers was terrible to see.
>
> Their clothing was in a deplorable condition, some of the children being literally sewn into their ragged little garments. There was hardly a child with a whole pair (of shoes).
>
> The state of the children was such that the school had to be fumigated after the reception.
>
> *From the National Federation of Women's Institutes survey report* Town Children Through Country Eyes *(1940)*

> The first night we slept on the floor of the church hall. The next day my sister and I were allocated to a Mr and Mrs Reece. At first it was quite frightening being separated from your mother and not understanding what was going on ... There were upsets sometimes. On one occasion we decided to go home to London. We followed the railway track. We thought it would take us back to London but after following it for about a mile we discovered it was a railway line used by the local mines.
>
> *Jim Woods was evacuated at five years old from London to South Wales*

> We were billeted in a manor house on a dairy farm. The parlour-maid, who was the one designated to actually look after us, used to beat you for reading in the morning. I can remember getting really severely beaten for reading 'Anne of Green Gables'. She didn't approve of working-class people reading, and anyway morning was for work, not reading ... The parlour-maid didn't want to look after us, so she used to get at me through my sister if I didn't do what she wanted. She used to hold her head under the water, that sort of thing.
>
> *Cynthia Gillett's war experiences appear in Jonathan Croall's book,* Don't You Know There's a War On? *(1989)*

Source: **www.spartacus.schoolnet.co.uk**

PART THREE

■ Evacuees' accounts of their experiences

> I miss my home in Tottenham and I would rather be there than where I am. I cannot find much to do down here. I miss my sister and my friends. I haven't any of my friends living where I live and I never know where to go on **Saturday and Sunday**, as I have no one to go with. At home I can stop in on **Saturday** if it is cold, but I have to take my brother out because the lady in this house goes to work and sometimes it is too cold to go anywhere. I miss my cup of tea which I always have at home after dinner. I miss my mother's cooking because the lady does not cook very well.
>
> *An extract written by a 13-year-old girl evacuated to Cambridge from London*

> I was an evacuee for six weeks. The main problem between evacuees and hosts seems to me to be the difficulty of adapting one to the other. **A few of the hosts treated their evacuees, mainly girls, as guests, or as they would their own children. But the majority treated the girls as unpaid maids ... A** great many hosts find it impossible to manage on the Government allowance and they grumble incessantly to their evacuees and demand a supplementary allowance from parents. When the parents explain that this has been forbidden, the hosts become extremely disagreeable, nag the evacuees, give them poor food and their meals separate from the rest of the family.
>
> *A-17-year-old girl evacuated from London*

> I was at primary school when war broke out, in **Nottingham**. As a small child I can remember the evacuees coming. We were horrible to them. It's one of my most shameful memories, how nasty we were. We didn't want them to come, and we all ganged up on them in the playground. We were all in a big circle and the poor evacuees were herded together in the middle, and we were glaring at them and saying, 'You made us squash up in our classrooms, you've done this, you've done that.' I can remember them now, frightened to death ... They used to be very quiet, and they only used to talk to themselves.
>
> *Kate Eggleston published these memories in* Don't You Know There's a War On? *by Jonathan Croall (1989)*

Source: www.spartacus.schoolnet.co.uk

1
They saw the new girl coming
So they clustered round the door
Blocked her path and threw her insults
Kicked her bag around the floor
Called her names, said she was ugly
What a weirdo, what a geek
Pushed and poked her as she shook there
She did nothing, did not speak.

2
And I watched them from the shadows
And I did not say a word
I just stood and watched the victory
Of the cruel and vicious herd
Fear and pity twisted in me
But my feet had turned to stone
My knees had turned to jelly
And I wished I was alone

3
And as I stood there watching
Past images of pain
Were flashing through my body
And crowding in my brain
The day they took my coat and threw it down the loo
The day they stole my money and filled my hair with glue
The day they locked me in a room and threw away the key
The day I bunked off school and hid till half past three

4
And I felt ashamed just standing there
Eye witness to her pain
I wasn't joining in with them
But felt bad just the same
I thought how I might help her
I thought what I might say
But my tongue was stuck inside me
As I turned my face away

5
I haven't seen the new girl since
She hasn't come to school
They say she might be moving
It's a shame, she looked quite cool
I might have had her as a friend
She might have been a mate
But I can't find that out now
'Cos I think that it's too late.

by Patrice Baldwin

Author's website: www.patricebaldwin.com

PART THREE

1

They saw the new girl coming
So they clustered round the door
Blocked her path and threw her insults
Kicked her bag around the floor
Called her names, said she was ugly
What a weirdo, what a geek
Pushed and poked her as she shook there
She did nothing, did not speak.

2

And I watched them from the shadows
And I did not say a word
I just stood and watched the victory
Of the cruel and vicious herd
Fear and pity twisted in me
But my feet had turned to stone
My knees had turned to jelly
And I wished I was alone

3

And as I stood there watching
Past images of pain
Were flashing through my body
And crowding in my brain
The day they took my coat and threw it down the loo
The day they stole my money and filled my hair with glue
The day they locked me in a room and threw away the key
The day I bunked off school and hid till half past three

4

And I felt ashamed just standing there
Eye witness to her pain
I wasn't joining in with them
But felt bad just the same
I thought how I might help her
I thought what I might say
But my tongue was stuck inside me
As I turned my face away

5

I felt all the injustice
Surge through me like a knife
What gave these no good wasters
The right to wreck a life?
I found my feet were moving
I felt my tongue break free
I turned to fetch a teacher
Knowing soon it could be me

continued

School Improvement Through Drama

6
But someone has to stop this
Someone has to act
Someone must stand up to them
And help break up the pack
If everyone does nothing
If nobody is strong
The mob will keep on ruling
It will just go on and on

7
They backed off when the teacher came
And out came all the lies
They hadn't kicked the bag around
Were only passing by
They gave me looks like daggers
Looks of hate both hard and long
But now I just felt dagger proof
And just thought, 'Bring it on!'

8
So I knelt and helped the new girl
Took her bag out of the bin
I told her I'd stay near her
Whilst she was settling in
And she gave a look of friendship
A look both soft and long
And I gave a look of friendship back
And we both thought, 'Bring it on!'

by Patrice Baldwin

Author's website: www.patricebaldwin.com

PART THREE

■ 'New pupil' role cards (fictional)

Sarah Smith
Sarah is moving schools because her parents have split up and she now lives with only her mother. Her mother decided to move to be nearer to Sarah's grandmother and to get some distance from her ex-husband. Sarah loves her mum and dad. She has had to leave her best friend at her old school. Sarah is friendly and pleasant but a bit nervous of children she does not know. She is a good friend.

Sylvia Galacska
Sylvia is new to living in this country. She has only lived in Poland before but her mother and she have come here to join her father. He has been living in England for a year and travelling to Poland some weekends to see them and take money home. He is a boat builder. Sylvia is pleased the family are together again as she has missed her father. She speaks quite good English as she has learned it at school. She knows there will be a few other Polish children in her new school but she has not met them yet. She hopes she will make new friends who are Polish and some who are not Polish.

Jane Simple
Jane hates her name. Children used to make fun of her name in her last school, where she was very unhappy and had no friends. She doesn't make friends easily. She is shy and pleasant but a bit of a loner. Jane is an only child. She has moved schools because her mother thinks it will help Jane if she makes a new start in a different school where no one knows her. Her new school has had a good recent inspection and claims to have no bullying. That is mainly why her mother has chosen it.

Peter Bailey
Peter is a sensitive boy. He is moving schools because he wants to go to a school that specializes in the arts. Peter dances well and plays guitar and violin well. He hates aggression and getting hurt and he hates sports. He does not enjoy playing with boys much. His best friend is a girl (Elinor) and she recently moved away. He misses her friendship. His mum and dad say he should try to make new friends who are boys in his new school but Peter finds it easier to get on with girls. He is very frightened of changing schools as he knows boys particularly can sometimes pick on him. He sometimes cries but tries hard not to. He hopes he won't cry in his new school.

■ **Real Victims' Voices**

The boys hid my bag so I couldn't find it at home time. They laughed at me when I started to cry.

My friends made me give them sweets. They say they won't be my friends if I don't. But they never give me anything.

I don't have any friends. At breaktime I just walk around the playground on my own. I would give the other children anything if they would be my friends.

One of the girls pokes me when the teacher isn't looking. It makes me cross and I slap her and then it's me that gets into trouble.

Sometimes the other children in the playground laugh at me because I give wrong answers. They don't do it in lessons because the teacher gets cross. But it hurts even more when we should be playing.

One of the boys said he would tear up my school book if I didn't give him money. I took some from my mum's bag, because I knew I would get in trouble with the teacher if my book is ripped.

PART THREE

■ Bullies' and Bystanders' thoughts (fictional)

I like being in a gang because it makes me feel powerful and important. I used to be bullied.

I pretend to like the people in this gang because I don't want them to pick on me.

My brother is in this gang and I am going to tell my mum about this when I get home. She will be mad about it.

I'm only watching so it's nothing to do with me really. I'm just glad its not me they are picking on today.

Oh no! Not them again. I hate this school. I just don't feel safe here.

I am going to do something about this. I'm going to ...

Artist: Chris Pepper
http://home.freeuk.net/chrispepper/index.htm

PART THREE

Drama Self Evaluation Framework

Name of school		Headteacher	
Teacher with lead/named responsibility for drama		Governor with designated/named responsibility for drama	
Date form completed		Date of next review	
Who has contributed to this review?		In brief, how was this review process carried out?	

Fully/Partly/Not in place ▶

1. ETHOS	EXAMPLES OF EFFECTIVE DRAMA PRACTICE	F P N	CURRENT PRACTICE, CHALLENGES AND IMPACT OF DRAMA IN SCHOOL (including where possible, measurable outcomes)	NEXT STEPS	WHO AND WHEN
1.1 The place of drama in the school	Drama is seen as directly linked to school improvement and is used as part of the planning and delivery of the whole curriculum across the school.				

	Drama is seen as a way to deliver on wider school objectives, e.g. improving pupil engagement and attitudes to learning, increasing confidence, improving writing, etc. Drama is within the current School Improvement and Development Plan as part of a broader priority or as a priority in its own right. Drama will be in our next SIDP.		
1.2 The support of Senior Management and governors	Drama is an agenda item at staff/SMT/governor meetings. There is a governor with designated responsibility for drama.		
1.3 The understanding and engagement of staff	All/some teachers/TAs understand and share ownership of the drama as pedagogy agenda and can demonstrate how it is applied and evident in their work.		
1.4 The understanding and engagement of parents	Parents have been informed that the school is developing and promoting drama as pedagogy. There is parental support for drama approaches as evidenced by parental comments and/or involvement.		

1. ETHOS	EXAMPLES OF EFFECTIVE DRAMA PRACTICE	F P N	CURRENT PRACTICE, CHALLENGES AND IMPACT OF DRAMA IN SCHOOL (including where possible, measurable outcomes)	NEXT STEPS	WHO AND WHEN
1.5 The wider involvement of external partners	The school is proactive in developing one or more partnerships to support drama in school hours, e.g. theatre educators or a playwright working in school. The school is proactive in developing one or more partnerships to support drama out of school hours, e.g. drama club provided by external providers.				
1.6 A culture that encourages pupils to have and develop their own drama ideas	All children are encouraged to believe in their own ability to make drama using their own ideas.				
1.7 A culture that values pupils and teachers as co-participants in drama	Teachers and TAs are fully committed to working in role alongside pupils in the drama. Pupils talk about their drama and are listened to by each other and by staff. The children's own ideas influence the shape, content, form and direction of the drama lessons.				
1.8 Opportunities to take part in a public theatre performance	Some children have opportunity to take part in performance for an audience, e.g. for the school or local community.				

School Improvement Through Drama

	All children have opportunity to take part in a theatre performance for an audience, e.g. for the school or local community.
1.9 Opportunities to see a public theatre performance	Some children have opportunity to attend a live theatre performance in/ out of school, e.g. visiting theatre company, visit a local theatre.
	All children have opportunity to attend a live theatre performance in/ out of school, e.g. visiting theatre company, visit a local theatre.

PART THREE

2. DRAMA ENVIRONMENTS AND RESOURCES	EXAMPLES OF EFFECTIVE DRAMA PRACTICE	F P N	CURRENT PRACTICE, CHALLENGES AND IMPACT OF DRAMA IN SCHOOL (including where possible, measurable outcomes)	NEXT STEPS	WHO AND WHEN
2.1 Indoor spaces that support drama	The school has a designated drama studio space regularly available (other than the classroom) for drama. This may be other than the school hall.				
2.2 Learning in and through drama outside the classroom	The outdoor environment is sometimes used by staff and pupils for drama activity and lessons.				
2.3 Visits that support the learning and teaching of drama/theatre	All classes make visits to venues that link to drama or where drama takes place, e.g. theatre, living history (museums), street carnival, etc.				
2.4 The use of display and performance to support and promote D4LC	Pupils are actively involved in the design and creation of displays that connect to their drama work. Aspects of their drama work have been shared with others through performance outside the drama lesson. Aspects of their drama work have been shared online, e.g. through the school website.				

PART THREE

2.5 Classroom layout that supports creative learning in and through drama	Layout supports rather than hinders collaborative, active and interactive drama for learning and spaces and physical resources are able to be used flexibly and safely.	
2.6 Finance	The school commits budget from core funds to drama. The school actively seeks additional funding to support the development of drama.	

3. DRAMA – CURRICULUM DEVELOPMENT AND DELIVERY	EXAMPLES OF EFFECTIVE DRAMA PRACTICE	F P N	CURRENT PRACTICE, CHALLENGES AND IMPACT OF DRAMA IN SCHOOL (including where possible, measurable outcomes)	NEXT STEPS	WHO AND WHEN
3.1 An integrated curriculum that teaches and uses drama	Drama is part of the planned creative curriculum for all children across the school. Drama is delivered discretely in its own right as well as through cross-curricular studies.				
3.2 Managing and organizing creative learning	Staff teach drama lessons. They are also willing to use drama strategies, conventions and approaches across the curriculum and not just as part of English lessons. Drama is evident as an approach in lesson plans and observations.				
3.3 Drama – curriculum exploration with external partners	External drama/theatre partners work in partnership alongside staff to help deliver the planned curriculum with a shared and agreed focus on learning and pupil creativity.				
3.4 Time is used imaginatively and flexibly to support drama for learning and creativity	Staff have the freedom to use lesson time flexibly when necessary in order to support and sustain creative thinking and the drama process.				

3.5 Creative approaches to cross-phase drama activity	Staff have the freedom and imagination to develop drama activity together across each other's phases and year groups.		
3.6 Drama linking to the real world	Staff make drama links with real or imagined businesses and enterprises, e.g. through Mantle of the Expert		
3.7 Culturally diverse drama/ theatre	Cultural diversity is valued and evident in the overall planned drama curriculum both in content and form, e.g. cultural mask work, world music, diverse origin of stories/myths/legends used for drama, culturally diverse theatre educators.		
3.8 Special drama/theatre events in the school calendar	All classes have the opportunity to attend live theatre each year. Drama/theatre events are part of the planned school curriculum. The school creates its own drama/ theatre events as part of the annual school calendar.		
3.9 Pupil involvement in decision making within and about drama	Pupils' comments and suggestions in drama and about drama are listened to and action taken where possible. The children clearly play an active role in shaping how their drama lesson develops (content and form).		

PART THREE

4. TEACHING CREATIVELY THROUGH DRAMA	EXAMPLES OF EFFECTIVE DRAMA PRACTICE	F P N	CURRENT PRACTICE, CHALLENGES AND IMPACT OF DRAMA IN SCHOOL (including where possible, measurable outcomes)	NEXT STEPS	WHO AND WHEN
4.1 Teaching drama – planning and collaboration	All school staff make use of 'in role' approaches and whole class drama across the curriculum. Experimentation and risk taking in teaching is encouraged and supported.				
4.2 Use of ICT to support drama	Staff make creative use of ICT in drama. The outcomes of drama are shared with others sometimes through ICT.				
4.3 Exploring creativity with drama partners	Staff are open to collaborative drama partnership work with other creative professionals, e.g. Drama ASTs, theatre educators, Leading Drama Teachers, playwrights, etc.				
4.4 Pupils' involvement in drama planning	Staff enable children and young people to contribute their ideas to drama teaching and learning.				

PART THREE

5. TEACHING FOR PUPIL CREATIVITY	EXAMPLES OF EFFECTIVE DRAMA PRACTICE	F P N	CURRENT PRACTICE, CHALLENGES AND IMPACT OF DRAMA IN SCHOOL (including where possible, measurable outcomes)	NEXT STEPS	WHO AND WHEN
5.1 Identifying pupils' drama strengths and potential	Staff and partners encourage and promote drama for all pupils. They recognize and enable the development of individual children's drama skills and talents.				
5.2 Modelling drama and creativity	All staff work in role at times and model creativity in and out of role through their speech, actions, attitudes and behaviours. They present themselves as drama-confident and creative people.				
5.3 Nurturing creative skills, behaviours and attitudes through drama	Staff use and develop children's creative and drama skills through planned and structured in-role activity that involves making meaning, performing and responding. Skills include: ■ Individual and shared improvisation and expression in and out of role ■ Questioning and challenging in and out of role ■ Purposeful problem solving individually and together in and out of role				

5. TEACHING FOR PUPIL CREATIVITY	EXAMPLES OF EFFECTIVE DRAMA PRACTICE	F P N	CURRENT PRACTICE, CHALLENGES AND IMPACT OF DRAMA IN SCHOOL (including where possible, measurable outcomes)	NEXT STEPS	WHO AND WHEN
	■ Creative thinking (making connections, seeing relationships, envisioning and making what might be, exploring ideas, keeping options open) ■ Information gathering and processing in and out of role ■ Reasoning and justifying in and out of role ■ Evaluating (reflecting critically on own and others' drama ideas, actions, performances and their impact) ■ Communicating (verbally and non-verbally) in and out of role				
5.4 Supporting personal, social and emotional development	Drama opportunities are planned and structured to support PSE development, e.g.: ■ Self-awareness ■ Self-esteem ■ Managing feelings ■ Motivation, application and perseverance ■ Enjoyment of learning ■ Empathy ■ Social skills ■ Team working				

5.5 Drama careers advice and placement (secondary)	The school's careers advice services represent careers linked to drama/ theatre and associated industries – the students meet and talk with professionals working in drama/ theatre about their career paths – work experience placements are negotiated with theatres and associated industries and enterprises.		

PART THREE

6. STAFF LEARNING AND DEVELOPMENT	EXAMPLES OF EFFECTIVE DRAMA PRACTICE	F P N	CURRENT PRACTICE, CHALLENGES AND IMPACTS IN SCHOOL	NEXT STEPS	WHO AND WHEN
6.1 Valuing teachers' drama talents	The drama talents of staff are recognized and staff are able to realize their creative potential within a teaching and learning environment.				
6.2 Performance management	During the setting of performance management objectives, drama as pedagogy is included (if necessary) as an area of teaching and learning and a drama teaching and learning individual teacher action plan is produced including drama.				
6.3 Staff CPD in drama	All staff have received continuous professional development on drama teaching and learning. Drama CPD is embedded in the INSET planning cycle of the school.				
6.4 Drama Learning and Teaching Support Networks	Teachers attend networks of drama teachers. Teachers network with other teachers of drama online. School initiates and/or co-ordinates networks of fellow schools and education professionals and best practice is shared and peer-to-peer support offered with respect to teaching and learning in and through drama.				

6.5 Reflective and collaborative drama practice	A culture of reflective drama practice is well established in the school. Cross-curricular studies working groups meet to develop ways of incorporating drama approaches into day-to-day teaching practice.		

7. DISSEMINATION AND ADVOCACY	EXAMPLES OF EFFECTIVE DRAMA PRACTICE	F P N	CURRENT PRACTICE, CHALLENGES AND IMPACTS IN SCHOOL	NEXT STEPS	WHO AND WHEN
7.1 Advocacy and dissemination	The school proactively advocates its practice in drama and drama approaches to teaching and learning through networks, events, publicity.				
7.2 Pupil-led advocacy	Pupils are active advocates for drama, e.g. through regular performances, presentations, and through pupil voice in a variety of media.				

PART THREE

■ References

1. Rose, J. (2008) *The Independent Review of the Primary Curriculum: Interim report.* Downloadable from http://publications.teachernet.gov.uk

2. Ofsted Report (2008) for Cecil Gowing Infant School, Norwich. www.ofsted.gov.uk

3. Norfolk County Council and National Drama, *Drama for Learning and Creativity (D4LC)* – action research log of a participating teacher.

4. Simpson, D. (2008) *Drama for Learning and Creativity (D4LC) Phase 2 Evaluation.* Downloadable from www.d4lc.org

5. Ofsted Report (2006) for Gt Hockham C of E Primary School, Norwich. www.ofsted.gov.uk

6. Norfolk County Council and National Drama, *Drama for Learning and Creativity (D4LC)* – headteachers' letters of application (2007). Website: www.d4lc.org.uk

7. DfES (2003) *Excellence and Enjoyment – A Strategy for Primary School.* Downloadable from http://www.standards.dfes.gov.uk

8. The Secondary National Curriculum (Key Stages 3 and 4). http://www.qca.org.uk

9. NACCCE (1999) *All our Futures: Creativity, Culture and Education.* DfEE. Downloadable from http://www.cypni.org.uk

10. Ofsted Report (2008) for Heartsease Primary School, Norwich. www.ofsted.gov.uk

11. General Teaching Council of England Survey of Teachers 2007. Downloadable from www.gtce.org.uk/research/tsurvey/survey07

12. Gardner, H. (1983) *Frames of Mind: The Theory of Multiple Intelligences.* Basic Books, New York.

13. Baldwin, P. (2004) *With Drama in Mind: Real learning in imagined worlds.* Network Educational Press, Stafford.

14. Harland *et al.* (2000) *Arts Education in Secondary Schools: Effects and Effectiveness.* NFER.

15. Great Britain Scottish Education and Industry Department Inspectors of Schools (1999) *Effective Learning and Teaching in Scottish Secondary Schools: Drama.* www.hmie.gov.uk/documents/publication/eltd-08.htm

16. Downing, D. (2003) *Saving a Place for the Arts? A Survey of the Arts in Primary Schools in England.* NFER.

17. Training and Development Agency (2008) *School Improvement Planning Framework.* Downloadable from www.tda.gov.uk/remodelling/extendedschools

18. Waters, M. (2006) *School Improvement Through Drama*, Birmingham Conference speech. Downloadable at www.d4lc.org

19. DfES (2005) Excellence and Enjoyment: Social and emotional aspects of learning. http://www.standards.dfes.gov.uk/primary/publications/banda.seal and http://www.nationalstrategies.standards.dcsf.gov.uk

20. Boal, A. (1992) *Games for Actors and Non-Actors.* Routledge.

21. Council for Subject Associations (CfSA) (2008) *Primary Subjects: Gifted and Talented.*

22. Council for Subject Associations (CfSA) (2009) *Primary Subjects: Learning outside the classroom*.

23. Reader, C. (1991) *A Lovely Bunch of Coconuts*. Walker Books.

24. Moreno, J. L. (1946) *Psychodrama* (2nd revised edition). Beacon House, New York.

25. Mosely, J. (1996) *Quality Circle Time in the Primary Classroom*, Vol. 1. LDA.

26. Baldwin, P. and Fleming, K. (2003) *Teaching Literacy Through Drama: Creative Approaches*. Routledge/Falmer.

27. Corbett, F. (2006) *School Improvement Through Drama*, Birmingham Conference speech.

28. Baldwin, P. (2008) *The Primary Drama Handbook*. Sage.

29. Tan, S. (2006) *The Arrival*. Lothian.

30. Claxton, G. (1997) *Hare Brain, Tortoise Mind*. Fourth Estate Limited.

31. Ofsted Report (2003) *Expecting the Unexpected*. www.ofsted.gov.uk

32. Turnbull, A. (1995) *The Last Wolf*. Hamish Hamilton.

33. Arts Council England (2003) *Drama in Schools* (2nd edition). www.artscouncil.org.uk/information

34. Welsh Assembly Government, *Teaching Drama: Guidance on Safeguarding Children and Child Protection for Managers and Drama Practitioners*. Downloadable from http://www.wales.gov.uk

■ Further reading

Ackroyd, J. and Boulton, J. (2001) *Drama Lessons for 5 to 11 year olds,* David Fulton Publishers.

Baldwin, P. and Fleming, K. (2002) *Teaching Literacy Through Drama: Creative Approaches,* Routledge.

Baldwin, P. (2004) *With Drama in Mind: Real learning in imagined worlds,* Network Educational Press.

Baldwin, P. (2008) *The Primary Drama Handbook,* Sage Ltd.

Bowell, P. and Heap, B. (2001) *Planning Process Drama,* David Fulton Publishers.

Fleming, M. (2001) *Teaching Drama in Primary and Secondary Schools – an integrated approach,* David Fulton Publishers.

Kempe, A. and Ashwell, M. (2000) *Progression in Secondary Drama,* Heinemann Educational Publishers.

Kempe, A. and Nicholson, H. (2007) *Learning to Teach Drama 11–18,* Continuum International Publishing Group Ltd, 2nd revised edition.

Neelands, J. (2004) *Beginning Drama 11–14,* David Fulton Publishers.

Neelands, J. (2006) *Improve Your Primary School Through Drama,* David Fulton Publishers.

Nicholson, H. (2000) *Teaching Drama 11 to 18,* Continuum International Publishing Group Ltd.

O'Neill, C., Heathcote, D. and Bolton, G. (1996) *Drama for Learning,* Heinemann Educational Publishers.

Toye, N. and Prendeville, F. (2007) *Speaking and Listening Through Drama 7–11,* Paul Chapman Educational Publishing.

Winston, J. (2000) *Drama, Literacy and Moral Education,* David Fulton Publishers.

Winston, J. (2004) *Drama and English at the Heart of the Primary Curriculum,* David Fulton Publishers.

Winston, J. and Tandy, M. (2008) *Beginning Drama 4–11,* David Fulton Publishers.

■ Index